EARLY YEARS

CHILD CARE AND EDUCATION

KEY ISSUES

Maureen O'Hagan BEd, MSc, MIHE, RGN, NNEB
Director of Quality Assurance,
Council for Awards in Children's Care and Education (CACHE), St Albans

Maureen Smith BEd(Hons), CQSW, RGN
Director of Curriculum and Assessment,
Council for Awards in Children's Care and Education (CACHE), St Albans

SECOND EDITION

Baillière Tindall

EDINBURGH LONDON NEW YORK PHILADELPHIA ST LOUIS SYDNEY TORONTO 1999

BAILLIÈRE TINDALL

An imprint of Elsevier Science Limited

© Bailliére Tindall 1993
© Harcourt Publishers Limited 1999
© Elsevier Science Limited 2002. All rights reserved

✠ is a registered trademark of Elsevier Science Limited

First edition 1993
Second edition 1999
   Reprinted 2001, 2002

0 7020 2373 6

British Library Cataloguing in Publication Data
A catalogue record for this book is available from the British Library

Library of Congress Cataloging in Publication Data
A catalog record for this book is available from the Library of Congress

Note

Medical knowledge is constantly changing. As new information becomes available, changes in treatment, procedures, equipment and the use of drugs become necessary. The authors and the publishers have, as far as it is possible, taken care to ensure that the information given in this text is accurate and up to date. However, readers are strongly advised to confirm that the information, especially with regard to drug usage, complies with the latest legislation and standards of practice.

Printed in China by RDC Group Limited
N/03

Contents

Acknowledgements

The authors and publishers wish to express their immense gratitude to the children, staff and parents of Hull University Union Day Nursery featured in Figures 1.2, 1.5, 1.14, 2.2, 2.3, 2.4, 2.5, 2.6, 2.7, 4.2 and 9.1, photographed by Sarah James.

Details of illustrations and Tables reproduced from other sources are as follows:

Figures 1.1 and 3.1: Harrison, K. 'Look! Look what I can do.' *In* Scott-Hughes, B. (Ed.) *Creative Action Ideas for Under Sevens*. London: BBC Books.

Figures 1.3 and 1.4: Atkinson, R.L. *et al*. (1990) *Introduction to Psychology*, 10th edn. Harcourt Brace (© Marcia Weinstein).

Figure 1.11: Foster *et al*. (1989) *Family-Centred Nursing Care of Children*. Philadelphia: W.B. Saunders.

Figure 1.12: Frantz, R.L. (1992) *The Origin of Form Perception*, © 1992 Scientific American, Inc. (all rights reserved).

Figures 1.13 and 8.3: Brown, B. (1990) *All Our Children*. London: BBC Education, courtesy of Luke Finn.

Figure 2.1: Sally and Richard Greenhill (photographers: Photo Library) in *Under Five and Under Funded*. London: Daycare Trust.

Figure 3.2: Whalley M. (1994) *Learning to be Strong*. Sevenoaks: Hodder and Stoughton.

Figure 3.5: *Language Matters*. 1988 Numbers 2 and 3. London: ILEA, Centre for Language in Primary Education.

Figure 3.7: Qualifications and Curriculum Authority. (1998) *An Introduction to Curriculum Planning for Under Fives*. London: QCA.

Table 3.1: Cambridgeshire County Council. (1996) *Framework for a Foundation Curriculum for Under Fives*.

Figure 4.1: Sally and Richard Greenhill (photographers: Photo Library)

Figure 5.1: Reynolds (1984) *Finding out about Child Development*. Cheltenham: Stanley Thornes.

Figure 5.2: Sally and Richard Greenhill (photographers) in Brown, B. (1990) *All Our Children*. London: BBC Education.

Figure 5.3: *Self-help Section of the Portage Checklist*. Windsor: NFER-Nelson.

Figure 6.2: Central Office of Information and Weller, B.F. (1980) *Helping Sick Children Play*. London: Baillière Tindall.

Figure 6.3: Kathleen Preston and Weller, B.F. (1980) *Helping Sick Children Play*. London: Baillière Tindall.

Figure 9.2 and 9.3: Barnaby's Picture Library.

Authors' acknowledgement

Thanks are due to all our students and colleagues with whom we have worked over the years.

Disclaimer

Please note that the views expressed in this book are those of the authors and are not necessarily the views of their employers.

Abbreviations used in book

ACE	Advisory Centre for Education
ACPC	Area Child Protection Committee
CACHE	Council for Awards in Children's Care and Education
CRE	Commission for Racial Equality
DfEE	Department for Education and Employment
EPO	Emergency Protection Order
EYCE	Early Years Care and Education
HIV	Human immunodeficiency virus
ILEA	Inner London Education Authority
LEA	Local education authority
NCC	National Curriculum Council
NNEB	National Nursery Examination Board
NVQ	National Vocational Qualification
OFSTED	Office for Standards in Education
OMEP	Organisation Mondiale pour L'Education Préscolaire
PTA	Parent–Teacher Association
QCA	Qualifications and Curriculum Authority
SAT	Standard Assessment Test
SEN	Special Educational Needs

Introduction

The first edition of this book was published in 1993 and has since become a major text in the field. It was designed to provide early years workers with a sound basis of knowledge and understanding linked to the National Vocational Qualifications (NVQs) in Child Care and Education. This is an opportune time to release a second edition of the book as the field of early years care and education has seen many changes over the past 5 years. There has been a change of government creating many new initiatives and changes in legislation, policy and practice. The content of the book is relevant to all early years workers who are working towards a level 3 qualification regardless of the setting they may be working in, i.e. group-based, home-based, statutory, voluntary or private.

The NVQs in Child Care and Education have been revised and are now NVQs in Early Years Care and Education (EYCE). This second edition is linked to the Early Years Care and Education NVQs and to the CACHE Diploma in Nursery Nursing (NNEB) which will be implemented nationally from September 1999. The revisions to both the NVQs and the CACHE Diploma are reflected in the content of each chapter and the explicit links are identified at the start of each chapter. This book will also be useful to those candidates who are undertaking the new CACHE Professional Development Awards.

Whilst not changing the basic style of the book, this edition provides updated material in all areas and has extended the scope of certain chapters; e.g. Chapter 1 covers child observations and assessment in greater depth, Chapter 4 on the curriculum reflects the introduction of 'desirable learning outcomes', Chapter 5 reflects the new attitudes towards children with special needs and Chapter 8 covers changes in the law.

Greater use has been made of scenarios and assignments which were so popular in the first edition and have been used by many NVQ candidates as a basis for extended pieces of work as part of their level 3 portfolios. Tutors have also found these useful to stimulate discussion and questioning.

To distinguish three distinct functions of the tinted panels you will come across in this book, we use three pictorial icons, as follows:

- at the start of each chapter the 'linking arrow' icon indicates links between the subject matter of the chapter and the NVQ units/CACHE Diploma modules listed below the icon
- in Chapter 1 a panel headed by the 'open file' icon presents an in-depth Case Study
- in most chapters the 'spectacles' icon heads short Scenario panels. These describe typical difficulties or crises that might arise in a child care setting and set out relevant questions for the NVQ student or early years worker, aimed at stimulating thought, observation, research or discussion.

The book aims to give candidates, students and practitioners greater theoretical knowledge and points them to further reading and study. Although the new edition's coverage is extensive, material on physical development and care is not included – a 'sister' book to this text, *Geraghty's Caring for Children*, 3rd Edition, by Maureen O'Hagan covers these areas in full. As always we would wish to encourage reflective practice and would urge readers to ensure that they are up to date in their thinking and can justify the provision that they offer. It is important that practitioners understand and incorporate into their work the underlying principles which underpin all work with children and their families. It is for this reason that the Statement of Underlying Principles from the National Occupational Standards is printed in full on page xiii.

We believe that the first edition of *Special Issues in Child Care* set the standard and paved the way for many other texts that were subsequently published. This new edition, *Early Years Child Care and Education: Key Issues*, does not compromise on the depth and extent of knowledge and understanding it expects readers to acquire as they work towards NVQ level 3, the CACHE Diploma or other relevant courses of study. Readers who are part of this occupational field will know that the work undertaken on a day-to-day basis is highly skilled and demanding and draws on an extensive knowledge base. There is no attempt to take a superficial look at complex issues and these are dealt with in depth. We owe it to the children and families who depend on us to make sure that we are an up-to-date, skilled and knowledgeable work force in order to provide the best possible service to our customers.

We would like to thank all those candidates, students, tutors and practitioners who have provided us with feedback on the first edition and have thus enabled us to provide a second edition which responds to readers' needs.

STATEMENT OF UNDERLYING PRINCIPLES

Links ➡

This section links with **all** the units of the National Occupational Standards in Early Years Care and Education

The following statement of principles is taken from the National Occupational Standards in Early Years Care and Education. The principles are the basis for good practice in child care and education. It is important that these principles are incorporated into the practitioner's everyday activities. The principles are not intended to be an 'add-on' but must be embedded in all aspects of a candidate's competent performance and in the knowledge component which underpins performance.

These principles draw on both the UN Convention on the Rights of the Child and the Children Act 1989, and also take into account the delivery of the School Curriculum and Assessment Authority (*now Qualifications and Curriculum Authority QCA*) 'Desirable Outcomes for Children's Learning'. They are based on the premise that the earliest years of children's lives are a unique stage of human development, and that quality early years provision benefits the wider society and is an investment in the future.

1. The welfare of the child

The welfare of the child is paramount. All early years workers must give precedence to the rights and well-being of the children they work with. Children should be listened to, and their opinions and concerns treated seriously. Management of children's behaviour should emphasise positive expectations for that behaviour, and responses to unwanted behaviour should be suited to the child's stage of development. A child must never be slapped, smacked, shaken or humiliated.

2. Keeping children safe

Work practice should help prevent accidents to children and adults, and should protect their health. Emergency procedures of the work setting, including record keeping, must be adhered to. Every early years worker has a responsibility to contribute to the protection of children from abuse, according to her/his work role.

3. Working in partnership with parents/families

Parents and families occupy a central position in their children's lives, and early years worker must never try to take over that role inappropriately. Parents and families should be listened to as experts on their own child. Information about children's development and progress should be shared openly with parents. Respect must be shown for families' traditions and child care practices and every effort made to comply with parents' wishes for their children.

4. Children's learning and development

Children learn more and faster in their earliest years than at any other time in life. Development and learning in these earliest years lay the foundations for abilities, characteristics and skills in later life. Learning begins at birth. The care and education of children are interwoven.

Children should be offered a range of experiences and activities which support all aspects of their development: social; physical; intellectual; communication; emotional. The choice of experiences and activities (the 'curriculum') should depend on accurate assessment of the stage of development reached by a child, following observation and discussion with families. Early years workers have varying responsibilities concerning the planning and implementation of the curriculum, according to their work role, but all contributions to such planning and implementation should set high expectations for children and build on their achievements and interests. Child-initiated play and activities should be valued and recognised, as well as the adult planned curriculum. Written records should be kept of children's progress, and these records should be shared with parents.

5. Equality of opportunity

Each child should be offered equality of access to opportunities to learn and develop, and so work towards her/his potential. Each child is a unique individual; early years workers must respect this individuality; children should not be treated 'all the same'. In order to meet a child's needs, it is necessary to treat each child with 'equal concern': some children may need more and/or different support in order to have equality of opportunity. It is essential to avoid stereotyping children on the basis of gender, racial origins, cultural or social background (including religion, language, class and family pattern), or disability: such stereotypes may act as barriers to equality of access to opportunity. Early years workers should demonstrate their valuing of children's racial and other personal characteristics in order to help them develop self-esteem.

These principles of equality of access to opportunity and avoidance of stereotyping must also be applied to interactions with adult family members, colleagues and other professionals.

6. Anti-discrimination

Early years workers must not discriminate against any child, family or group in society on the grounds of gender, racial origins, cultural or social background (including religion, language, class and family pattern), disability or sexuality. They must acknowledge and address any personal beliefs or opinions which prevent them respecting the value systems of other people, and comply with legislation and the policies of their work setting relating to discrimination. Children learn prejudice from their earliest years, and must be provided with accurate information to help them avoid prejudice. Expressions of prejudice by children or adults should be challenged, and support offered to those children or adults who are the objects of prejudice and discrimination. Early years workers have a powerful role to play in nurturing greater harmony amongst various groups in our society for future generations.

7. Celebrating diversity

Britain is a multi-racial, multi-cultural society. The contributions made to this society by a variety of cultural groups should be viewed in a positive light, and information about varying traditions, customs and festivals should be presented as a source of pleasure and enjoyment to all children including those in areas where there are few members of minority ethnic groups. Children should be helped to develop a sense of their identity within their racial, cultural and social groups, as well as having the opportunity to learn about cultures different from their own. No one culture should be represented as superior to any other: pride in one's own culture and social background does not require condemnation of that of other people.

8. Confidentiality

Information about children and families must never be shared with others without the permission of the family, except in the interest of protecting children. Early years workers must adhere to the policy of their work setting concerning confidential information, including passing information to colleagues. Information about other workers must also be handled in a confidential manner.

9. Working with other professionals

Advice and support should be sought from other professionals in the best interests of children and families, and information shared with them, subject to the principle of confidentiality. Respect should be shown for the roles of other professionals.

10. The reflective practitioner

Early years workers should use any opportunity they are offered or which arises to reflect on their practice and principles, and make use of the conclusions from such reflection in developing and extending their practice. Seeking advice and support to help resolve queries or problems should be seen as a form of strength and professionalism. Opportunities for in-service training/continuous professional development should be used to the maximum.

1: THE DEVELOPING CHILD

Objectives

- Importance of child development
- Critical periods
- Cognitive development
- Perceptual development
- How children learn
- Piagetian theory
- Critique of Piaget's work
- Language development
- Symbolic representation
- Emotional development
- Attachment theory
- Self-esteem
- Fears and anxieties
- Social development
- Socialization
- Moral development
- Observation, assessment and record keeping

Links

This chapter has links with:
- NVQ (EYCE) Units: C4, C5, C8, C9, C10, C11, C14, C15, C16, C17, C18, C25; M7, M8; E1; P2, P7.
- CACHE Diploma Modules A, E, H, L, R, S.

Introduction

The study of child development is relatively new and much of it is derived from aspects of different disciplines, such as psychology or biology, which have been drawn together to provide a multi-disciplinary, holistic view of the child. Most of the research named in this chapter has taken place within the western, industrialized nations and the results cannot always be applied to other cultures and societies, particularly those which are very different in ideology, family patterns and child-rearing practices.

How children grow and develop underpins all work with young children, and it is essential that all who work in this field have a good understanding of child development. Although this chapter does not consider research methods and their validity, it is important to understand that research does not necessarily provide 'the truth' but will reflect the design of the research and the theoretical perspectives behind the work. There are different theories of development that can be confusing, but certain commonly-accepted principles need to be known and understood in order to work effectively. It is therefore necessary to draw out from the various perspectives those elements which early years workers use and find useful in their everyday work. The chapter aims to cover aspects of children's social, emotional, cognitive, moral and language development, but does not consider physical care and development. As child development studies form a large and important area for early years workers, it is recommended that particular areas of interest be followed up using the references at the end of the chapter.

Assignments are not included for this chapter as it is assumed that readers will wish to undertake observations and assessments on the developing child. Suggestions for observations are included at the end of the chapter.

Figure 1.1
'Look what I can do!'

Normative measurement

Although development is often assessed through measuring how a child performs compared with the 'norm', e.g. using age-related development scales, it is important to recognize that this method has pitfalls and can be judgemental resulting in children being labelled 'backward' or 'deficient' in some way. It is important to emphasize that all children develop at different rates and it is difficult to assess what the norm actually is as there are no hard-and-fast measures against which a child can be judged. It is essential to take into account the social and cultural context within which the child receives care and education, and the child's individual needs. The use of normative measures does, however, provide a broad framework, which is helpful to workers in making assessments of children's progress. In view of this, the chapter considers 'norms' of development linked broadly to the age/stage of the child.

Integrated development

Although the chapter looks at aspects of development separately, it is important to stress that children develop in an integrated and holistic manner; e.g. if children's physical development is impeded, then their capacity to explore the world will be affected and this affects their learning. If children have poor self-esteem, this will affect their ability to take risks, e.g. having enough self-confidence to climb to the top of the climbing frame or to undertake new physical challenges. Lack of self-confidence and self-esteem will also affect the child's capacity to learn and to relate to others. All these developmental threads are closely linked and interdependent. Workers with pre-school children usually aim to promote the all-round development of the child.

Stages and sequences in child development

Although there are a variety of viewpoints concerning the developing child, there is a good deal of evidence that children's developmental patterns follow the same sequences but at different rates; e.g. nearly all hearing children pass through a 'pre-linguistic' stage which includes babbling, imitating and practising sounds which form the basis of their first words. However, babies vary considerably in the time they take to reach the stage of word production. Most will reach this stage at around their first birthday, but some will talk earlier and others later. All will have gone through the pre-linguistic stage.

Critical periods and emergent skills

One of the most exciting and rewarding aspects of caring for young children is to see them grow and develop. As children mature and pass through the various stages of development many researchers think there is a 'critical' time when a child is most ready to develop particular skills or concepts. A 'critical' time is thought to be when a child has physically or mentally matured to the point they can move on in learning and development. In order to do this they will need an environment that allows them to do so and opportunity to practise, e.g. children may be ready to walk at around 15 months: their nervous systems, muscles, balance and co-ordination have developed sufficiently and they are confident in movement. If they are then kept indoors and sit in a buggy all day, they are unlikely to walk. This is an obvious example but there are other aspects of development which are much more subtle. Through careful observation and assessment, staff must be aware of what stage children have reached in their development, take note of their emerging skills, and provide support for them, which will encourage the next phase of learning. This requires sensitivity by the adult and an awareness that it is possible to hold back children who are ready for further learning. This is most likely to occur when adults measure a child's progress against developmental scales linked to age and do not allow for individual differences or assume that a child cannot learn a new skill or concept because research shows that the 'average' age of doing so is different from the child's. In viewing development, it is essential to be aware that children's progress is not always clear-cut and there will always be overlap between stages. You will notice that children practise emerging skills over and over again, and the secret of effective work is to identify these and to plan activities, experiences and routines which stimulate and encourage these aspects of development. The adult's role in promoting development is very important and is considered further in this chapter. The skills of observation and assessment are vital tools in identifying a child's stage of development and judging how best to provide for them, and are considered at the end of this chapter.

Cognitive (intellectual) development

Cognitive or intellectual development covers thinking, reasoning, problem-solving, memory, aspects of perception through the senses, concept formation, concentration, attention, and many other mental functions not all of which can be dealt with here. All aspects of development are linked, but there is a particularly strong link between cognitive and language development as each is thought to influence the other directly. When the various components of cognitive development are put together they constitute what is usually called 'intelligence'.

Intelligence testing

Earlier this century there was a great emphasis on intelligence and intelligence testing, e.g. the work of Alfred Binet leading to Stanford–Binet tests. These tests were supposed to measure how intelligent a person was and to predict future achievement. The 11+ examination that decided if children should go to grammar schools was widespread in the UK until the 1960s. Research at that time revealed that this exam was not so much a fair assessment of 'intelligence' as a selection based on culture and social class. Children from working-class homes, regardless of their potential ability, did not do so well at these tests because the language and concepts tested were often middle-class and beyond their experience. Testing children in this way led to 'labelling' them either bright and intelligent or otherwise. Further research (Rosenthal and Jacobsen, 1968) showed that such labelling leads to adults having lower expectations of the children and the 'self-fulfilling prophecy', i.e. children fulfil those low expectations and do not reach their full potential.

Later work has challenged the idea that it is possible to test intelligence fully, and that the best that can be done is to test certain components such as memory span or number ability. This can only test a sample of any individual's abilities and major decisions should not be taken on such limited evidence. Many workers or researchers do not agree with tests on the grounds that 'intelligence' as a separate concept is not open to definition, and testing is socially biased. Some educationalists and psychologists consider there are advantages to using tests that are especially designed to be bias-free as they can be used to assess a child's particular abilities and whether extra help is required. It is worth noting that there are difficulties in producing bias-free tests and it is arguable whether they are possible at all.

Nature/nurture debate

There is considerable discussion concerning whether intelligence is determined by genetic inheritance or by the environment in which a child is brought up. Binet, for example, thought that intelligence as such was fixed at birth and depended on inheritance. Other educationalists and psychologists feel that the environment and educational experiences to which a child is exposed are more important than genetic inheritance.

Research on identical twins who are brought up separately has been used to study which of the above factors is most important. These studies generally support the idea that a good deal of intelligence is inherited, but some studies have been criticized as being biased and unscientific. There have been other studies that stressed the importance of the environment in determining intelligence. Partly as a result of these, workers from the 1960s onwards introduced compensatory education programmes designed to benefit the poor and socially disadvantaged; e.g. Headstart in the USA worked with parents and children and has led on to the High/Scope Curriculum (see Ch. 3).

The evidence for either side is not clear-cut, and on balance it seems that both factors play a part. However, it is unlikely that any child's potential will be reached in an environment that is uncaring or unstimulating. In general, it is more important in early childhood to create an environment that maximizes opportunity and development for all, rather than attempting to create an elite group and concentrating on the academic prowess of its members.

Creativity and imagination

Creativity is often linked with 'intelligence', but research has shown that creative people are not always those who score highly in intelligence tests. Intelligence tests usually measure the ability of a subject to solve problems and give 'correct' answers in a particular manner which eliminates alternatives – this is known as convergent thought. Creativity might take many forms such as art, music or sculpture or the ability to solve problems in unusual and different ways. This latter type of ability is linked with the ability to think divergently and consider new options. Scientists, engineers and mathematicians, as well as artists and writers, need to be capable of divergent thought.

Workers with young children need to encourage children's creativity and imagination. This is discussed further in Chapter 2. Children need open-ended problems that will encourage them to think in a variety of ways. Where children are regularly given 'closed' tasks such as painting within the lines (not the child's lines), using a template, or sticking a pre-cut piece of paper on a card to take home, this discourages their own creativity. Workers need to concentrate on activities that allow children to develop their creativity and to concentrate on the process of creating and not on the end product. In order to encourage creativity children should be encouraged to explore and play with materials and activities with no right or wrong answers and where all results are acceptable. Modelling or painting is a good example where children's efforts should be valued regardless of the end product. If children's creativity is stifled through a diet of activities that are adult centred and 'closed', they may not learn to trust their ability to draw or make things and could develop negative attitudes about themselves. Although this applies to all children, highly creative children can find themselves particularly frustrated and unhappy in a restricted environment and as a result will under-achieve and not develop to their full potential.

Sensory learning

Babies and very young children learn through their senses, i.e. sight, smell, touch, taste and hearing. In the early years a rich diet of sensory experience is needed. Good quality sensory experience attracts the child's attention, lets the child enjoy the experience and encourages further learning. Sensory experience should be available for the child at the time and level it is required. Too much sensory stimulation is as bad as too little and workers should observe and assess the child's requirements; e.g. in encouraging sensory development through hearing, young children need quiet periods as well as noise which means monitoring even sounds provided by musical mobiles and background music. Children need to hear single sounds and loud and quiet sounds to learn to discriminate between them; they need to hear high-and low-pitched sounds and a wide range of different sounds. Very often linking sounds with appropriate pictures reinforces the learning.

Attention and concentration

If children are to learn effectively, it is important that they can concentrate and attend. Children should be encouraged to concentrate and adults should expect them to be able to attend for periods of different lengths depending on their stage of development. In the 'Effective Early Learning' Project (Pascal and Bertram, 1997) Dr Christine Pascal used the following observational scales which can assist staff in measuring concentration.

Adult–Child Engagement Scale
This scale assists adults in assessing the provisions in the nursery and whether adults are sensitive to the children and encourage independence and motivation.

Leuven Involvement Scale
This scale assists adults in measuring how involved children are and the level of involvement.

Undertaking these types of measurement helps to assess the overall provision and the needs of individual children.

A choice of activities that interests children and enables them to succeed will encourage concentration. Expecting very young children to concentrate for long periods is not appropriate and adults need to be sensitive and notice when children's concentration is waning. Sometimes it is in order to suggest a few more minutes at an activity whereas at other times children need to be able to move on to something else. Forcing children to concentrate on activities where they have lost interest will lead to the child becoming bored and frustrated and can lead to behaviour problems or lack of interest in learning. Often having an adult nearby and sometimes directly involved or assisting in an activity can help a child to concentrate. Praise and encouragement should be freely given.

Children's concentration will vary from day to day; they may be tired, unwell, tense or unhappy. This does not necessarily mean there is a problem but persistent lack of concentration should be monitored and investigated.

Some children have particular needs or learning difficulties and may be labelled 'hyperactive' or be diagnosed as having attention deficit disorder. There is some evidence that hyperactivity and food allergies are linked but some children are hyperactive for no known reason and may or may not improve as they get older.

Memory and recall

In addition to encouraging children's concentration it is important to encourage memory and recall. This enables a child to make the most of learning opportunities. Memory games such as Kim's game are fun and can be developed to encourage memory and recall. There are many other memory games using words, objects or cards. Questioning children in a non-threatening way about something they have experienced or asking them to re-tell stories can also be useful. Get into the habit of doing this in everyday situations by asking 'What did we do yesterday?' or 'Whose birthday was it last week?'

Bruner (1980) describes 'iconic thinking' where children are reminded of their prior learning and experiences. There are many ways in which children can be reminded such as the use of objects, interest tables and books. Adults should draw children's attention to the links with the past and help develop memory and encourage children themselves to make the connections.

Perceptual development

Perception is how persons extract information from the world around them. Studying how babies perceive the world around them has led to some important findings, especially with regard to their emerging abilities. Studying how babies perceive the world allows us to understand how we might best provide for their needs. Research has revealed that babies are far more active and sophisticated in their interpretation of events and more able to make use of the world around them than had ever before been realized. In view of this it is important that workers provide not only a loving and caring environment but also a stimulating one. This involves meeting the babies' physical needs, giving consistent care, developing firm attachments between babies and carers and surrounding them with appropriate levels of sensory stimulation in the form of light, colour, sounds, smells, tactile experiences such as massage, textures to feel and explore and adults to talk to them and with whom they can respond.

Perceptual development of young babies

- All senses are working at birth.
- Face, hands, abdomen and soles of feet are more sensitive to touch.
- Newborns can feel pain.
- Babies of a few hours old will orient to direction of sound. At 2 weeks they will stop crying and attend to human voice. Babies quieten to low sounds such as whispers and are alert to higher frequency sounds. At 1 month, they will recognize different speech sounds. At 3 months, they will imitate low- or high-pitched sounds. At 4 months, babies can link familiar sounds with objects, e.g. mother's face with voice. From around 5 months, babies begin to respond to their own name.
- Babies can distinguish mother's smell from others.
- Babies prefer sweet tastes, especially breast milk.
- It is thought that newborns do not at first see in colour. Their focus is poorly developed but they can focus best on objects about 8 inches away. They will track movements of objects and people. They are light sensitive and seem to prefer the human face. Babies scan with their eyes and focus on the edges of objects. They appear to copy facial expressions. From 2 months on, there is evidence of depth perception that is related to size constancy. If this does not occur, babies would not be able to perform simple acts such as reaching out for objects, as they would not be able to judge distance in relation to size. At about 4 months, babies can discriminate between two- and three-dimensional objects, and they can focus on their hand whilst sitting or lying and on an image of self in a mirror. At 5 to 6 months, they prefer complex things to look at and enjoy bright colours. From 6 months on, babies can focus on small objects and are more able to follow rapid movements.
- Object constancy or the recognition that things exist when out of sight occurs from 8 to 12 months.

Figure 1.2
Baby looking in a
mirror.

How children learn

Learning is a controversial area of development and there is a variety of different perspectives. The importance of play in children's learning is covered in Chapter 2, but it is widely understood that one of the principal means by which young children learn is through talk, play and social interaction.

Learning theory

One view of human development and learning is based on the idea that learning as such cannot be measured, only the resulting behaviour. Psychologists such as Skinner who take this line are called 'behaviourists' and they believe that learning takes place through conditioning or through observation of role models. Although there are variations within learning theory, the main points are as follows.

Classical conditioning (Pavlov)
The work of Pavlov on the behaviour of dogs is a famous example of classical conditioning. Pavlov discovered that if a light was flashed before a dog was fed, the dog would learn to associate the light with food and eventually would salivate in anticipation of being fed in response to the light alone. This learning was based on association of an event with a particular result often linked with a reflex action.

Operant conditioning (Skinner)
Research with humans is more difficult than with dogs and the concept of operant conditioning is more relevant. This is also learning by association, but it is the

association of a behaviour with the consequence of that behaviour. Operant conditioning suggests that learning takes place as subjects' responses to various stimuli are either rewarded or punished. This is called either positive or negative reinforcement. Behaviour can be changed over time by rewarding a person via a variety of reinforcers such as praise, food, toys or a hug. Unacceptable behaviour may be modified or changed by offering rewards for change, withholding rewards or avoiding unpleasant happenings, e.g. a child who persistently demands attention at the expense of other children might find this behaviour is largely ignored whilst any positive behaviour is rewarded. As the main purpose is to gain adult attention this acts as a negative reinforcer for the demanding behaviour, but as positive reinforcement to encourage good behaviour. Active punishment such as smacking is not considered an effective means of changing behaviour as it does not promote something positive in place of the negative.

Social learning theory

Social learning theorists such as Bandura (1973) (and see 'Social Learning' section, p. 38) emphasize the effects of social forces and believe that children can learn through imitation and modelling their behaviour on important people in their lives. This theory stresses the importance of role models for children's learning. Learning theory offers a clear idea of learning but does not adequately explain the complex beings that children are. Children often experiment and play in new ways not because they will get an external reward but because they enjoy what they are doing. This theory does not explain where new behaviour that has not been observed, imitated or reinforced comes from. However, different professional groups involved in child care and education often use the concept of modifying behaviour through reinforcement and modelling. This is discussed further in Chapter 9 on children's behaviour.

Piaget's theory of cognitive development

Jean Piaget (1896–1980) has been a powerful influence on our understanding of children's development, and his work has been widely used by educationalists and many who work with children. His theory of cognitive development is complex and is discussed here in outline only. Although there has been criticism of the theory, much of it remains as important guiding principles for workers with young children.

Piaget believed that children were active agents of their own learning and that a major task for them was to develop an ability to organize experiences and learn from them in a way which enables them to make sense of the world. He believed that intelligence consisted of the ability to make adaptations to the environment by taking in information, processing it, and then using it appropriately (assimilation). Some children would be able to do this more efficiently than others. The early phases of this process occurred through reflex activity such as searching for the nipple, combined with the child's inborn strategies for exploring the world (seeing, hearing, touching, smelling, grasping and sucking). Piaget felt that new information taken in by the young child would then require change or modification of existing mental concepts or categories/maps (schemas) through a process of 'accommodation', e.g. a toddler may have been used to drinking out of a red cup and has a schema that says 'all cups are red'. When presented with a yellow cup, the child has to learn through assimilating the new information and changing the existing schema to accommodate the new information, which says 'cups may be yellow.' Each child has to achieve a balance or equilibrium in learning through this process. If there is too much new information assimilated, and the child does not have time to deal with it, i.e. to experiment, explore, practise and become familiar with it, the child will become confused and over-stimulated. When this happens the process of accommodation cannot occur efficiently and the child's learning is impaired.

As well as schemas, Piaget describes other mental structures called 'operations'. These enable us to combine schemas in a logical manner and make links between different areas of experience. Using the above example, a child may have a schema for drinking cups which involves them being red; the schema will change to cover yellow cups at this level. As the child grows and develops, it will realize that cups may be different colours, shapes, sizes and materials and used at different times for different purposes. This involves combining schemas for shape and size, and imagining different varieties of use through the use of mental 'operations'.

Conservation

According to Piaget, children initially judge the world around in terms of what they see, and do not understand the underlying principles that are apparent to older children and adults. At around the age of 7, they gradually begin to understand that objects and events are not always exactly what they seem. One aspect of their ability to do this is called 'conservation'. It is a difficult concept and the following practical examples are those that it is possible to try to carry out with children.

Conservation of mass (Fig. 1.3).   This can be demonstrated by using two balls of clay or Plasticine that the child agrees are the same. One of these balls is taken and rolled into a sausage shape in front of the child who is then asked if they both have the same amount of clay. Most children under 6 or 7 years will say that the sausage shape is larger: the children are not able to 'conserve' mass.

Conservation of number (Fig. 1.4).   The child is shown two rows of buttons and agrees they contain the same number. One row is spread out to make a longer row and the child is asked which row now contains most buttons. According to Piaget, children under 7 are likely to say that the spread-out row has more buttons.

Conservation of length, area, quantity, weight and volume develop and can be tested in similar ways.

Reversibility/transformation

Reversibility is a key concept linked with the ability to conserve. Children learn that when materials have been changed they can be changed back again.

Figure 1.3
Conservation of mass.

Figure 1.4
Conservation of
number.

Piaget's stages of cognitive development

A key aspect of Piaget's theory is the four stages of development through which all children pass. Children in each stage have particular capabilities beyond which they should not be expected to function. Piaget's stages are:

Sensori-motor stage (birth–2 years)
Learning through the five senses and through movement. Egocentric, cannot de-centre. Object permanence by the end of the first year.

Pre-operational stage (2–6 or 7 years)
Child can now use symbols such as language to stand for other things. Thinking is still tied to concrete, real life objects and events and what is seen. Child cannot comprehend abstract concepts. Pre-operational thought is rigid: things are seen in black and white. 'Moral realism' means children expect everyone to share their view of right and wrong which is itself based on what actually happens rather than motives for behaviour. Child cannot classify by more than one feature until around 4 years and sees everything from its own point of view. Reasoning is often illogical, e.g. children hurt themselves against a toy and proceed to smack the 'bad' toy. This assumption that objects have consciousness is called animism and can be the root of many fears.

Concrete operations stage (7–11 or 12 years)
Thinking is becoming more rational but child still needs to be able to see and manipulate objects to help check what it is doing and thinking and finds it difficult to think in the abstract. Child can see things from others' points of view, but egocentricity persists as the child tries to make difficult facts fit into its own ideas rather than changing its own viewpoint to accommodate the facts. Child can take into account several features of objects and events at the same time and group objects by several common features, can solve several conservation tasks and understands reversibility and transformations. Child recognizes there is more than one solution to a problem and has better understanding of some abstract concepts. Understands quantity and one-to-one correspondence.

Formal operations (around 12 years of age)
Stage extends and develops throughout adulthood. Characterized by the ability to think logically and in the abstract. The period of change from concrete to formal operations takes some years, and it is not clear whether all adults complete the transition.

Critique of Piaget's work

Piaget's work was a major breakthrough in our understanding of the developing child, and this must not be underestimated. However, work by a variety of researchers has challenged or built on some of his methods and conclusions, e.g. the work of Vygotsky, Bruner or Donaldson.

Some criticisms of Piaget's work are:

- Piaget took as his starting point what children could not do, rather than what they could do.
- Piaget emphasized the role of the intellect but did not adequately consider the impact on it of other areas of development such as language or emotional development.
- Piaget underestimated the social and cultural context in learning and cognitive development. Modern research has stressed that learning occurs within the context of everyday social interactions.
- Individual differences between children are not adequately considered and there is no clarity on the overlap between stages.
- Children, much younger than Piaget indicated, can de-centre (take into account several aspects of an object or event at the same time), conserve and understand reversibility and also demonstrate other cognitive skills. This is thought to be due to the manner in which the original experiments were done and the language used. It is thought that children did not understand the tasks, not that they could not do them.
- Children under 7 are capable of some logical thought when they fully understand what is being asked.
- Very young children are capable of seeing some things from other points of view.
- Piaget's idea of fixed stages of development has been largely superseded by the idea of sequences. This means that children's learning in any particular area will follow the same basic order, and use the same rules and strategies for learning. Workers with young children need to 'tune in' to these sequences in order to provide individual children with correct educational experiences, not those based on the assumption that children cannot move on in their learning because they are tied to a particular age or stage.
- Restricting the view of the young child as a learner not capable of logical thought or understanding complex issues could artificially restrict the curriculum offered and lead to lower expectations.
- The role of experience and adult support in learning is much more important in an individual child's progress than Piaget had allowed for when discussing stages of development.
- Piaget's work indicated that the child would learn from its own inner motivation, and stressed the role of discovery learning which involves a child finding out for itself. This idea of the 'solitary' learner has been challenged by recent work, which stresses the importance of the adult or other children in supporting learning.

Social constructivist model of learning

This model of how children learn uses elements of other views drawing particularly on the work of Vygotsky and Bruner and aspects of Piaget's work. This model of learning is the one most favoured by early childhood educators in the UK today. The model stresses that the child learns through interaction with its environment, usually through talk and play. It emphasizes the importance of the child's social world and the role of the adult in supporting learning and providing an effective learning environment. This model of learning encourages adults to intervene in children's play and learning and requires skilled and supportive adults who understand how children learn and develop.

The main features of this models are:

- *Children are active learners not passive recipients of information.*
- *Adults need to observe and assess children's stage of development.*
- *Based on their observations adults support children's learning.*
- *Adults intervene and extend learning and do not leave children to get on with it.*
- *Adults need to create learning opportunities for children based on the child's emerging skills.*
- *Adults need to listen and talk to children.*
- *Parents and a wide range of other adults are important players in creating a learning environment.*
- *Adults and children work together in developing learning.*

Concept formation

A major task for the development of thought is the formation of concepts – these are cognitive categories that help organize experience and acquire new areas of knowledge and understanding. The way young children form basic concepts is linked to their perception of the world and other cognitive tasks such as the ability to conserve or classify. Children who can conserve are able to develop accurate concepts in such areas as those mentioned below. Children have to learn to concentrate and to discriminate which features of a situation are important, and this demands developmental 'readiness'. They must also have real experience of as wide a variety of materials and objects as possible to consolidate and extend their learning. This is best done through opportunities to play freely but in a carefully structured environment. This is one of the reasons that the early years curriculum stresses active learning using concrete experiences and encourages children to handle objects and materials. In doing this they explore the properties of new or unfamiliar items, solve problems and modify their existing schemas.

Basic concrete concepts such as eggs, chairs or dog are understood by very young children through the adult labelling the object consistently and the child understanding as much about the object or event as possible. It is much later, at around 7 years onwards, that the child can then place eggs into the inclusive category of 'food', or dogs under the classification 'pets' and then the wider classification of 'animal'.

Children in their early years learn about the properties of objects such as colour and shape and relational concepts such as over/under, inside/outside. Children under 6 or 7 years do not usually have a firm grasp of counting and number: this means understanding what numbers really mean, not just rote counting, e.g. six will remain six in every situation. This is learned through trial and error and experience in different situations with a variety of materials. More difficult concepts such as 'time' or aspects of number such as subtraction take longer to grasp firmly and reliably. Often, children seem to understand the idea of 'soon' or 'next' but they are not able fully to appreciate all that this means in terms of the passage of time. Children are around 8 years of age before they really understand the passage of time, and even then it is at a simple level. They are around 12 years before they understand time, speed, distance, age and their interrelationships.

Abstract concepts such as honesty, peace or justice and complex physical concepts are likely to take much longer to establish, and many children are into adolescence or adulthood before they are understood. Evidence from various sources indicates that some adults never reach this level of higher-order thinking. It is important, as always, that workers with young children are aware of where the child has reached in terms of concept formation. Once this is identified, appropriate experiences and activities to support concept learning can take place. Modern research stresses the role of the adult in supporting children's conceptual development far more than Piaget recognized. Adults must support concept formation through their talk and interaction with children. Children need adults to help them to understand concepts and require many opportunities to handle materials, to practise using objects and to talk and discuss.

Stages of cognitive development 0–7 years 11 months

Age/Stage	Key features
1–3 months	Learning through senses and own movement. Early concepts beginning to develop. Sensitive to light. Recognizes and imitates low- or high-pitched sounds. Can tell own mother by smell. Imitates facial expressions, likes human faces and turns towards them. Recognizes bottle. At 3 months, plays with own fingers.
3–6 months	Shows excitement at approaching adults or familiar welcome sounds. Enjoys contact and looks around. Watches adults carefully and with purpose at 6 months. At 4 months can link mother's voice with her face. At about 5 months, enjoys bright colours and complicated objects to look at and concentrate on. Reaches for objects and judges distance in

relation to size. Shakes rattle at 5–6 months and passes objects from hand to hand. Learns the difference between two- and three-dimensional objects. Learns people are permanent before objects, i.e. that they continue to exist even if the baby cannot see them. Can track objects well and co-ordinates seeing, grasping and mouthing. Develops favourite tastes. Expresses pleasure by smiling and laughing.

6–9 months   Understands signs, e.g. a spoon means food, a coat might mean going outside. Objects are now recognized as permanent. Holds objects and bites them, puts objects into mouth. Tries to grasp spoon or cup. Imitates simple actions. Watches as ball rolls away. Holds toys. Visually very attentive to happenings taking place.

9–12 months   Memory develops. Can anticipate the future and own routine. Imitates sounds and actions. Claps hands and waves 'bye bye'. Gives toys on request. Puts objects in and out of container. Less mouthing of objects. Points at objects or persons.

1–2 years   Helps when dressing. Indicates when wet or soiled. Drinks from cup and uses spoon. Explores properties of toys and objects. Throws things to the ground repeatedly. Intensely curious and needing constant supervision; constantly explores environment. Less mouthing of objects. Hand preference emerging. Points finger at things wanted and demands satisfaction. Enjoys sound-making toys, colours, picture books. Follows adults and imitates domestic activities. Simple role-play. Wants things immediately and is not able to defer gratification. At 2 years will scribble. Enjoys picture books and recognizes fine details. Names body parts. Follows simple instructions. Beginning to see the differences between things but usually concentrates on one thing at a time.

2–4 years   Becomes symbol user. Language develops. Imaginative play strongly features and continues to develop. Can represent events and objects through drawings and models. Remains curious about world and constantly exploring. Sees similarities. Between now and 7 years developing understanding of transformation and reversibility (processes can be reversed). Understanding of time, i.e. past/present/future is beginning to emerge with ideas of deferring wishes to future. Can discuss recent events. Asking many questions. Demands stories and wants favourites over and over again. Tells own stories, sometimes confuses fact and fiction. Animism (objects have feelings). Subject to irrational fears. Tells rhymes and songs. Can count by rote. Knows full name and address. Remains strongly self-willed. Shows appreciation of humour. Plays with wide range of toys, construction, creative, basic materials. Concentration-span growing. Finds difficulty in seeing the world through others' points of view and usually concentrates on one aspect of a situation. Beginning to consider others (start of moral development) and how others can feel hurt.

4–7 years   Plays co-operatively. Imaginative play continues to deepen. Language development continues. Literacy (talking, listening, reading writing), numeracy and conceptual development feature strongly. Thinking becomes more co-ordinated as language develops and more complex and inclusive concepts form; e.g. animals form a class which encompasses dogs, tigers and many others. Moral development continues as child works out right from wrong and develops concepts such as forgiveness or fairness. Increasingly sees others' points of view and shows concern. Can still have some difficulty telling fact from fiction.

Development of language and communication

The development of language is an important milestone for the growing child and a major achievement. Language and the use of symbols help children to communicate their wants and needs to the outside world. They help to extend their experience beyond their immediate environment, and to express their feelings. Play and the ability to talk and interact verbally with others offer the child a powerful means of learning. The development of language is closely linked to children's thinking and conceptual development. Children who are confident communicators are empowered as they can express their feelings freely, can negotiate their wishes and needs and develop self-confidence and self-esteem. Adults should always respect a child's right not to communicate whilst being sensitive to the reasons. It may, for example, be that a child wishes to communicate but is having difficulty as a result of sensory impairment whilst other children may wish to be silent until they feel more confident in a new situation.

There are four main ways in which language is used:

1. *Listening and understanding (receptive speech). Children always listen and understand language before they use it.*
2. *Talking (expressive speech).*
3. *Reading.*
4. *Writing.*

These four are closely linked, and the last two depend on success in listening and talking. In the case of sensory impairment, different strategies are used to facilitate reading and writing. This section will consider only receptive and expressive speech; Chapter 3 looks at reading and writing and contains references for further research.

Children can communicate in different ways other than through spoken language, e.g. non-verbal communication such as body language and facial expression, crying and gestures. Children who have some difficulty in language may rely on non-verbal methods and need help in developing language skills. Sensory impairment such as hearing loss may severely affect the development of spoken language. Children may learn other methods of communication such as signing which are valid forms of communication.

Origins of speech

Linguists and psychologists have studied the origins of speech and language in children and have very different views on how it is acquired. Learning theorists think it is learned through imitation, and in part this is true, but this does not explain the child's capacity to create and invent entirely new sentences they could never have heard before. Chomsky (1968) stated that children have an inborn capacity to acquire language, and that part of the process of successful acquisition is associated with hearing language used. Their 'language acquisition device' sorts out the appropriate set of rules for the language they hear.

Backing up this argument, there seems no doubt that when children begin to speak they use grammatical 'rules' to create an infinite variety of new sentences and phrases. Proof of this also lies to some extent in their usage of 'virtuous errors'; e.g. they may have learned that plurals often end with an 's', therefore the child will apply the rule to make sheep into sheeps. This shows that they are not merely repeating what they have heard but are attempting to apply rules in their speech.

Language and thought

Piaget's view was that children's language development was constrained by their stage of cognitive development. In other words, language would not proceed ahead of the child's basic thought processes as the two are closely linked. Others, such as Vygotsky and Bruner, suggest that it is as children talk and interact with others that they progress in language and thinking.

Baby talk

Adults often speak to babies in a particular way. This involves using short sentences, simple language structures, repetition, a higher pitch than normal and a slower rate of speech which emphasizes content words. This way of talking to babies has been called baby talk, 'motherese', caregiver language and is now often known as child-directed speech. A key feature is the expectant pause when adults wait for the child to communicate and vocalize back to them. Babies and young children are thought to attend more closely to this type of speech and learn from repeating the grammatical patterns. Adults often imagine what they think the child is saying or interpret facial expressions or slightly modify and expand a child's own speech and repeat it back to the child and this helps to further language development, e.g.

Baby　Looks at teddy and says 'Ta ta.'
Mother　Pause, then 'Yes … here's your teddy.'

Baby Pauses and looks again at teddy. Points and says 'Ta ta ta.'
Mother Responds to imagined or implied request from baby, 'Yes … Mummy wants
　　　to kiss teddy.'

This kind of turn-taking response using slow, high-pitched, repetitive speech encourages children to talk and enjoy interactions with adults. It is also important to allow babies time to listen and to respond and to allow them to listen to a range of different sounds and pitches. Babies enjoy listening to rhymes, handclapping, bells and other interesting sounds and soon learn to associate the sounds with the objects or people.

Language and social context

During the 1960s and 1970s there was a linking of failure at school with the way in which children used language. It was thought that working-class children used a restricted language code which prevented them understanding and taking advantage of school opportunities (Bernstein, 1961). School staff, who were likely to be middle class, were thought to use an elaborated code of language which gave middle-class children an advantage in educational terms. As a result of this type of research, compensatory education attempted to provide a linguistically enriched environment for working-class children without always recognizing that the children's own language and culture were important and valid in their own right. Associated with this was an assumption that the reasons for educational disadvantage were rooted in the home. Modern research has found that children's language develops in much the same way regardless of home background, and that listening to stories and participating in everyday conversations are crucial factors in the development of language and literacy (Wells, 1985, 1987).

Bilingualism (English as an additional language)

Many children in the UK today speak more than one language. Such children may use English at school and a different language at home with their family. There is rarely a complete balance between the two. Settings must ensure that children are not labelled as having poor language skills just because they do not speak English fluently. Children may well be fluent in their home language but speak rarely at school or nursery. There is often a silent period before a child learning a second language, which is the dominant language, feels confident enough to communicate. Sometimes an older child who is bilingual can help this transition in school or nursery by acting as a role model for the younger child as well as by helping to interpret. In some early years settings, workers see their role as teaching the child English and gradually phasing out the home language (transitional bilingualism). However children need to be fluent in their home language in order to become literate in English and there are many advantages in being fluent in more than one language. To encourage children to develop bilingually can be a means of showing respect for and valuing their home culture, which raises the self-esteem of both the children and their families.

Children who achieve a broad balance of fluency in more than one language have the advantage of familiarity with more than one culture and can learn to respect both. Being bilingual does not seem to affect literacy skills and seems to increase creativity and divergent thinking. Bilingual children are often more sensitive to situations as they are more used to interpreting sounds and intonations.

Egocentric speech

This is the 'talking away to themselves' with which those who care for young children are so familiar. Psychologists and linguists have different views on the purpose of egocentric speech, which can be short sentences or 'telegraphese', that accompanies play or a long and complex egocentric monologue. To assess whether true egocentric speech is being heard, it is useful to listen and to ask oneself at what or whom is the language aimed? Egocentric speech is usually aimed at the child itself.

It can be very enlightening to 'listen in' on children's egocentric conversations, as often deep or hidden feelings may manifest themselves. Talking to themselves is a form of externalized thinking through which children regulate and plan their own behaviour. It usually accompanies play, but can occur when a child feels frustrated. Egocentric speech is often stimulated by the need to solve problems that are difficult to 'think through'. As the child's thinking becomes internalized there is less need for egocentric speech and it eventually disappears.

Promoting language development

Children need a language-rich environment from their earliest days. This can be through songs, rhymes, stories, actions and talk in everyday activities. When children experience this they are able to use language freely and to enjoy it.

Providing a language-rich environment

- Record examples of children's language either on tape or in written records and note progress.
- Draw children's attention to environmental print such as advertisements and signposts.
- Use print in the nursery for labelling areas, topics, interest tables, including the child's own name.
- Provide a 'graphics' area where writing and mark-making is encouraged.
- Use the environment of the nursery to provide writing paper and implements, e.g. by the telephone in the home corner.
- Write down the children's own stories at their dictation.
  Regularly share stories, both read and told from the earliest months of life.

- Allow the children to make their own books.
- Be able to change and adapt stories, rhymes and songs to avoid stereotyping and encourage participation by all, including children who have sensory impairment.
- Use a range of songs, rhymes and finger plays to extend language.
- Use books and language activities from a variety of languages and cultures.
- Use stories, rhymes and conversations in community languages for children whose first language is not that of the setting, and encourage other children to participate.
- Use community language resources such as older siblings, parents, community workers and libraries.
- Use visual aids such as puppets, masks and telephones.
- Use audio equipment and encourage children's independent use of it.
- Provide a stress-free environment where children do not feel pressurized to talk or 'perform', and are not criticized when they make mistakes.
- Provide practical situations where it is expected that children communicate.

Interacting to promote development of language

- Utilize a child's non-verbal communication.
- Reflect language and non-verbal communication back to the child through speaking, listening, writing (e.g. writing down the child's own stories) and reading as appropriate.
- Remember to keep parents informed and maintain confidentiality.
- Use one-to-one, small and large group language opportunities according to the child's confidence and abilities.
- Use simple, clear language with lots of repetition (see 'baby talk' above).
- Use language opportunities in games, activities and routines.
- Encourage child–child conversations as well as child–adult.
- Praise and encourage, give positive feedback.
- Use both direct questions: 'Where is Jane going?' and indirect: 'Does anyone know why Jane is going outside?'
- Use open-ended sentences that do not require 'correct' answers, and give time for children to reply.
- Give time and opportunity to verbalize feelings, and where necessary provide appropriate vocabulary in a sensitive way.
- Listen carefully and responsively to children and feed back corrections to their language in natural conversations.

Observing and assessing

- Carefully observe and assess children's stage of language development, including listening, speaking, reading and writing, including mark-making.

• Note during everyday activity whether the child has a hearing difficulty.
• Assess when children might need help from speech therapists or other specialists.

Stages of language development

Pre-linguistic stage

Age	Key features
1–3 months	Cries when hungry or has discomfort. Orients to sounds and is startled by sudden noises. Appears soothed by human voice, especially mother's. Coos when contented (occurs in deaf babies).
3–6 months	Babbles and coos. Vocalizes vowels and consonants and syllables: 'ba ba ma ma'. Laughs out loud. Cries when upset or hungry. Searches for source of sound. Responds to tone of voice.
6–9 months	Continues to babble and imitate speech sounds. Uses long, repetitive strings of sounds: 'mememe adadad' (deaf children usually do not use repetitive, tuneful babble). Babbling more linked to the language of the parents rather than 'universal' sounds. Will shout and vocalize in order to communicate.
9–12 months	Continues to imitate speech sounds. Uses 'jargon' which is strings of sounds that go up and down like conversation. Shows understanding of 'bye bye', simple instructions such as 'give it to me'. Also understands simple words in context: 'cup' or 'teddy'. Uses most vowels and consonants. Understands, and perhaps names, 'mama' or 'dada'. Points to objects.

Linguistic stage

Age	Key features
12–15 months	More 'jargon'. Uses gestures and understands 'no'. Less likely to cry for attention and more likely to vocalize. Has 2–6 word speech vocabulary and understands many more.
15–18 months	Uses 6–20 words. Points to parts of body. Points at pictures and may label. Uses gestures widely and 'jargon'. 'Echolalia' which is echoing prominent word or last syllable. Enjoys

	rhymes and tries to sing. Uses holophrases that are single words with different expression to mean different things.
18 months–2 years	Uses around 50 words and understands many more. Beginning to put words together, e.g. 'dada come'. This is known as 'telegraphese'. Refers to self by name. Asking for names of objects. Joins in songs, rhymes, finger plays. Obeys simple instructions such as 'close the door'. Echolalia remains.
2–3 years	Develops large vocabulary and understands more. Beginning to use plurals and pronouns but makes 'virtuous errors', e.g. mouses instead of mice. Egocentric speech during play. Holds simple conversations. Asks questions using what, where and who. Loves stories, especially when repeated over and over again. Can use short sentences, including adjectives. May stutter when excited.
3–4 years	Speech inflections are more adult. Large vocabulary and uses grammar correctly in most cases. Still has problems with sentence structure and pronunciation and uses infantile form. Can have quite complex conversations, especially about past events. Asks many questions using why, when and how. Still enjoys and repeats songs and rhymes. Enjoys jokes and nonsense talk. Confuses fact and fantasy in stories. At 4 years, gives own name, age and address.
4–5 years	Speech usually correct and becoming more sophisticated. Asks meanings of abstract words and uses them and other interesting words but not always correctly. Understands and then uses adverbs and prepositions. Talks freely and uses imagination. Answers questions in detail and can elaborate.

Figure 1.5
Child drawing with
large crayons.

Symbolic representation

Although language itself is a form of symbolic representation, there are many other ways in which children make one thing stand for another. Children also communicate symbolically through dramatic play, music and movement and construction, and adults have an important role in encouraging this.

The development of children's drawing follows broadly the same universal sequence from scribble to line to drawing, and is an important indicator of the child's internal world, a kind of 'visible thinking'. Drawing can also help a child to express feelings and happenings that are too difficult to put into words.

It is likely that a child will be able to scribble from 1 year onwards and reach the 'realism' stage of clearly representing what is seen at about the time they are in the first years of formal school. Only at the latter stages of this sequence can we be certain that children have a clear internal picture of a person in relatively correct proportion. This also indicates a developing sense of self and an ability to observe the world. The stages are as follows:

1. *Scribble stage.* At first the child will hold a crayon or pencil and move it backwards and forwards. These will develop into multiple and circular scribbles where, as well as backwards and forwards, the crayon is lifted from the paper and moved in different directions.

Figure 1.6
Scribble stage.

2. *Schematic stage.* Marks inside circle and circle crossed with lines. Sun designs.

Figure 1.7
Schematic stage.
Marks are made
inside a circle and
sun designs.

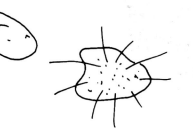

3. *First representation.* This is usually a face.

Figure 1.8
First representation.
'My Mum and me,'
drawn by Kelly, aged
4 years.

4. *Heads and bodies.*

Figure 1.9
Heads and bodies,
drawn by Daniel,
aged 5 years.

5. *Realism stage.*

Figure 1.10
Realism stage.
'My flats,' drawn by
Liam, aged 5 years.

Social and emotional development

The basis of healthy social and emotional development is a positive self-image and good self-esteem. For these to develop satisfactorily children need a basis of love, encouragement and acceptance through which to face the outside world and to make positive and fulfilling relationships. How well a child relates to others depends to some extent on the development of trust that comes through having early basic needs for food and comfort met in an atmosphere of unconditional love and care. This is the kind of loving acceptance which does not depend, for example, on a child's appearance or behaviour, and where carers value individual children for what they are. This is particularly important during the first years of life, as the quality of a child's first relationships will affect all subsequent relationships. Although these needs are often met within the traditional nuclear or extended family, these are not the only effective structures that can provide emotional and physical security for our children. Today there are a whole range of different relationships and family structures within which children thrive. It is clear, however, that children do best in a small family-type group rather than a large institution where close and intimate bonds cannot be formed. This is discussed further in the section on attachment (p. 28).

Stages of social and emotional development

Age	Key features
1–3 months	Babies respond to human contact, particularly that of primary carer through smiling, quietening and body responses. Gazes at human faces.
3–6 months	Responses are more sustained. Preference for the primary carer is growing. Smiles at most people. Vocalizes and enjoys turn-taking communication.
6–9 months	Fear of strangers appears, and distress at separation from primary carer or carers. Interacts in different ways with family members.
9–12 months	Fear of strangers appears to increase although this depends on the setting, e.g. whether known carers are present. Will use a 'comfort object' such as a piece of blanket, familiar toy or dummy, or thumb to suck. Capable of different emotions, e.g. rage. Seeks attention.
12–15 months	Emotionally unstable and needing reassurance. More demanding, assertive and independent. Temper tantrums may start. Early toilet training may set up anxiety.
15–18 months	Resists changes in known routines. Can be defiant. Does not see others as individuals. Still careful with strangers but showing some interest also. Beginning to distinguish 'you' and 'me'.
18–24 months	Increasing independence brings with it strong emotional feelings. Anger and frustration lead to more tantrums. The increase in language and symbolic thought allows some feelings to be expressed through imaginative play. Does not like to be told 'no' and will express rage at being thwarted. Shows pleasure in own possessions. Can distinguish between self and others but remains self-centred. Follows carers around and is more social.
2–3 years	Becoming more stable, equable and confident but still mood swings from positive to negative and will vary between being dependent and clinging, to being rebellious and unco-operative. Can experience sibling rivalry. Needs support and reassurance in transition to nursery but is learning to separate from carers. Has sense of own identity, knows name, place in family, gender. Has irrational fears.
3–5 years	More stable and emotionally secure. Enjoys helping at home or in the nursery and enjoys adult approval although sometimes

difficult and cheeky. Can be friendly and caring to younger children and animals with occasional aggressive lapses. Although much more independent, the child still needs adult support to cope with difficult situations. Well-developed imaginative play helps to cope with strong feelings. Still fears loss of parents or carers.

5–7 years Becoming increasingly confident and independent. More aware of right and wrong and will feel guilty if behaving in unacceptable fashion. Often argumentative and dogmatic.

Emotional development

Promoting emotional development

The adult can support the child's healthy emotional development as follows:

- Assisting the child to develop independence and trust and confidence in others through encouraging firm attachments or emotional bonds with a small number of adults who give consistent care.
- Promoting the development of the child's self-confidence and self-esteem through giving praise, encouragement and positive messages.
- Caring for and supporting the young child as the child struggles to establish control of powerful feelings and gain overall emotional balance.

Attachment theory

Introduction
Babies are vulnerable, and their development is dependent on receiving adequate love and care. Research has indicated that forming close emotional bonds with adults who remain consistent in the child's life forms the basis of healthy emotional development. In the first years of life a baby will form an enduring emotional attachment or bond with those who give love and care.

The work of John Bowlby
The work of Bowlby (1975, 1979) has been influential; his main hypothesis is that babies will do best if they receive consistent care from one adult carer, usually the mother. If the child receives care outside the home from other adults, then, suggests Bowlby, the child suffers maternal deprivation, and this will ultimately harm the child's emotional development and may lead to higher levels of delinquency in later

life. This work seemed to be supported by work such as that of the Robertsons (1969). In this piece of work, the child's reaction to separation from his mother was starkly recorded in a very moving way, but of course this does not demonstrate that good bonds cannot be made with other important adults. The work of Bowlby and the stages of loss and grief are discussed further in Chapter 6.

Modern views of attachment theory

Modern practice is based on the conclusion that babies will make attachments to a small number of adults but there is a definite hierarchy to these bonds some of which will be closer than others. The processes of feeding, bathing and cuddling, and the responsiveness of the carers to the developing child give opportunity for this bond to become strong. Babies are able to thrive and develop even when cared for by several adults,

Figure 1.11
Attachment.

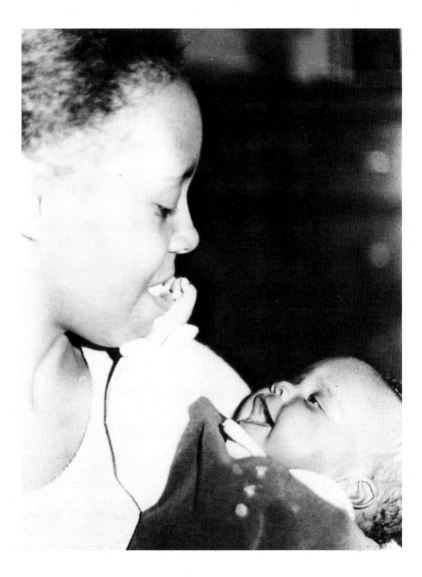

but this care must be stable, of high quality and consistent in order to promote emotional health and good overall development (Hennessy *et al.*, 1992). However, there does not need to be a biological link in order to make effective attachments. It is important that attachments are encouraged with other family members, close friends and other carers. This will make it possible for mothers to leave their babies knowing that they will experience minimal distress. If, as indicated, a baby can make several attachments, then there is much less pressure upon mothers to stay at home. There is an obvious political and ideological point to make here: if mothers do not harm their children by going out to work, and they wish to return to employment, then there should be adequate, high quality child care provision to facilitate this. Work such as Bowlby's has given us tremendous insights into the needs of babies and young children for consistent care, but has also been used to justify keeping mothers in the home and reducing state child care provision.

Not all cultures make provision for babies and toddlers from this point of view. Rouse and Griffin in Pugh (1992) describe how Japanese child development experts, in a discussion on spoiling children, describe the attachment-like behaviour of mothers as 'narcissistic, over involved investment in children'. They report that in China group day care is viewed as beneficial because children can get away from the dangers of spoiling in a single child family and that in Italy stress is laid on the environment, the peer group and the team of educators rather than an individual key worker. Rouse and Griffin state that they would welcome more research into these alternative philosophies but they also say:

> Educators are required to make a commitment of attachment to children they nurture, to be open to intimacy, not only with the children but with other members of families ... people selected to be educators should therefore be adults capable of attachments to children without clinging suffocating closeness. They must not be compensating for their own unresolved early experiences of separation and instability.

To encourage the formation of healthy attachments adults need to respond promptly and appropriately to the baby's signals. As well as giving physical care to meet basic needs, babies respond to sensory contact and develop socially through turn-taking communication between themselves and their carers.

From the earliest weeks of life, a baby can recognize its primary carers, usually the parents, and begins to respond positively to their voices and presence. Where there are problems in establishing emotional bonds with primary carers for whatever reasons, it is likely that the baby may not be so emotionally secure and well settled. However, babies are all different: some are able to tolerate delay and frustration better than others, and it is a mistake to assume that all babies who seem fretful and difficult have not received sensitive care and handling. Ainsworth *et al.* (1971) devised 'the strange situation' test, a technique for assessing the quality of attachment, by looking at responses at the time of reunion. Although this test has limitations, it is still widely used and can help with the assessment of babies' attachments.

Separation anxiety

During the first few months of life a baby will smile and make eye contact, attempt to reach out and to babble in response to people around. Although the process of bonding is gradual, by around 8 months most babies will be firmly attached to their primary carers. They will become increasingly distressed at separation and will demonstrate fear of strange adults, although they are less likely to demonstrate fear of unknown children at this stage. This is known as 'separation anxiety'. Research in Uganda found that, on average, babies from the Ganda tribe were showing separation anxiety by 5 to 6 months. This was attributed to the fact that these babies spent far more time in close contact with their mothers: the babies slept with their mothers, were carried in a sling and rarely separated even for short periods.

At around 2 years of age, fears of separation and strange adults tend to diminish, although this depends on the individual child and circumstances. Children who have had a secure base and firm attachments are generally confident and willing to explore the world around as well as being able to give and receive affection. However, they still experience temporary shyness and difficulties with separation. When starting playgroup or nursery it is often the well-attached child who displays initial clinging behaviour before settling in well and taking full advantage of the opportunities offered. At the age of 3 to 5 years, these children become more independent and begin to make attachments to other children and adults who spend time with them. However, the initial primary attachments, usually with parents, remain very important, and when these are secure and positive, the child is likely to develop a good self-image.

Comfort objects

Babies become attached to favourite comfort objects such as soft toys or blankets. They can sometimes be seen staggering along with a large blanket in one hand whilst sucking the thumb of the other. These are usually abandoned when the child has no further use for them and it is generally better to allow this to happen naturally. Winnicott (1974) described these as transitional objects. He believed children needed transitional objects to help them through the realization that they were a separate person. The transitional object represented the mother or carer when they were not there and gave comfort to the child. Transitional objects are a source of comfort to the young child when separated from its mother or carer and can help the settling-in process. Settings should try to accommodate the child's need for its comfort object.

Babies prefer human faces

Research has shown that babies have an inbuilt preference for relationships with human beings rather than objects (Fantz 1961, and see below). It has been found that babies prefer round shapes and especially the human face. Other experiments have been carried out to test babies' reactions to speech as opposed to other sounds, and also to test if very young babies prefer their mother's voice or smell to that of others. Most babies preferred human contact and particularly their mother's presence. This indicated that the process of attachment or expressing preference for primary carers does start within the first weeks of life.

Figure 1.12
Infants' viewing
preferences for
faces.

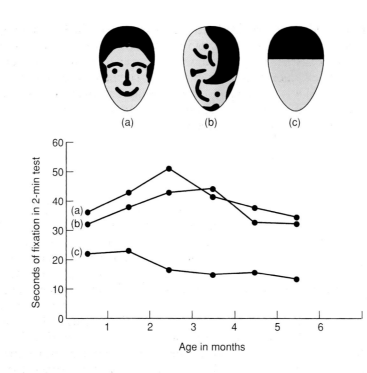

Poor attachments

There are many reasons why parents/carers may have poor attachments to their children. The source of this can sometimes be traced to separation soon after birth, or if the baby is unplanned and unwanted. Some babies are harder to love than others: they may cry a lot or seem to give little back to their parents who may themselves have unrealistic expectations. Research into babies with handicaps shows that it is sometimes difficult for parents to bond with apparently unresponsive or unlovely babies, although most do so satisfactorily. Social conditions and stress can sometimes play a part. Some parents simply have too many personal difficulties, may be mentally ill or may themselves have received poor parenting. It is important to note that most parents do bond with their children and care for them lovingly, despite difficulties. The quality of bonding is variable, and all workers with young children and their families should note where attachments seem weak and undeveloped.

Babies who are not developing firm attachments will feel insecure and appear fretful and difficult. In extreme cases, where very little love and contact are made, they will become emotionally 'starved' and exhibit bizarre behaviour such as head-banging or repetitive movements. Babies in large institutions with minimal attention will lie for hours doing these things or just gazing into space hopelessly, sometimes whimpering but not bothering or having the energy to cry, having already learned that their needs will not be met. Sometimes parents or carers cannot discriminate between signs of hunger, fatigue and other distress, and the baby may be left in a distressed state for some time. As the child gets older, it is less confident and may not leave its mother's side to explore and experiment or show any emotion if she leaves the room. As a result, these children are less likely to take advantage of the learning opportunities in their environment, their all-round development may be held back and they will be less likely to make trusting relationships. In extreme cases, children may exhibit 'indiscriminate affection' where they make superficial contact with whoever is available and show no fear of strangers. It does seem that, to some extent, early deprivation can be overcome when children do receive consistent loving care, but it is difficult to assess the long-term effects.

Self-esteem

For many children, the development of a positive self-image is difficult, but if they do start life with a good degree of confidence and self-esteem, they will be better able to cope with what lies ahead. Development of this good self-image depends on a child receiving positive messages about its own worth and loving acceptance when mistakes are made. If a child receives negative feedback such as important adults continually criticizing behaviour or is called clumsy, stupid or skinny, it is likely that the child will believe itself to be less than worthwhile. Often children with the poorest self-image are those who have been abused or neglected. Also, whilst many children receive positive images regarding themselves from their own family, there are situations which occur where this may become damaged. Children who receive negative images regarding their skin colour, language, cultural background, social class, gender, disability, or physical characteristics will develop poor self-esteem, and measures have to be taken to minimize the damage. Children also learn through identification with positive role models, and it is important both that significant adults in their environment are able to provide these and that they are available in books or through contact with visitors to the nursery; e.g. if girls can see older girls or women achieving success in a leadership role, they are more likely to feel that they too can be leaders.

Signs of poor self-esteem can be:

- *Lack of confidence*
- *Clinging behaviour*
- *Not willing to take risks and rise to challenges*
- *Aggression, attention-seeking or withdrawal*
- *Self-destruction behaviour*
- *Self-denigration.*

Poor self-esteem leads to a child not realizing its potential for learning, development or self-fulfilment. It is vital that those who work with young children and their families recognize the importance of their role in helping to build self-esteem. This is not always easy, as workers themselves often have to struggle with these issues in their own lives.

To encourage self-esteem:

- Children should be valued for who they are, not what they look like or can do. It is important to praise and encourage children and not to criticize in a destructive manner.

- Discriminatory attitudes and behaviour should be challenged. Discussions and activities regarding gender, race, disability and family grouping should be planned and everyday opportunities taken to strengthen anti-discrimination.
- Materials, activities and resources should reflect positive images of all children regardless of ethnic origin, gender or disability.
- Strategies for raising parents' self-esteem should be planned such as encouragement in decision-making, inclusion in activities and valuing their contributions.
- Children should be offered choices in their daily lives and opportunities to feel in control of their environment, within the limits of safety and consideration for others.
- Self-help skills should be encouraged as should personal independence.
- Children should be encouraged to play and be helped by professionals such as psychologists if they are unable to play because of serious damage to their self-esteem.
- Children should be given an opportunity to succeed in what they are setting out to do, and unrealistic expectations should be avoided.
- Children should be encouraged to express, discuss and control their feelings. Opportunities should be taken in everyday situations such as when an aggressive incident occurs. Adults can ask probing questions in conversational style: 'How did that make you feel?'; 'Why do you think you hit him/her?'
- Behavioural boundaries should be set and consistently applied so that children are not confused and uncertain regarding what is expected of them.
- Children should be encouraged to communicate their feelings appropriately through language and positive activity. Adults may need to model the appropriate vocabulary.
- The environment should be carefully organized to allow children maximum autonomy and independence. This means they are encouraged to make choices for themselves and do not have to depend on adults to get things for them; e.g. if they wish to play outside, they do not have to ask for adults' permission but find the boots and coats for themselves and only ask for help if really needed.
- Children should receive consistent care, preferably using a key worker system (where a very small number of named adults are responsible for the total care of the child). This enables attachments to be made.
- Children's basic needs for food, rest, shelter, love, care and stimulation should be met.
- Children and families should be shown respect in order to develop self-respect.

- Planned activities and experiences reflecting the points above and designed to encourage self-esteem should form a part of the curriculum and daily routines for young children.

Powerful feelings

There are aspects of children's lives which do provoke powerful feelings in them, e.g. major transitions such as weaning, toilet training, arrival of siblings or separations such as illness or starting school. Helping children to cope with these events and to develop in a stable and positive manner requires adults to provide a safe base of love and acceptance from which children can feel secure. From this position of safety it is easier for a child to cope when feeling out of control. The behaviour resulting from feelings such as anger, temper tantrums and jealousy is covered in Chapter 9. It is important that adults do not have different expectations regarding expression of feelings according to gender or other stereotypes, e.g. girls may cry but boys may not. All children should be encouraged to express their strong feelings in appropriate ways.

Ways of helping children to cope with powerful feelings

It is important to give the child appropriate language to express feelings and a range of appropriate equipment, materials and activities to facilitate imaginative play. As adults support this type of play, it allows children to experience powerful and potentially destructive feelings in a safe environment, e.g. the child who is feeling jealous of a new baby will often express negative feelings towards a doll or soft toy. This can give adults an insight into those feelings and an opportunity to support the child and channel the aggression. Channelling aggression can take many forms. For some children, vigorous outdoor play will help, while others find pummelling clay or dough offers a release. Certain toys such as a hammer and pegs also give the child a chance to express anger or frustration.

Fears and anxieties

Children often experience a range of fears and can easily become anxious. Babies and toddlers can be frightened of strangers and of losing their primary carer. They can also show fear of loud noises, high places, sudden movements, strange places or animals. Young children's fears are very real and must be taken seriously. It is easy to laugh at a child's fear of disappearing down the bath drain along with the bath water, but it is kinder and more sensible to recognize the fear and devise strategies for overcoming it. Many children are frightened of the dark and it is important that they are given night lights and not ridiculed or terrorized.

Childhood fears are often irrational and adults must be patient and sensitive in handling them. It is usually better to face the fears and discuss them appropriately with the child. If children feel defenceless, they may be overwhelmed by feelings of hopelessness, and adults must endeavour to give them the inner resources to cope.

Imaginative play can offer the child an opportunity to 'play out' fears; e.g. if the child has had painful experiences at the doctor's surgery or in hospital, the setting-up of a hospital corner with appropriate resources gives the child a chance to explore feelings; here the child can pretend to be the powerful adult and to give the painful treatment. This kind of role play helps to express fears and to control them.

Magical thinking

Children under school age can mix fact and fantasy very easily and many engage in 'magical' thought in which they feel that they can alter reality by their thoughts and wishes; e.g. children who are jealous of one parent may feel it is their fault if the parents separate. Their thoughts and feelings are very real to them and 'magical' thinking can leave them feeling guilty, frightened and insecure. As well as this, a child can believe itself to be a person or thing, and can act with conviction and authority within that role. It has been known for children taking on a 'super-hero' role to believe themselves capable of jumping from windows without hurting themselves. Where children have real and persistent difficulties sorting out reality from fantasy they may need specialist help.

Imaginary friends

Sometimes children will invent an imaginary friend who expresses all the unpleasant and guilty feelings that the child cannot, or who is simply a companion to them. This is a perfectly normal happening which children eventually outgrow. There is concern, however, when a child is unable to distinguish fact from fantasy in an extreme manner and, again, adults need to be sensitive and able to assess when this is happening.

Emotional stress

Children who are experiencing pressure in their lives which leads to emotional stress will react in various ways. They can become withdrawn and introverted or conversely very noisy, aggressive and attention-seeking. Children under stress often regress and exhibit babyish behaviour. If they are clean and dry, they may start soiling or bed-wetting. They may refuse to eat or demand a bottle. Excessive thumb sucking, masturbation or other comfort habits may also occur (see Ch. 9). Adults need to be sensitive to the child's needs, note sudden or gradual changes and be able to assess when these occurrences are temporary during a difficult period for the child or whether they are symptoms of a more serious, underlying problem. Either way children need help, and action should be taken involving parents and professionals as necessary. This will involve investigating the cause of the distress rather than concentrating on the symptoms.

Social development

Closely linked to emotional development and the making of attachments is the young child's social development. As good attachments are made, so the baby begins to interact with the world around in a social manner, through reaching, smiling and babbling. Social development covers:

- *Socialization*
- *Cultural development*
- *Relating to others*
- *Developing social skills.*

Socialization

Every society has its own code of acceptable behaviour based on its values and beliefs. Within that society there will be variations that usually stem from religious, cultural or environmental factors and family beliefs concerning what is appropriate and acceptable. According to the Oxford Dictionary, culture refers to the customs and traditions of a particular group. Children's development takes place within a particular culture and early learning occurs in that cultural framework. Children's attitudes, values and behaviour are greatly influenced by the culture of their family group as well as other aspects of their environment. Culture is a dynamic concept always changing and developing and is passed on from one generation to the next through the process of socialization.

It is important when caring for and educating young children to recognize and value their cultural background and inheritance. Workers in the early years field should understand that their own culture may be different from that of the children in their care and this can sometimes cause difficulties; e.g. during religious festivals such as Christmas some families may not wish their child to participate. These wishes should be accommodated sensitively and settings should not assume that all children will join in.

Every child has to learn what the code of acceptable behaviour is and to base its behaviour and attitudes on the example of significant adults in the world around. As well as this children must learn their own role within this bewildering set of expectations. This process is called socialization. It is considered essential that children are socialized into the values and behaviour of their society in order to maintain stability and order. Where this can be seen to be beneficial to all members of that society and is based on mutual respect and consideration this is acceptable to most people. However, it is also the case that children can be socialized into accepting values that might be seen to be against human rights. There is widespread discrimination on the basis of skin colour or gender in many societies and this is perpetuated through the attitudes and values transmitted through socialization.

Socialization is an enormous piece of learning for the child, and although it is difficult to divide up, the following are useful ways of viewing the process:

- Learning to behave in socially-approved ways. This involves the child knowing what is approved and modelling their behaviour on these lines.
- Playing approved social roles, including gender roles. This involves children learning what their role is and how it is customary to behave, e.g. being a daughter, pupil, brother, friend.
- Developing appropriate social attitudes. This is helped if children like and trust people and enjoy joining in with groups.

Agencies of socialization

There are many socializing influences on young children, but most can be grouped in the following broad categories:

- *Families*, whose influence remains throughout childhood and often into adulthood.
- *Schools* or other forms of day care and education become more important as the child grows older and relates to other significant adults.
- *Friends* and friendship groups become increasingly important influences throughout childhood and adolescence.
- The *media* become increasingly influential as the child grows up. Children watch a good deal of television and some spend long periods of time playing computer games; this can be seen reflected in their play.

Social learning

There are many different points of view concerning how children become socialized. One influential view is held by social learning theorists, who feel that children learn who they are and what is expected of them through observing others and their experience of the way adults interact with them. They respond to important adults in their lives by modelling their behaviour upon those adults. It is pointless telling a child what to do and expecting the child to behave appropriately if the adult concerned consistently does something different for the child is much more likely to copy the adult's behaviour than listen to the adult's words. Attitudes may also be learned, such as when a child is told to love and care for granny, but picks up the tension and upset in the family if granny is coming to visit. This learning, whether good or bad, will be stronger if it is positively reinforced, e.g. when a child is aggressive to another boy and the carer rewards this aggression by comments such as, 'Good boy, you really showed him what a wimp he is.'

Bandura (1973), a social psychologist, tested children to see how they modelled themselves on adults. Three groups of young children watched a short film with three different endings. Each group saw an adult attacking a 'bobo' doll. The adult would hit and punch the doll, sit on it, and kick it whilst shouting aggressively. The different endings were seen by different children: the first group saw the adult being rewarded for his aggression; the second group saw the adult punished; and the third or control group saw no reward or punishment given to the adult. After watching this the children were given the opportunity to play with a bobo doll and their behaviour recorded. Those who had seen the aggressive adult being rewarded and the control group were equally aggressive to the doll. Children in the group who had seen the adult punished were significantly less aggressive. Bandura concluded that through watching the films children had learned new ways of being aggressive and had become more so.

It is difficult to be certain how far Bandura's finding would be true in a less artificial situation and there are many criticisms of this type of experiment, but there are lessons to be learned from it. Bandura suggested that for children really to learn from models they will need to be seen as powerful, competent and similar to the child and have a good nurturing relationship with the child.

Attachment to adults

Most research shows that early socialization takes place through attachments to parents/carers. Good attachments lead to effective socialization as children soon learn what pleases their carers and in general try to behave positively. If attachments are poor there is less incentive for children to try to please, as their efforts are often ignored or misunderstood. Where children experience many separations from their carer, this can lead to poor attachments and problems in socialization. If children cannot interpret their carer's expectations, either because they are unable to respond because of learning difficulties or as a result of sensory impairment, then there may also be difficulties in socialization.

Attitudes and prejudice

Attitudes and prejudice are formed early in the process of socialization, as are stereotypes of black[1] people, women and other groups. All workers with young children must avoid stereotypical assumptions, which, in the case of black children, for example, are often negative and lead to poor expectations of those children. Research by Rosenthal and Jacobsen (1968) and others has shown that where expectations are low, children often perform badly (the self-fulfilling prophecy).

Gender roles

Children usually know what gender they are between the ages of 2 and 3 years, although they may not be certain if their gender is permanent. During the whole of the pre-school period they are learning through the various agencies of socialization what it means to be masculine or feminine and are beginning to associate each with

[1]   The term black will be used in this chapter and in Chapter 8 as a shorthand for describing those people who are seen by white society as being black in colour and who are discriminated against on the grounds of colour even though not all of these people would describe themselves as black. This term will predominantly cover those people of Afro-Caribbean, African and Asian origins.

various characteristics and valuing each differently. Girls are often taught through socialization that it is better to be pretty and passive, and wrong to be noisy, dirty or inquisitive. Some theorists think these differences are due to biological reasons but much research disproves this. Work has been done which shows that carers react very differently towards boys and girls. Boy babies are given more attention and they learn to demand more; they are also played with in ways that are likely to encourage assertiveness and independence.

Gender stereotyping prevents boys and girls developing as whole people and restricts their choices, e.g. girls may not feel free to tackle woodwork or are intimidated by the boys when they try to use outdoor equipment. Boys may be teased when they show interest in music or dancing. Stereotypes of masculinity and femininity are reinforced through the media and often encouraged by peer pressure. Schools and other institutions are beginning to be aware of the damage that is done through gender stereotyping and some are taking measures to counteract it. Girls are being encouraged to be more assertive and adventurous and to tackle traditional male subjects such as technology and engineering and boys are being encouraged to become more caring and reflective. Gender stereotypes are thought to be implicated in boys' current underachievement in schools although they are not the only reason. There is still a long way to go in supporting both boys and girls to be able to make choices which do not reflect gender stereotypes.

Figure 1.13
Boys bathing 'babies'.

Children and race
Research (Milner, 1983) shows that by the age of 2 years children notice differences in skin colour, and between 3 and 5 years they attach a value to that colour. Through the media, family, their peer group and the world around them they receive messages, both non-verbal and verbal, that children with white skin are more beautiful and valuable than those with dark skin. Many workers have experience of very young children trying to scrub their skin white. Workers can do much to aid developing aware-

ness of race by reinforcing positive messages concerning black skin using whatever resources are available. Confronting racism amongst and against children and acting as a positive role model are very important.

Relating to others

The basis of healthy social development is the establishment of trust which occurs as the babies' needs are met in the earliest months of life. Babies begin to associate interaction with adults as both pleasurable and as a means of removing their frustration, whether caused through hunger, discomfort or feeling alone.

Part of social development is the baby's response to its primary carer, usually the mother. Research has shown that babies under 6 months will explore and play with toys but their reactions to their mothers are quite different. With her, babies hold what could best be termed a 'conversation' which involves encouraging communication by means of making responsive sounds and elaborate body movements. This communication was not linked primarily with the satisfaction of needs but seems to be a mutually enjoyable activity performed just for the pleasure of it and it is known as 'interactional synchrony'. Social interaction is important because it is part of how children discover who they are and what they can do.

Babies begin to show some interest in other infants as young as 6 months of age. They will smile at each other and explore the other's face and body much as they would an object or plaything. As they become older they become more interested in making social contacts with other children, but how soon real social interactions take place depends on the amount of time they spend with other children and their early experiences and individual personality.

The following table indicates the sequence of social development in play between birth and 7 years. All children are likely to go through these stages but some will take much longer than others and will require greater adult support. The age at which children reach each stage can vary widely depending on individual children and their experiences. Each stage is not clear-cut and, for example, children capable of co-operative play may still prefer to play alongside others (parallel) or alone.

Social participation in play 0–7 years	Approximate age
Solitary play (child plays alone)	0–2 years
Spectator play (child watches play of those around)	2–2$\frac{1}{2}$ years
Parallel play (child plays alongside others not with them)	2$\frac{1}{2}$–3 years
Associative play (a child is beginning to interact with others)	3–4 years
Co-operative play (children playing together co-operatively with shared goals)	Possible from 4 years on

During the pre-school years play will become more socially-oriented and children will begin to demonstrate more pro-social behaviour. At the age of 2 to 3 years, when they are entering nursery or playgroups, children's social development depends on the home and environment. If, for example, they live in high-rise flats, with little opportunity to play with other children or meet other adults, they are likely to take some time to settle in at nursery and will need to be given space before they are ready to play with other children or even begin to understand how to share. It is a mistake to expect children of this age to find it easy to share toys and playthings and the demand to share often leads to conflict and tension. It is much better to avoid confrontation with a child by introducing distractions. Many children of 3 or younger do seem able to show caring behaviour towards other children showing distress even though they are not ready to play with them. However, young children under 2 to 3 years tend to see the world only through their own needs and views; e.g. a 2-year-old observing another's distress might offer a favourite toy, assuming that what would comfort them would also comfort others.

Most children will be developing greater social awareness between 3 and 4 years of age. They will enjoy imaginative play in small groups or in twos and can be heard talking to one another and developing their play in a more co-operative manner. These relationships tend to be fleeting but children do express a preference for certain friends and play regularly with them. At this stage there is usually, but not always, some preference for play with children of the same sex, but there is still a good deal of mixed play.

By the time children are established at primary school they should have well-developed friendships which can be remarkably enduring. These will be characterized by an ability to develop complex co-operative play and supportive attitudes towards one another. By the time children are 7, and often well before this age, they play almost exclusively in separate boy/girl groups.

Difficulties in relating to others

Children whose language development is delayed, have sensory impairment or who are difficult to understand will sometimes find social relationships problematic, as may those who do not speak the language of the setting. Children in this situation may retreat into themselves and become isolated or conversely become aggressive and attention-seeking. Such problems require prompt help from staff, parents and professionals.

Some children are much more socially popular than others. Often these children are friendly, supportive and outgoing, physically larger, taller and more attractive than their peers. They may also be more successful at school and good at specific tasks or games. Youngest children in families also seem to be more popular. Conversely, children who are physically unattractive or emotionally immature, less friendly, more aggressive and critical are those who will be less popular and even isolated from friendship groups. Children of this age and younger already place a value on skin colour and ethnic or gender group, and children may be more or less popular, valued and likely to take risks or to become leaders as a result of these early attitudes and prejudices.

Figure 1.14
Children playing
together.

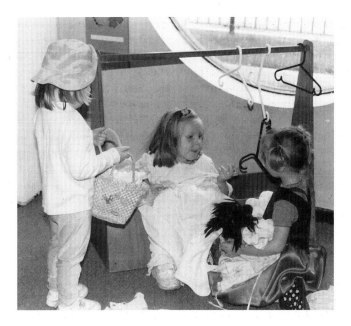

Where children are having difficulty relating to others it is important that correct assessment and monitoring take place. If the difficulties are superficial and reflect immaturity or lack of experience, they are often easily rectified. If they indicate a more serious underlying cause, this will have to be identified and appropriate help sought. Children will often reflect in their social behaviour problems in the family and it is important that parents feel free to discuss these issues.

Developing social skills

Social skills are those aspects of learning, behaviour and development which help children to be accepted into the wider world. In some instances it is accepted that these will depend on personal values, e.g. what constitutes 'good manners' will vary from culture to culture. Universally accepted social norms such as consideration for others are important. These involve learning to share and take turns, being positive in play and relationships, and developing basic skills such as dressing and undressing, using appropriate language, keeping clean, using the toilet, and acceptable mealtime behaviour. If children cannot cope, they often become unpopular and ridiculed by other children. Helping children to develop social skills which allow them to become independent and accepted by their peers and adults is a vital aspect of care and education which, if ignored, causes children's self-esteem to suffer. This is particularly difficult if parents are careless or unaware concerning their children's hygiene or appearance and have not prepared them to mix with others. In these cases, particularly, it is important to involve parents in the work with the children.

It is essential to recognize the social and cultural differences amongst families, and workers need to show sensitivity in handling such situations; e.g. some children may be used to eating with their fingers at home as this is their cultural norm. Workers should not assume that this indicates children who have not learned to use cutlery which is the 'correct' way to do things, but should devise strategies along with parents to ensure that other children do not ridicule this behaviour. At the same time, it will be helpful for the child to learn to use cutlery, but not with an assumption that this is the only acceptable way of eating.

Children who have problems, for whatever reason, need to be given adequate support and guidance as to what is acceptable behaviour. Providing good role models of behaviour is far better than criticizing children and holding unrealistic expectations. Adults working and playing alongside children help them to understand by example what is acceptable social behaviour. Children should be encouraged and their achievements praised without concentrating on the negative. A consistent routine enables children to develop basic skills in self-care. Collaborative approaches that involve children working together also provide good learning opportunities.

Moral development

This is the development of conscience and ideas of right and wrong. There are different views as to how this occurs according to the particular school of psychology involved. Views on how children learn to be considerate, thoughtful and socially aware will determine how workers deal with issues of discipline and punishment as well as how day-to-day situations are handled; e.g. Bandura and the social learning theorists consider moral development to be linked to what children learn through observation and modelling, whereas Piaget felt that pre-school children judge things superficially without reference to motive and are not able to separate right from wrong in a adult way. It seems much worse to them accidentally to break ten plates when being helpful, than deliberately to break one plate when being naughty. Children of this age believe that rules are fixed and unchangeable and that the number of plates broken determines the level of punishment meted out. Piaget thought that as children mature, usually from 7 to 8 years of age, they learn that rules can be broken and that punishment is not inevitable. This leads eventually to a mature understanding of moral concepts and the development of conscience.

Kohlberg (1969) built on Piaget's views and went further in defining six stages of moral development. The highest of these stages was that of 'post-conventional morality'. This involves awareness of high moral principle; not everyone reaches this stage. Kohlberg's theory has proved controversial and led to other ways of looking at moral development; e.g. Gilligan (1982) takes a feminist perspective that challenges some of the more orthodox approaches. Other theorists believe that Kohlberg's descriptions relate to the values of western society and are not innate stages of development as he claimed.

Criticism of Piaget's views is similar to that of his description of cognitive development: namely that he underestimates the child's capacity to think logically, and in this case to understand motive and to think morally.

Discipline and boundary-setting

Young children need a firm structure of rules and boundaries as they develop their own 'internal' sense of right and wrong. After the age of 7 the child is increasingly likely to have a more adult way of making moral decisions. As children grow up, it is important for them to develop their own internal sense of right and wrong which grows out of their relationships and experiences. Sometimes children are given different sets of expectations at different times, and those who care for them are inconsistent in setting boundaries for behaviour; this leads to confusion for the child who simply does not know how to respond. Extreme punishment will lead to a child being insecure, fearful, and lacking trust. It does not lead to a well-adjusted and socially competent child. These issues are further discussed in Chapter 9.

Observations, assessments and record keeping

This section covers:

- *Record keeping*
- *The rights of children and families concerning observation and assessment*
- *Issues to think through before undertaking an observation*
- *The reasons for the observation and assessment*
- *Validity and reliability*
- *Styles of observation*
- *Pointers towards good observation technique*
- *Methods of observation*
- *Objectivity*
- *The language of observation*
- *Recording the observation*
- *Assessment.*

Introduction

This section provides some basic information concerning record keeping and the skills of observation and assessment, but it is recommended that further research and reading takes place.

Record keeping

Different types of records are kept in early years settings. These will vary in content, style and format according to the needs of the setting, parents' needs and the requirements of external agencies such as courts, doctors or schools. Detailed records are necessary for registration under the Children Act 1989 and for Office for Standards in Education (OFSTED) inspections as well as being good practice. Generally each child has its own records which are a developmental record of early childhood that can be passed on to the parents, school or other agency as required. Records are confidential material which should be treated carefully and only shared with others on a 'need to know' basis. Records should be clear and non-judgemental. Most parents are anxious to know how their children are progressing and will be happy to share in record keeping and updating.

Records contain various items of information. These may include observations and assessments, diaries, examples of the child's work, test results, parental contributions, notes, and medical and background information. Children may wish to add to their own portfolio as they get older.

There is no right or wrong way of keeping records. Some settings will have computerized records but many will use paper-based systems. Some settings use daily diaries for individual children whilst others will record information less frequently. Many settings will have different record systems for different types of information.

Good practice indicates that records should as a minimum contain the following information about each child:

- Full name, address and date of birth
- Gender
- If parents/carers agree, information on siblings, family structure, health status, disability, language, religion, ethnic origin, culture
- Names, addresses, work and home phone numbers of parents and carers (this could include photographs)
- Emergency contacts and information on those authorized to collect the child
- Address and phone number of general practitioner and health visitor (social worker where appropriate)
- Consent forms for outings and administration of medicines
- Any individual contractual arrangements.

Records should:

- *Be up to date and comprehensive*
- *Be available to staff on a 'need to know' basis*
- *Be consistent in format, clear and easily understood*
- *Be based on accurate, valid and reliable information*
- *Be available for parents*
- *Contain relevant information that parents and/or other agencies wish to have*

- *Contain samples of children's work such as paintings and examples of mark-making*
- *Contain relevant information on the growth, health and development of the whole child*
- *Cover significant achievements and milestones.*

Records may be used in a variety of situations ranging from routine assessments to circumstances where children's futures are being discussed and decided, e.g. in court cases or in case conferences. It is important to ensure that your records are accurate and comprehensive and are dated and signed.

Observations

The rights of children and families

All child observations and assessments used within the setting should be confidential and stored in a safe place. Where observations are undertaken by candidates on placement they should not identify the child or use the family name and false names are not appropriate. Candidates should use identifiers such as letters or numbers, e.g. child x.

Parents and children have rights and these should be considered when observations and assessments are planned. Parents and children or those who have parental responsibility should know when observations are planned and in most cases their permission to observe and record should be sought. When observing and assessing children, remember that parents and children themselves can give valuable information.

Issues to think through before undertaking an observation

You need to be able to use a range of methods of observing and assessing children based on the needs of a particular situation. This means that before you start you should know:

- *The reason for the observation*
- *The most appropriate type and method to use in the particular circumstances*
- *The limitations of type and method used, i.e. its validity and reliability*
- *The most appropriate way of recording the observation*
- *How to avoid bias and be as objective as possible*
- *The rights of children and parents concerning observation and assessment*
- *How to use the information gained about the child or children to make the assessment*
- *How to confirm your assessment, e.g. through further observations, using information from other sources.*

The reasons for the observation and assessment

Observing children and assessing their individual needs form the basis of good practice. As you observe young children and record your observations, you will increase your understanding of the developing child and learn to make valid and reliable inferences about the children in your care. Inferences are the conclusions, judgements or deductions you make about the child as a result of your observation and which form the basis of your assessment. In order to provide a quality service for children and families, staff require the skills of observation and assessment in order that detailed information about each child is available to assist in planning the provision for that child or group of children. Observations of children tell you about their world and their stage of development. Vygotsky (1978) talks about the 'zone of proximal (potential) development'. Vygotsky's writings suggest that there is a gap in what the child currently does on its own and what it could do in a supportive environment. Bruner's research on how adults 'scaffold' children's learning is discussed elsewhere in this book. Bruner and Vygotsky both indicate that careful observation of children is needed to enable adults to know when and how to intervene and to provide for children's learning and development.

Observations and assessments may be required in many different situations of which the following are examples:

- *To learn more about the children in the setting*
- *Mild/serious concern about a particular child's development or behaviour*
- *Routine assessments*
- *As part of a baby diary*
- *Structured assessment/profiles, e.g. in cases of special needs*
- *Assessments for purposes of the case conference or court*
- *Students for learning purposes*
- *To assist with developing care plans and planning individual programmes*
- *To facilitate curriculum planning*
- *To understand how children use their environment*
- *To provide a more effective environment*
- *To confirm or contradict other assessments*
- *Health surveillance*
- *To encourage parental involvement*
- *To help identify good practice*
- *To facilitate transfer to other settings*
- *To measure reaction to change of key worker.*

Validity and reliability

Observations and assessments must be:

Valid – this means that the results must be able to be checked and audited to ensure they really are accurate and not the result of a random chance.

Reliable – this means bias-free and consistent in use across time.

Styles of observation

Participant. Observations carried out whilst involved in caring for/educating children. This type of observation is best carried out by skilled and experienced workers who can observe as part of their normal practice with children. Usually this type of observation is supplemented by non-participant observation if further information is required. Participant observation is sometimes used when workers wish to change an aspect of a situation and to measure a child's reaction to the change.

Non-participant.   Observations carried out whilst not involved in caring for/educating children. These enable observers to concentrate fully on the observation and are the most suitable for those developing the skill.

Snapshot.   Descriptions that capture what a child is doing at a particular point in time.

Longitudinal.   Observations over a period of time.

Pointers towards good observation technique

- Get permission from parents to observe their child explaining why you are undertaking the task and how the results will be utilized.
- Be clear about why, what and how you are observing.
- Check that you have everything you need, to avoid moving once settled.
- Be as unobtrusive as possible.
- Avoid eye contact (except in participant observation) with those you are observing.
- Be aware of factors in the environment which might affect your judgement or upset the children, e.g. change of routine.
- Be aware that children will vary in their responses from day to day according to a variety of environmental factors such as who is in the room with them, the temperature etc.
- Decide if the observer will interact with the child to encourage or to guide or if the observer will remain detached. Record the observer's interactions.
- Minimize distractions such as interruptions from other staff or children by carefully planning the observation, informing staff, ensuring cover and explaining to the children.
- Leave the detailed interpretation until later.
- Check that your previous knowledge or reports from other workers do not influence your observation, descriptions or interpretations.
- Remember that being observed can change the children's behaviour.
- Remember that children and parents have rights and their feelings should be considered.
- Remember that your observation and assessment should be unbiased and will be read by other people.

Methods of observation

There is a wide range of methods available for observing children and the method selected for a particular observation will depend on its aim and purpose and how the findings will be used. There are also constraints; e.g. if you have responsibility for a child or group of children it may not be possible for you to undertake non-participant observations. All methods of observation have their strengths and weaknesses and decisions on children's progress should draw from a range of information not just that which is gained through one or two observations. Remember children can be distracted easily and external factors may break their concentration.

Narrative methods. These are observations of children that describe in narrative (an ordered account of connected events – Pocket Oxford Dictionary) form what is perceived by the observer, usually in the sequence in which it happens. This type of observation requires fluent language skills. Narrative methods include:

Anecdotal records. These are brief accounts written soon after an activity or incident occurs. These can be recorded at the end of a session, are easier to manage as they can be done by participant observers and can cover individual or groups of children. Anecdotal records rely on what has been selected by the observer to be significant and are therefore appropriate for more skilled observers as they are open to be less objective. Anecdotal records rely on memory and may miss out vital information. Although requiring significant skills, this type of observation is widely used.

Running records. These records stem from non-participant observation, which involves descriptions of the child that record what they said or did in sequence as it occurs. This is a useful method for students and others new to observing and assessing children, and as it describes what happens as it happens it is less likely to be biased in what is recorded. (Some bias is inevitable in all observation and assessment.) Running records are most successful with individual children rather than groups and can capture unexpected events. Recording may be time-consuming and it can be difficult to draw out conclusions and inferences from a mass of data (information).

Diaries or log books. Information comes from a day-by-day account of the child/children's behaviour or activity which can include running or anecdotal records and examples of children's work. Diary records can give background or context and can be very effective in giving a full picture over a period of time but they are also selective in what is recorded and can be biased. Staff may use the diary system to involve parents who may participate in the recordings. Diary records require persistence and a consistent approach to recording. They are useful for reviewing progress.

Detailed recordings. These observations focus on specific areas of development or play. Recordings can be open-ended or closed categories but are usually complex, requiring concentration and skill. Detailed recordings are generally non-participant. They can provide rich, detailed description and although they can be used for groups of children they are most effective with individuals.

Checklists.   The observer records the behaviour or development by ticking off the item as it is demonstrated on a checklist. These can be checklists which have been professionally prepared by, e.g. psychologists, paediatricians, local authorities and schools or can be devised by workers for their own needs. Decisions about children's progress should use other types of observation in addition to checklists to confirm the findings.

Checklists can only give worthwhile information if they are:

- *appropriate – cover the areas you want, fit your purposes*
- *valid – appropriate, the form in which they are presented and the way they are used can be justified by the circumstances*
- *reliable – bias-free, consistent in use.*

Checklists are quick to use and can be used in a variety of settings with more than one child. They record a clear picture of the presence or absence of particular behaviours or development. Checklists can be used in participant and non-participant observation. Checklists can cover several developmental areas and types of behaviour giving a useful picture of the child and can be used to measure against the 'norm'. Checklists are often over-simplistic, focus on what a child cannot do and miss important factors, e.g. the details and context of the observation such as whether the child is tired or the room is too hot. The content can sometimes be unreliable, inappropriate or not valid. Checklists may not allow for the fact that the absence of a behaviour does not mean that a child cannot perform. Measurement against the 'norm' must take account of the differences in rates of development and should not label children.

Charts and pre-coded categories.   These are observations that are recorded into a pre-written format. They are not the same as checklists as they allow the observer to enter a wider range of data. They do however share many of the strengths and weaknesses of checklists as described above. Many of these observational formats should only be used by experienced professionals as the information gained is highly confidential and must be used with caution.

Examples are:

- *Family trees and genograms* record the child's family history and can be used to help understand the child's genetic background and inheritance.
- *Growth charts* measure height and weight.
- *Maps of the child's environment* record in a diagrammatic form all the significant people, activities and organizations in the child's environment.
- *Flow charts* can be useful in depicting a sequence of events such as a daily routine.
- *Sociograms* record how children relate to one another in a group and can be presented in diagrammatic format. In Figure 1.15 it is clear which children are most popular and which are less popular or

isolated. Such findings need to be checked and re-checked using further sociograms and other methods.

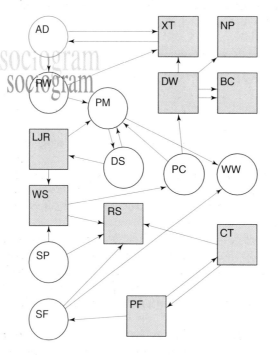

Figure 1.15
Sociogram. Friendship preferences of a group of 4-year-olds. Circles are girls; squares are boys.

Tracking.   This involves drawing a simple map of the setting and tracking the movements of one child or a group over a period of time. The tracking should include some notes that refer to what the child is doing during the tracking process. Tracking can be simple or complex and can show:

- *how the child uses its environment*
- *how long the child stays in each area*
- *the degree of involvement with the activities or with other children or adults*
- *levels of concentrated play or flitting*
- *barriers in the setting and whether the environment requires changing*
- *areas children avoid*
- *how adults might be deployed.*

Tracking will often reveal interesting patterns of behaviour which require investigation using different observation methods.

Target child.   A specialized form of observation which focuses on one child in a group or situation. Target child observations use complex coding systems within pre-coded categories which save time and mean that the recordings can contain more detail of activities and language. Target child observation may require some narrative observation and recording.

Graphs.   These are not direct observational material but can be used to present data gained from observing children. They will require supporting information, which explains their use. Graphs indicating height and weight of individual children are frequently used as are simple bar or pie charts that are developed with the children, e.g. a group's food preferences.

Sampling methods.   These include:

- *Time sampling.* Observing and recording what a child is doing at regular intervals during a set period of time, e.g. every 15 minutes over a morning. It is important to note that the validity of time sampling will increase if records are kept of the context of the behaviour, e.g. 'At 11.45 a.m. child X was playing on his own with the sand. He was using shells to make a beach and concentrating hard. Suddenly, he screamed and threw sand onto the floor.' This gives an accurate picture of what child X actually did but omits to describe the context, which was that he had been told by the worker to leave his play and wash his hands for lunch.

  Time sampling can also look at particular areas of the setting such as the construction area and help judge the extent of its use and if it is used equally by boys and girls. It can be difficult to interpret a jumble of information from a time sample and as this method relies on the observer to record the significant activity or behaviour, it is open to bias.
- *Event sampling.* This involves observing and recording particular events such as temper tantrums or acts of aggression when they occur over a set period. Event sampling tells you how often the behaviour occurs, how long it lasts, what are the causes or triggers and how serious it is. It can assist in changing attitudes to particular children who have, for example, been labelled as aggressive, by objectively assessing the extent of the aggression. Event samples can be difficult to sustain when the behaviour is infrequent.

  Sampling methods are quick and efficient and provide useful ways of testing assumptions about children by careful observation and recording and are reliable over time. More than one child can be observed at a time and records could be made at the time or shortly afterwards. However concentrating on particular events or times could in itself prove biased and lead to labelling a child by not considering the whole picture. In addition, sampling breaks up the natural continuity of behaviour.

Example of headings used in sampling observation

Type of observation
Name of observer
Date and setting

Who present
Name/DOB/age of child
Parent's permission gained
Reason for observation
Time period or event sampled

Figure 1.16
Example of time
sample format.

Date & Time	Context	Behaviour/activity observed	Comment

Figure 1.17
Example of event
sample format.

Date & Time	Trigger or cause	Behaviour	Duration	Severity	Comments

Objectivity

Whilst it is very difficult to be completely objective when observing, you should be aware that your own views and expectations may affect how you record and interpret your findings. No two people will see the child in exactly the same way and it is important to ensure that observations are as objective as possible. Observations should be as free from bias as possible in order to be valid and reliable. **Conclusions should not be drawn from one observation only and confirmation should be sought from other staff and professionals.**

The language of observation

You should record accurately what you see, hear and experience as you observe and not attempt to draw inferences or conclusions at this time. Describe what you see and avoid using judgemental or imprecise terms such as 'poor', 'naughty', 'badly behaved', 'silly', 'sweet' and 'cute'.

Remember you are not here to make judgements which 'label' a child and the language you use when recording your observations can help to avoid bias.

Recording the observation

It must be emphasized that although every situation is different, observations should exclude unnecessary, speculative comment about children and families. The following are likely to be necessary points to record:

- *Details of the setting, numbers of adults, children, equipment and activities available*
- *Date and time of day*
- *Detail of the individual child as appropriate (this might be a thumbnail sketch or a detailed description including family background)*
- *Purpose/intention of observation*
- *Actual observation/data recording, including children's activity on and off task as required*
- *Interpretations/conclusions*
- *Recommendations for further action.*

Recordings can be written or oral using audio or videotapes. Word processors and computers are useful tools. Diagrams, charts, drawings and photographs can enhance the observation and assessment.

Assessment

The purpose of gathering observational information is to make an assessment of the child based on that observation. As has been stressed in this section, assessment of children draws from many sources, and observational data, although very important, needs to be backed up by other information, e.g. from other workers. Your data should be discussed with appropriate persons and parents, compared, cross-checked and further assessments done where necessary. When assessing children and families, care should be taken that comparisons against 'the norm' take into account individual variation within the wide range of normality. Assessments should actively consider possible forms of bias related to such factors as gender, race, disability, culture, religion, social class and family pattern.

In some cases such as court reports, it may be appropriate only to record what children actually say and do and how they behave, including changes over time. In some circumstances, again including court reports, it is necessary to state your professional opinion but it must be based on accurate records that you can utilize to justify your view.

Assessments should:

- remain confidential and be shared only with those who need the information
- be shared with parents (unless there are specific reasons not to do this)
- consider the rights of children and families
- note possible cultural, racial, social and gender-based influences on children's responses to structured assessment situations
- accurately reflect your observation findings
- state whether the aims of the observation have been met
- not be judgemental and negative

- not make inferences or judgements unless they can be supported, e.g. by other professionals, parents or reference to theory or recognized 'norms'
- carefully detail any supporting information from relevant and reliable sources and ensure it is authentic
- use language carefully, avoiding generalizations and assumptions that cannot be substantiated, especially about children's backgrounds. Never use unjustifiable phrases such as 'she is quiet because she is an only child' or 'he does not join in because his family does not speak English'
- lead to a recommendation for how your practice with this child should be modified, how the curriculum offered could be changed
- encourage reflection on your effectiveness and that of the setting.

As you become more skilled at observing and assessing children and making inferences based on your observations, your confidence in your own professional judgement will grow and the service you offer to the children and families will improve.

Example of an observation

There is no right or wrong way of observing and recording as each depends on the specific circumstances. The following is an example of a real observation from a first-year candidate in a practical training placement undertaken on the request of the placement. A useful training exercise is to read the observation and evaluate its content as follows:

- *Is the observation useful?*
- *Does it fulfil its aims?*
- *Is it comprehensive?*
- *Has it recorded appropriate and sufficient information?*
- *Have you developed a 'feel' for this child from reading the content?*
- *Is the language used appropriate?*
- *Is the technique used appropriate?*
- *How does it meet the requirements of the 'Assessments should' list above?*
- *Are its inferences (conclusions) appropriate and valid?*
- *How could it be improved?*

Case Study

Observation

Type	Narrative – Running Record Non-Participant
Purpose	To observe Tom B to see how involved he is with nursery activity after staff noticed he was very withdrawn after a period in hospital
Child's name, DOB, age	Tom B DOB 15 June 1993, aged now 3 years 11 months
Name of Observer	Ms S
Permission	Obtained from grandparent
Location	Home corner Blue Room XYZ Nursery
Date and time	10.05–10.20 a.m. May 30 1997
Those present	Ms H, Tom's key worker; nursery officer; Mr G, nursery assistant; Ms S (the observer) and three other children in the room (2 boys and 1 girl) all aged between 3 and 4 years. None of the children has identified special needs and all are fluent in English. This group of children has been together for nearly 3 months and all have full-time places.

Other information

The room is well equipped in workshop style with a range of activities available. Children have free access to a range of activities and help themselves to items on low shelving. The home corner is well equipped with dressing-up clothes and equipment for domestic play. One section is laid out as a shop selling fruit and vegetables, including those used in cooking ethnic meals. There are various cooking pots in the 'kitchen'. The back door to the room is always open to an outdoor area into which the indoor themes are extended.

Background.   Tom has been in the nursery for 8 months after moving to the area. He spends a good deal of time with his grandparents and enjoys their company. Tom is an only child and both his parents work full time. He is usually happy to come to nursery and not distressed when left by his parents or grandparents. He has had the same key worker throughout.

Tom is a small, slight boy with dark hair and green eyes. 6 weeks ago, Tom was admitted to hospital with breathing difficulties and although now recovered he appears after 3 weeks back at nursery to be very withdrawn and not playing with the other children in the home corner. To encourage him to join in, his key worker is working hard with Tom, including spending time in the home corner with a small group of children and intervening to include him, provide props and suggest roles he could play. This observation is to check his progress and the effectiveness of his key worker's intervention.

Observation

Tom has been playing with small construction on and off for most of the session. He has been concentrating hard and talking to himself although it was difficult to hear his speech. After he leaves the construction Tom walks around the room not settling. Ms H asks Tom if he wants to go into the shop and buy some fruit and vegetables. He says no but after a few moments he leaves the construction and walks slowly over to the home corner. He goes inside, and starts to talk to Ben whilst standing by the plastic fruit and vegetables. He is frowning and picks up an apple and says 'I'm a Daddy and I like apples. We have them at my house.' Ben grabs the apple from Tom and says 'We have red ones.' Elsa comes in and picks up a bunch of grapes. She says 'Do you want to buy these?' 'No,' says Tom. 'I'm not going shopping today. I haven't got a bag.' 'Bye bye,' says the girl. 'You go out of my shop if you haven't got a bag.' Tom leaves and heads towards the student who is assisting with dough modelling. Tom sits down and picks up the dough banging it up and down on the table but not trying to model. He twists around on his chair and looks back at the home corner. Hamid comes across to Tom and joins in with the dough banging. Hamid shows Tom how to press model cars into the dough to make an image. Tom takes Hamid's car and presses the car into dough whilst making car noises. Hamid leaves Tom and moves to the student. Tom watches Hamid and the student for some time then leaves and walks across to the home corner. Ms H offers Tom a bag for his shopping and says 'Why don't you go and see if you can buy anything in the greengrocer's?' Tom smiles and enters the home corner with his bag. Elsa is still playing with the shop and asks Tom what he wants to buy. Tom looks carefully at the fruit and concentrates on his reply. 'Apples and bananas – two and three.' 'That's 2p,' says Elsa. Tom offers imaginary money.

Evaluation

Tom appears to be able to make contact with other children and to initiate pretend play. However he required an adult to point him to the home corner and to suggest that he plays there. His first reaction was 'no'. Tom still appears to lack confidence in his ability to enter a role fully and responds by leaving the home corner when another child tells him to do so even though he keeps looking towards the home corner and seems to wish to return to play. Ms H intervened and provided Tom with a prop (bag) to help him continue and this appeared to work.

Tom also played with the car and dough and began some pretend play although this did not last long and was not developed.

This observation demonstrates that there is an improvement on Tom's observed behaviour of 3 weeks ago when he refused to enter the home corner except with an adult and never took on a role. O'Hagan and Smith state that pretend play 'encourages developing language using new forms of speech and vocabulary'. Most children of Tom's age enjoy role play and it is important to keep encouraging this aspect of his development as it should help him to be less withdrawn and to 'play out' his problems.

It is important that Tom continues to be encouraged in his pretend play, especially role play where he appears reluctant to take on roles. His improvement should proceed with continued support but needs to be monitored. Suggest that Tom is encouraged to use the dressing-up clothes linked to the theme of bears which is just starting in the nursery as well as continuing to develop domestic role play. Although there has been a project on hospitals fairly recently, it might help Tom to have the opportunity to play using hospital props, even incorporating this into a theme for the nursery. It would be useful if further observations could be undertaken in 3 and 6 weeks' time to check his progress.

Reference
O'Hagan, M. and Smith, M. 1993 'Special Issues in Child Care.'

Suggestions for observations and assessments

The suggestions below relate to a few of the many situations and circumstances which may be observed. Every situation will be different and the observation technique may be adapted accordingly. A commonsense approach should be taken to decide the type, form and reason for observing. However, inferences should always be confirmed by others and/or relate to a particular theoretical framework.

1. To measure the physical development of a child against normative scales

Devise a checklist for physical development for a particular age range. Observe one child and measure physical development against the checklist. Make brief notes of what you observe.

Evaluate your observation, stating what further assessment is needed. What inferences have you drawn? How should provision be adapted?

2. To check a child's use of room space, which activities are used and levels of concentration and interaction

Draw a diagram of the room indicating the various activity areas. Observe one child over a period of 30 to 45 minutes, tracking the use of space and involvement in activities. Note the track taken on the diagram. Record separately what the child did in each area.

Evaluate how the space was used, the child's involvement with other children or adults, the levels of concentration and interest per activity visited. Decide the value of the information you have recorded. What inferences can you draw? Are these backed up by other information? From what source? Is the source reliable? What have you learned about the child or the room or any of the activities? What are the next steps for this child and for the setting?

3. To find out which children are accepted or not accepted amongst their peers using a sociogram (most useful with slightly older children)

Find out who the children in the group enjoy playing with. (Speak to the children if necessary and if they are mature enough to understand the question and answer sensibly). Check their answers are consistent by asking them again the following week. This will identify reasonably enduring relationships. Draw a diagram indicating each child's choices. You will soon notice children who are very popular and those who are isolated. In your evaluation, ask yourself why are some children isolated? What effect is this having on their development? What can be done to draw them in? Why are some children more popular? Can you use these children to help with those who are isolated?

4. To assess a child's physical skills (gross motor, balance, co-ordination) and to plan an appropriate programme

Observe one child in the following areas:

- *Gross motor skills, e.g. running, jumping, skipping, climbing*
- *Confidence in movement*
- *Balance.*

Assess the child's physical skills. Compare with other children of the same age and normative scales. Plan a programme for this child linked to your findings.

5. To test colour identification of six colours in a group of 3-year-olds

Draw a bar/pie chart of your results. What do these results tell you? Does your group need more work on colour identification? Plan a programme that will enhance this area of learning.

6. To observe a baby at bath-time

Write a running record of the baby at bath-time. Include the adult preparation. Note the appearance of the baby and the process of bathing, the condition of skin and nappy area, the toiletries and equipment used, the baby's reactions to its carer, the language and interaction, the enjoyment of the water, any distress, where the baby's attention was focused, use of bath toys, baby's movements and signals to its carers. Your conclusion and evaluation will depend on your findings but will largely focus on what you have learned about baby care and development.

7. To observe and assess a child's aggressive outbursts

Undertake an event sample preferably over one morning and one afternoon session (the more event samples the better as this means your findings are more valid and reliable). Draw up a pro-forma for recording in advance of the planned observation. This means you will have to stay near to the target child for most of the session or ask other staff to alert you when such an outburst seems imminent. Note any aggressive outbursts and record them. Record the happenings immediately prior to the outburst for possible causes (triggers or antecedents), the time of day, extent, length and nature of the event and who was involved. Include how staff dealt with the outburst and how other children coped. Your evaluation will draw inferences on the causes of the outburst, if the same staff or children are involved, if the outburst is related to tiredness, does it occur predictably, can it be linked with anything in particular? You may find the child has been labelled as aggressive and your observations do not bear this out.

8. To observe the large construction area of the nursery to assess its use by girls

Undertake a time sample over one morning and one afternoon session (or whatever is possible – the more sessions the better as this means your findings are more valid and reliable). Draw up a pro-forma for recording in advance of the planned observation. Over your chosen session or period of time you will need to note who is playing in the construction area and draw up a graph of use by girls and boys. If boys dominate the area, you will need to identify an action plan to encourage use by girls.

9. To assess a child's ability to 'conserve' volume, number and/or mass

Before making this observation re-read the section in this chapter on 'Conservation'. Work with children in the age range 4 to 7 years. Using Plasticine, dough or clay for testing conservation of mass, show the child two equal-sized balls and gain their agreement that these balls are the same size. Roll one of them out into a sausage shape and ask the child if they are still the same size. A child who cannot yet conserve will say that the sausage shape is bigger. Follow this principle using a row of buttons for number and water for volume. In your evaluation, test whether your findings match Piaget's stages. Give a reason for your finding. Test other children to confirm your findings. What do your findings indicate about Piaget's stages?

10. To observe babies of different ages when separating from their carer

Observe a baby being left by its carer. Carry out this observation with a young baby aged 6 months and a toddler aged 14 months. Observe carefully the baby's reactions, i.e. facial expression, body language, crying and the carer's reactions and method of handing over the baby What have you learned about attachment theory? If the baby is given to the key worker, does this make a difference? What are the most effective ways of comforting a distressed baby? What settling-in procedures are needed for babies? How can the carer best be reassured?

11. To observe the language and interaction between a caregiver and a baby learning to use language

Observe a baby and its mother (or key worker) engaging in child-directed language. Note down the language used and sounds made. How does the adult modify the type of speech used and how does the baby react?

REFERENCES AND FURTHER READING

Ainsworth, M.D. *et al.* (1971) Individual differences in strange situations behaviour of one year olds. *In* Schaffer, H.R. (Ed.) *The Origins of Human Social Relations.* New York: Academic Press.

Ball, C. (1994) *Start Right.* London: Royal Society of Arts.

Bancroft, D. and Carr, R. (1995) *Influencing Children's Development.* Oxford: Open University Press/Blackwell

Bandura, A. (1973) *Aggression: A Social Learning Analysis.* Englewood Cliffs, NJ: Prentice Hall.

Bee, H. (1992) *The Developing Child.* New York: Harper Collins.

Belsky, J. and Rovine, M.J. (1988) Non-maternal care in the first year of life and the security of infant-parent attachment. *Child Development* **59**: 157–167.

Bernstein, B. (1961) Social class and linguistic development. *In* Halsey, A.H., Floud, R. and Anderson, L. (Eds) *Education, Economy and Society.* New York: C.A.

Bowlby, J. (1975) *Attachment and Loss. Vol. 1: Attachment.* Harmondsworth: Pelican.

Bowlby, J. (1979) *The Making and Breaking of Affectional Bonds.* London: Tavistock.

Brown, B. (1990) *All Our Children.* London: BBC Education.

Bruce, T. (1987) *Early Childhood Education.* Sevenoaks: Hodder and Stoughton.

Bruner, J. (1980) *Under Five in Britain: The Oxford Pre-school Research Project.* Oxford: Grant McIntyre/Blackwell.

Bruner, J. (1990) *Acts of Meaning.* Cambridge MA: Harvard University Press.

Chomsky, N. (1968) *Language and Mind.* New York: Harcourt, Brace and World.

Cox, M. (1992) *Children's Drawings.* Harmondsworth: Penguin

Davenport, G.C. (1988) *An Introduction to Child Development.* London: Unwin Hyman.

Donaldson, M. (1978) *Children's Minds.* London: Fontana/Collins.

Donaldson, M., Grieve, R. and Pratt, C. (1983) *Early Childhood Development and Education: Readings in Psychology.* Oxford: Basil Blackwell.

Equal Opportunities Commission

An Equal Start: Guidelines for those Working with the Under Fives. Manchester: EOC.

Falhberg, V. (1982) *Child Development.* British Agencies for Fostering and Adoption.

Fantz, R.L. (1961) The origin of form perception. *Scientific American* **72**: (May).

Fatchett, A. (1995) *Childhood to Adolescence: Caring for Health.* London: Baillière Tindall

Flanagan, C. (1996) *Applying Psychology to Early Childhood Development.* London: Hodder and Stoughton.

Gilligan, C. (1982) *In a Different Voice: Psychological Theory and Women's Development.* Cambridge, Mass.: Harvard University Press.

Goldsmiths College (1993) *Principles into Practice (PIP)* Research project. London: Goldsmiths College.

Henessy, E., Martin, S., Moss, P. *et al.* (1992) *Children and Day Care: Lessons from Research.* London: Paul Chapman.

Kellog, R. (1970) *Analysing Children's Art.* Mayfield Publications USA.

Kohlberg, L. (1969) *Stages in the Development of Moral Thought and Action.* New York: Holt, Rinehart and Winston.

Landers, Cassie (1995) Childhood trainers guide to the development of the young child. *In Enhancing the Skills of Early Trainers Pack.* Bernard van Leer Foundation/UNESCO Holland.

Lee, V. and DasGupta, P. (1995) *Children's Cognitive and Language Development.* Oxford: Blackwell/Open University Press.

Lindon, J. (1993) *Child Development from Birth to Eight: a practical focus.* London: National Children's Bureau.

Milner, D. (1983) *Children and Race: Ten Years On.* London: Ward Lock Education.

National Commission on Education. (1993)

Learning to Succeed. London: Heinemann.

Oates, J. (Ed.) (1995) *The Foundations of Child Development.* Oxford: Blackwell/Open University Press.

Open University School of Education. (1991) *Working with Under Fives.* Milton Keynes: Open University Press.

Pascal, C. and Bertram, T. (Eds) (1997) *Effective Early Learning.* London: Hodder and Stoughton.

Piaget, J. (1926) *The Language and Thought of the Child.* New York: Harcourt, Brace.

Piaget, J. (1962) *Play, Dreams and Imitation in Childhood.* London: Routledge and Kegan Paul.

Pugh, G. (Ed.) (1992) *Contemporary Issues in the Early Years.* London: Paul Chapman with the National Children's Bureau.

Robertson, J. and J. Film Services. (1969) *John: Young Children in Brief Separation.*

Rosenthal, R. and Jacobsen, L. (1968) *Pygmalion in the Classroom.* New York: Holt, Rinehart and Winston.

Rouse, D. and Griffin, S. (1992) Quality for the under threes. *In* Pugh, G. (Ed.) *Contemporary Issues in the Early Years.* London: Paul Chapman with the National Children's Bureau.

Rutter, M. (1981) *Maternal Deprivation Re-assessed.* 2nd edn. Harmondsworth: Penguin.

Rutter, M. and Rutter, M. (1992) *Developing Minds.* Harmondsworth: Penguin.

Skinner, B.F. (1953) *Science and Human Behaviour.* New York: Macmillan.

Tizard, B. and Hughes, M. (1984) *Young Children Learning: Thinking and Talking at Home and at School.* London: Fontana.

Vygotsky, L.S. (1962) *Thought and Language.* New York: Wiley.

Vygotsky, L.S. (1978) *Mind in Society.* Cambridge, Mass.: Harvard University Press.

Wells, G. (1985) *Language, Learning and Education.* Windsor: NFER/Nelson.

Wells, G. (1987) *The Meaning Makers.* Sevenoaks: Hodder and Stoughton.

Winnicott, D.W. (1974) *Playing and Reality.* Harmondsworth: Penguin.

Wolfson, R. (1996) *From Birth to Starting School: Child Development for Nursery Nurses.* London: Nursery World.

2: Promoting Children's Learning Through Play

Links

This chapter has links with:
- NVQ (EYCE) Units: C1, C2, C3, C4, C8, C9, C10, C13, C14; M7; E3.
- CACHE Diploma Modules B, D, H.

Introduction

This chapter is not about the philosophy of play but takes as its start point a commitment to play as the young child's right and principal means of learning and self-expression. Research into play has shown that a 'commonsense' approach to children's play is not enough, and that workers with young children must understand the central importance of the play experience for a child in order to nurture and provide for it effectively.

The importance of play

Deprived of play the child is a prisoner, shut off from all that makes life real and meaningful. Play is not merely a means of learning the skills of daily living. The impulse to create and achieve, working through play, allows the child to grow in body and mind ... Play is one of the ways in which a child may develop a capacity to deal with the stresses and strains of life as they press upon him. It acts too, as a safety valve, allowing him to relive and often come to terms with fears and anxieties which have become overwhelming.

OMEP (1966)

Figure 2.1
Playing together

Defining play

Play is difficult to define. When children play it is a very complex series of events and cannot be compared to adult 'play' which is a description of recreational activity. Play occurs at different levels and is of varying quality. High quality play will mean the child is deeply involved, learning, developing and practising skills. High quality play will not just happen but needs to be structured, i.e. it requires adults to make provision tailored to the child's needs and often involves adults actively demonstrating playful behaviour.

In the past, play has been seen as the child's way of getting rid of surplus energy or as a preparation for life. This chapter takes the view that play is more than that and should be valued for itself. The subject of children's play is a political one. If play is seen as something that children do anyway and exists to occupy their time when they are not working or engaged in formal learning, this will affect the curriculum offered to young children and the play provision made for them. Equally if play is seen as centrally important for learning, it will be given greater value and will form part of the learning curriculum.

Children learn and are motivated through their play and play can involve intense concentration and commitment of time and energy. In other words, although it is play it is not always 'fun' in the accepted sense. Children learn about themselves and their world through the medium of play but it is not the only way they learn, e.g. learning through modelling (copying) behaviour of important adults. Modelling behaviour is not learning through play but the development and consolidation of the learning may well be through role play. Play has a key role in enhancing a child's whole development including basic skills, concepts, ideas, feelings and moral and spiritual values.

Through play, children are helped to develop physically, and are encouraged to explore, experience, discover, practise skills and ideas, and interact socially. Play acts as an outlet for feelings and concerns. Playing goes ahead of serious 'doing' as children experiment and become confident with new skills and concepts. Play acts as an integrating mechanism for every aspect of experience. Through play, children create other worlds where they can test out reality and discover who they are. In play children's self-esteem grows and develops as they can succeed in what they do.

Adults working with young children should avoid using language in ways that devalue what the child is doing in play by separating what is seen as 'work' from what is seen as play; e.g. adults often say 'When you have done this [a set task], you can go and play.' If play is seen as separate from 'work' for young children, this can lead to an unnatural division in that it rejects the important principle that play is the main vehicle for children's learning. This message is particularly important now when a more formalized curriculum for very young children is being introduced by some settings as a response to changes in attitudes and government policy. This is covered in more detail in Chapter 3.

Tina Bruce (1991) has attempted to identify what is 'pure' play and uses the term 'free-flow' which has no neat definition and is closely linked to 'imaginative, free or creative play' but not exclusively so as this type of play acts as a catalyst for other activities. Bruce identifies the need for children to 'wallow in ideas, feelings and relationships' and to become 'technically proficient' through free-flow play.

The following equation states the essence of free-flow play (Bruce, 1991):

free-flow play = wallowing in ideas, feelings and relationships + application of developed competence, mastery and control

The important message is that children should be given support and resources for their play and that the play experience should be highly valued and central to their care and education.

Perhaps the most useful way of defining play in a practical sense is by looking at its commonly accepted characteristics. Play:

- *is usually pleasurable.*
- *is spontaneous although it may be stimulated by an adult.*
- *usually concentrates on a process not a product.*
- *has no explicit rules and no right or wrong way of performing.*
- *is an activity where children have ownership of what takes place.*
- *is when a child is a willing and active participant.*
- *builds on the child's first-hand experiences – a child cannot play by proxy.*
- *builds on and extends a child's learning.*
- *demands hands-on activity which is immediate and relevant.*
- *of any quality does not happen automatically.*

Using the list above we can see that, for example, building an imaginary building with blocks is play whereas although television may stimulate play, watching television is a passive activity which cannot be described as play. Listening to stories is likely to involve children more directly, depending on the telling, but is also not play in an active sense.

Who plays?

As soon as babies begin to explore and interact with their environment they begin to play. Often their first plaything is their carer's face or mother's breast. As children develop, they learn to play with their own hands and to explore objects around them using all their senses. Playing and interacting with the world helps them learn where they end and the world begins. Every healthy child is predisposed to play and learns to play through interaction with others and the world around them. The child's play experience will vary with the child's background and culture. Where a particular culture does not consider children's play to be important this affects the time available for play and the resources allocated, and means that the children themselves will not value play. When children do not, cannot or will not play, e.g. those who have been abused or lost trust in adults, there is usually cause for concern and the child and parents or other carers will need professional help. Play takes energy and sick or tired children will play less. Some children are simply too busy to play as their lives are full of activity. Most children need time and space to themselves to develop and learn how to play and need a flexible routine where there is a balance of adult-structured and open, less-structured situations where they are left alone to experiment and to discover but where adult support underpins their experience.

Scenario 2.1	

Hannah is 3 years old. She lives at home with her mother, older sister Katherine aged 5, and baby brother, Phillip, aged 6 months. Hannah's father has recently moved out of the family home after a difficult period of arguing and bickering with her mother. Hannah spends three mornings a week in a local nursery.

Hannah is often aggressive in her play, both to the equipment and to other children.

What play provision might help Hannah to cope with the situation at home?

Theories of play

There are several competing theories of play that the practitioner can draw upon. Some of these contain minor differences within a particular theoretical perspective.

Psycho-analytic theories

Psycho-analytic theory derived from the work of Freud or later thinkers such as Winnicott (1971) who view play as the means by which children are helped to cope with their anxieties and fears, and by which they are able to integrate and interpret both positive and negative experiences. Freud saw play also as a means of children fulfilling their deepest wishes. Play is thought to be used by the child to gain mastery over painful anxieties, and this has been viewed as a basis for the development of therapeutic play therapy techniques.

Cognitive development theories

Cognitive theorists such as Piaget (see Ch. 1) also stress the importance of play as an integrating mechanism that helps children to come to terms with the world. Piaget viewed play as a process in which the child is active and through which the child learns. He felt that play went through stages of development, e.g. the young baby will play using the senses and its own activity (sensori-motor play). Children of 18 months to 5 years will engage in symbolic play where they make one thing stand for another, e.g. pretend play using language and other forms of representation. Piaget felt that through practice play develops finally into 'play with rules' which is a higher level of co-operative play when children are able to make and use rules in group play situations.

Piaget has been criticized as seeing play in a narrow form: merely practising and perfecting new skills rather than acquiring them through play. Others see play as much more important in the acquisition of new information and the construction of new concepts and ideas.

Structured (guided) play

High quality, structured play opportunities are the bedrock of most early years provision but this does not mean that children play to order and are not allowed to choose their own activity. Structured play is where the play environment is carefully structured to provide (a) a balance and range of play opportunity and (b) adult support and resources tailored to the needs of individuals and groups of children. There will be occasions when adults are more directive in moving particular children towards certain types of play experience and other occasions when children choose freely. Play within a well-structured environment is not superficial, time-wasting, and repetitive but is quality play which draws on many of the 'characteristics of play' listed earlier in this chapter.

Children benefit from exploring and examining materials selected by them and which they can use in play. The Oxford Pre-School Project (Sylva, Roy and Painter, 1980) compared children in Oxford pre-school centres with children in Miami. The children in Oxford were presented with a large range of equipment and materials from which to select whereas the Miami centres offered a more limited range of equipment at any one time chosen and set out by the teacher even during free play periods and with a greater emphasis on the three 'R's. The findings of this investigation revealed that the Miami children were less intellectually involved in their activity despite its apparently more formal educative nature.

Scenario 2.2

You are a childminder caring for 2 children, aged 2½ and 3 years. Both children enjoy simple pretend play but you feel that they are not developing and extending this type of play.

Describe three strategies you could use in the home to offer increased pretend play opportunities. What props would assist in these strategies? How could you use books and stories to enhance the pretend play?

When to intervene

Adults play a key role in ensuring that high quality play experiences are available. This is best done through careful observation and assessment of the children's needs. Adults will need to be aware of children's emerging skills and where they are in Vygotsky's 'zone of proximal development' (see Ch. 1). Children who are left to occupy their time without support or resources often 'play' in a superficial and repetitive way. Adults should intervene sensitively not to dominate the play nor necessarily to change its direction, but to extend it and offer resources and support which enable the children to develop and elaborate their play experience.

Scenario 2.3

Two boys, aged 3 and 4 years, have built a long line of blocks across the carpet. They are beginning to make a square enclosure, but are in dispute about whether to do so or not. One of the boys wants to build the line of blocks till it reaches the wall. The other would like to finish the enclosure and make it into a garage. Tempers are beginning to fray. An adult appears on the scene and suggests that if they do not stop squabbling the blocks will be put away.

(a)   Is this the most useful form of intervention?
(b)   How else might the adult intervene to help with the dispute?
(c)   How might the play situation be extended to satisfy both boys?

Types of play

Play can take many forms, and many so-called serious learning activities become enjoyable play events for children. Play is often categorized into types, and this can be a useful method of making sense of the variety of activities that are called 'play'. The following sections list the main categories of play although the lists are not exhaustive. More usually, too, children's play will encompass several types of play within one activity, e.g. a child will construct a road or bridge with bricks and this then becomes a part of imaginative play; children playing with basic materials such as sand and water often use imaginative and investigative play.

Vigorous physical play

Movement provides a very natural way for children to learn. Workers need to observe children closely and note how they move their bodies as much can be learned about a child's self-esteem, confidence and cognitive skills from this.

Activity involved				
Crawling	Balancing	Rolling	Rough and tumble	
Running	Hopping	Cycling	Digging	Twisting
Jumping	Skipping	Kicking a ball	Pushing and pulling	
Climbing	Chasing	Throwing		
Scrambling	Sliding	Catching	Stretching	Dancing
Lifting	Carrying	Arranging objects	Grasping	Releasing

Development/behaviour encouraged

- Overall health, physical development and body functioning, e.g. encouraging healthy blood circulation and controlling body weight
- Skills in mobility, e.g. gross motor, balance and co-ordination
- Large muscle development
- Agility
- Spatial awareness (underneath, through, over, under, different perspectives)
- Directional awareness (sideways, backwards, forwards)
- Body awareness (how it feels to be upside-down)
- Physical challenges
- Learning to take risks and pushing/extending physical development to its limits
- Self-confidence
- Social relationships, turn-taking and helping others. Release of tension
- Practical concepts of area, energy, weight, forces, mass, inertia
- Temporal awareness, estimating speed, slowness, quickness.

Resources/equipment/environment

- Open space as large as possible within bounds of safety
- Safe surfaces with mats as appropriate
- Places to 'hide', trails to follow, tents and shelters
- Indoors or outdoors, e.g. themes in the nursery extend to the outdoor area in a seamless progression
- Organizing the environment so that the outdoors can be used whatever the weather through providing boots, gloves and waterproofs in the winter and sun hats and skin protection in the summer.
- Natural or manufactured equipment
- Climbing frames, swings, slides, ropes
- Bicycles/trikes, scooters
- Playground markings to enable controlled steering and awareness of direction and to assist in ball or traditional games such as hopscotch

Figure 2.2
Playing outside

- Large construction
- Trees, tree trunks, logs, rocks, boulders, stepping stones, tyres, bridges made of crates, planks or nets
- Different levels and gradients
- Different surfaces, e.g. rough, pebbly, smooth, grass, sand, bark, mud
- Earth/sand to dig
- Balls, hoops, ropes to climb, skipping ropes
- Wagons, carts and wheelbarrows to push and pull, and transport objects of different weights and sizes
- Barrels and tunnels
- Large-scale writing equipment such as large paintbrushes and water.

Creative play

Activity involved
Drawing   Junk play   Sewing
Painting and other creative activity with tools or fingers
Cutting   Printing   Threading   Modelling   Cooking   Puzzles   Sticking
Collage   Lacing

Development/behaviour/learning encouraged

- Hand–eye co-ordination, manipulative skills
- Representation of different types (making something that stands for something else)
- Creativity, divergent thought
- Sensory learning
- Self-expression, emotional release, sense of achievement
- Discovering the properties of different materials
- Learning about colour, textures, shapes, patterns, two- and three-dimensional experiences
- Confidence, satisfaction and self-esteem through achievement
- Greater freedom to experiment as the process of doing is more important than the product which should not be judged against a pre-determined adult standard or model.

Resources/equipment/environment

It would be impossible to itemize everything that could be used in creative play as almost anything could. The environment should be encouraging, clean, well-presented and well-maintained with a choice of materials. Children should be provided with overalls and facilities to wash. Wherever possible a workshop approach should be used where adults are available to facilitate a child's creative play, but not to dominate or impose their own ideas of how things should be done at the expense

Figure 2.3
Creative play.

of the child's creativity. Materials should always be accessible to children so they are not dependent on adults. The following items constitute a basic list for creative play:

- *Paints, crayons, pens, and brushes of different colours and sizes*
- *Paste, glue, paste/glue spreaders*
- *Sponges, scissors, rulers, staplers and sticky tape*
- *Paper of all colours, shapes, textures and sizes*
- *Tissue paper, card, corrugated paper, crepe paper, coloured foil*
- *Straws, string, beads for threading or lacing*
- *Sewing equipment*
- *Material for collage*
- *Junk which should be sorted and graded*
- *Cooking equipment, bowls, rolling pins, wooden spoons, scales, cookers and cutlery.*

Play with basic or natural materials

Activity involved

Play with:

Dough	Clay	Plasticine	Sand	Sawdust	Straw	Cornflour
Peat	Earth	Water	Ice	Snow	Wood shavings	Grass cuttings
Soap flakes						

Looking after pets, insects and plants
Gardening activities
Natural environment
Woodwork

Development/behaviour/learning encouraged

- *Knowledge and understanding of the world*
- *Manipulative skills, small muscle development*
- *Sensory development*
- *Exploration/investigation of natural materials and their properties*
- *Release of tension through hammering, pummelling, squeezing*
- *Soothing and relaxing in water play*
- *Basic science and mathematical learning such as capacity, volume, change of state, e.g. whisking eggs*
- *Life cycles*
- *Care of other living creatures*
- *Hygiene*
- *Planting and growing*

> • *Enrichment of play through use of 'organic' material, especially useful for children in hospitals or restricted urban environments.*

Figure 2.4
Water play.

Resources/equipment/environment

It would be impossible to itemize everything that could be used in play with basic materials as almost anything could. The environment should be encouraging, well-presented and well-maintained with a choice of materials. Children should be provided with overalls and facilities to wash.

- Indoors and outdoors
- Tools for use with clay or dough, shapes, rolling pins, boards
- Woodworking equipment, bench or table, nails, hammers, vice, saw, wood off-cuts
- Sieves, colanders, different-sized containers and jugs, tubing of different diameters for water play, food colouring, liquid detergent/soap for bubbles, items for floating and sinking experiments
- Buckets, spades, containers with holes, shells, boats, shapes, moulds, sieves, combs, wheels for sand play
- Zoo and farm animals, dinosaurs and other models to set up play scenarios in water or sand

Figure 2.5
Sand play

Symbolic (pretend) play

Activity involved

Role play when children act the role
of another person using pretend items
to represent real

Advanced fantasy play such as playing
out stories

Socio-dramatic play when children in
groups take on roles and co-operate
together

Using props such as dressing-up
clothes, play telephones, puppets, masks

Domestic or house play

Doll play

Pretend play around painful situations
such as going to the dentist or
accommodating a new sibling

Small-scale toys to create their own
world

Development/behaviour/learning encouraged

- Developing an inner 'thought' world through reliving and
  reorganizing experiences

- Coming to terms with the world around and understanding everyday events, trying out new ideas, practising new words and behaviours in a 'safe', pretend situation
- Exploring own feelings and experiencing those of others through acting out roles such as mothers or teachers
- In pretend play, functioning at a more advanced level than would be the case in everyday life
- Facilitating symbolic and creative thought
- Experiencing being a 'leader' or person with authority
- Learning to care for others who are smaller or weaker
- Developing language using new forms of speech and vocabulary
- Acting out painful or difficult situations and coming to terms with their own strong emotions
- Relieving stress and aggressive feelings
- Developing imagination and fantasy worlds and learning the difference between these and the real world
- Talking and communicating through an intermediate object such as a telephone or puppet (often a very successful way of encouraging a shy or withdrawn child)
- Early mathematics through grading and sizing materials such as plates or dolls' clothes
- Early literacy through provision of writing material, e.g. for shopping lists or message-taking, labelling of storage drawers, shelves, play equipment
- Co-operative/collaborative play with others and increased social skills
- Domestic play can help to counteract gender role stereotyping.

Resources/equipment/environment

- Space should be allocated for a pretend play area, more than one if possible
- Pretend play can be both outdoors and indoors and equipment can be placed outside
- Outdoor areas such as sand pits can become building sites or even ships with a little adult help
- Pretend play areas such as dens or small corners where children can escape from view and where they feel safe – this enriches language and encourages high quality pretend play
- Dressing-up clothes – should be easily accessible, graded and sized and include a wide variety of everyday clothing from a variety of cultures such as hats, shawls, trousers, dresses, skirts, saris, shalwar-khamis
- Other dressing-up materials, e.g. animal or clown costumes or attractive pieces of cloth of all sizes and possibilities
- Home corners with a wide range of real, yet child-sized, equipment from a variety of cultures which acts as a link between home and the care/education environment

- Material for other pretend play areas such as hairdressers, building sites, garages, offices, hospitals, dentists, clinics and shops
- A selection of small-scale toys such as garages and cars, road layouts, train sets, and dolls' houses.

Figure 2.6
Pretend play.

Construction play

Activity involved

Exploring and experimenting with construction of all types
Making towers, roads, bridges, houses with blocks

Learning to use Lego and similar types of construction toys, at first to familiarize and acquire the technique then actually to make something

---

Development/behaviour/learning encouraged

- Large and small muscle development
- Manipulative skills
- Imaginative use of construction
- Emotional release (building up and knocking down)
- Sense of achievement
- Spatial awareness
- Mathematical learning and language through measuring, lining up, counting, estimating and assessing

- Design and elements of technology
- Co-operative play
- Can help to counteract gender role stereotyping, especially for girls.

Resources/equipment/environment

- Space to use construction. Some items should be available at a table, others should be in a safe floor area not used as a passageway. Avoid uncarpeted areas and cover tables with blankets to minimize the potential for noisy play that can disrupt concentration
- Large construction can take place outdoors, always on a safe surface
- Large and small blocks, wooden or other material, all shapes, colours and sizes
- Lego and similar construction toys
- Junk
- Large and small boxes.

Figure 2.7
Construction play.

Games play

Games playing takes many forms, from simple peek-a-boo or I-Spy through to complex invented games, board games or sports-based games which take place in a playground. Although many modern researchers and practitioners would not agree, according to Piaget and Vygotsky, games with rules are the pinnacle of children's play experience towards which they develop during the pre-school years. In these early years, children learn what rules are, who makes them, how they can be safely broken and their overall purpose.

Scenario 2.4

You are a newly-registered childminder caring for a baby of 18 months and a child of 3½. You are aware that you need to purchase extra play materials and equipment for the children in your care, yet you are working to a strict budget.

Looking at what is available from shops and catalogues and considering other items that might be available from other sources, select six items that you feel would be most useful in promoting good quality play. Justify your purchases in terms of their value to the children's development and learning.

Games playing introduces children to their culture, whether it is through playground games which may have their roots in history but have evolved to suit the times, or the highly competitive games which prevail in our culture and suggest to children that to win is all-important. Games imply rules and turn-taking, and in this sense help children to develop socially. Children also have to learn to cope with losing in competitive games but should not be placed in situations with which they cannot cope. Help should be given in a positive manner to children struggling to accept the reality of losing.

Playing board games is usually an enjoyable experience for children and one from which they can learn, or extend and consolidate learning; e.g. a learning theme on food may use a simple, home-made board game based on the story of 'The Very Hungry Caterpillar'. Mathematical skills, and concepts such as counting, one-to-one correspondence, matching and seriation are also part of playing board games such as the above or snakes and ladders or ludo. Children have to learn to cope with losing in competitive board games, and that is why it is often better to make simple, home-made games which can be adapted to ensure that no-one loses too badly! Children will, of course, often make their own rules that are kept to in a rather erratic way. Young children will vary in their capacity to lose a game and many will find it very painful.

Messy play

This is an unfortunate title and sometimes leads to a misunderstanding of the value of messy play. Many types of play will come into this category which has a tremendous value for children. Playing with earth, sand and water can be delightfully messy, as can finger-painting. Children enjoy playing with cornflour and water or whipped-up soapflakes and many children spend lengthy periods just feeling and exploring the textures. Messy play allows children to explore through their senses a variety of interesting textures, colours and smells without being thought 'naughty'. Some children find it difficult to enter wholeheartedly into this play for a variety of reasons but they should be given overalls and sensitively encouraged to do so; e.g. children vary enormously in their initial reactions to cornflour and water play – some look at the mixture with suspicion and say 'yuck' while others delve straight in. Most children enjoy this play and find it tension-releasing, soothing and satisfying. Messy play is particularly important in today's urban environment where children seem surrounded by clinical, dehumanized buildings where cleanliness is valued and there is nothing messy yet safe to explore. Hospital play-workers find safe messy play an important antidote to the extreme environment found in a hospital. Children are often worried about being dirty and their own bodily functions and can be highly embarrassed, especially in a hospital setting. Children involved in messy play, touch and explore organic materials, and this seems to help them cope with this kind of urban sensory deprivation.

Super-hero play

Super-hero play (for example, pretending to be Batman or the latest, popular TV characters) is common at the nursery/reception stage and usually influenced by watching television. This pretend play is often carried out by boys who perceive themselves as powerful beings taking on the characteristics of their heroes. All that is needed for this play is a piece of material large enough to be tied around the neck as a cape and perhaps some kind of weapon. Although boys particularly enjoy this play, it is very stereotyped and aggressive and usually excludes girls who are portrayed in a rather patronizing and passive manner by these programmes. It is difficult to deal with this and it is almost impossible to discourage it completely; however, attempts should be made to interest boys in other forms of pretend play wherever possible.

Scenario 2.5

A group of 3- and 4-year-old boys is spending a good deal of their time rushing around the nursery pretending to be super-heroes. They enjoy this play and use any props that come to hand, e.g. hats, cloaks, and sticks Their play is very repetitive and they are reluctant to settle down to any quieter activities or to allow others to join in. Some of the younger children are beginning to be afraid of them.

How would you deal with this situation? Describe how you would ensure that this group was able to settle to other activities? What positive action would you take to ensure that other children were not frightened?

Computers and video

No chapter about play can avoid talking about computers and video games. Children are very restricted in modern society and do not enjoy the freedom to play in the streets and countryside, as did previous generations. As a result children spend a lot of time indoors without the company of their peers. A good deal of time is taken up watching television or video or playing computer games with an increasing passivity and lack of involvement with other people. Although this is often seen as a problem for older children, many younger children are heavily involved with computer games which are often targeted towards them. In addition many computer games are war-like, militaristic and violent and encourage a sexist stereotyped view of the world.

Computer use also has some advantages such as learning keyboard skills, using the Internet and playing games which can benefit children in various ways, e.g. developing hand–eye co-ordination and increasing access to information. However these activities cannot be described as 'play'.

Computers are a multi-million pound industry and can bring enormous benefits for children of all ages in supporting learning and bringing enjoyment. The issue for early years workers is to encourage a balanced use of computers and ensure that children wherever possible spend most of their time in 'hands on' play in real-life situations.

Exploratory/experimental play

Young children have an innate curiosity and a fierce determination to explore the world around them. Adults should not discourage this but should ensure that the environment is safe. Play should encourage exploration, discovery and experimentation. With babies and toddlers this is very clear as they go through the stage of 'being into everything'. Their curiosity seems insatiable and they need a constant supply of new and ever more interesting materials to explore. Abbott (1994) commenting on the work of Hutt (1989) states that 'Hutt showed clearly that exploration is a powerful forerunner to full blown play'. Good practice in early years work indicates that children must be given time and opportunity to explore and investigate the world around them.

With older children this intense curiosity, although present, is often less obvious. In a nursery it can often be seen in, e.g., scientific investigative play with mirrors, lenses circuits, magnifiers, and magnets, growing things and keeping pets. Children also enjoy technological investigative play with, e.g., windmills or hoists and pulleys, or a table with articles such as old telephones or clocks to dismantle or make up using tools such as screwdrivers. The use of information technology might also come into this category as many young children are computer-literate and enjoy experimenting with various pieces of software. As children explore and investigate they store away

Figure 2.8
Observing the
world outside.

the information and experience gained for later use; the more experiences they have, the more their learning will be generalized to cover other situations and events.

Treasure basket and heuristic play

Research has confirmed that very young babies are highly curious and motivated to learn (Goldschmeid 1989) and shows that babies as young as 6 months who can sit but are not mobile enjoy 'treasure basket' play. This involves young babies making a selection from a 'treasure basket' of everyday natural (not plastic) objects which are new and interesting to them. Objects should be safe to handle and mouth, e.g. shells, fir cones, apples, lemons, spoons, wood and leather objects, textile or fur. Babies can show amazing powers of concentration but their lack of mobility means they cannot retrieve dropped objects until they have become more mobile.

Goldschmeid also describes 'heuristic play' also known as learning through exploration which occurs usually in the second year of life and is linked to increasing mobility. Children at this stage are constantly putting objects in and out, filling and emptying, fitting one inside another. To satisfy children at this stage requires a wide variety of different objects (not toys) with which they can experiment and expand their skill. These objects can include containers of different sizes and lids, woollen pom-poms, ping pong balls, large hair curlers, corks, large buttons, wooden clothes pegs and many other everyday items. Most settings providing heuristic play do not provide this type of play each day but find about two to three times per week is effective. This may change according to the interest of the children and the availability of

Scenario 2.6

You are a senior worker in a baby room with 8 babies between 6 months and 2 years. The babies are well cared for but often seem bored and fretful. There is no formal planning for play and learning in the baby room and provision is a very 'hit and miss' affair. You have been asked by the nursery manager to introduce a more planned and structured approach to play and early learning experiences for these babies.

Plan how you would introduce this more structured approach to play and early learning. How would you prepare the staff to ensure they understood your goals? What equipment and activities are you likely to use and why? How would you evaluate whether your changes were effective?

materials. Heuristic play has no success or failure/right or wrong way to perform. In heuristic play, children learn by observing the characteristics of the objects and what they can or cannot do and there is no pre-determined result as with many manufactured toys.

Outdoor play

It is important that children have continuous access to outdoor play and it is not confined to set times and good weather. Children can wear boots and warm clothes and careful organization can allow for adult supervision in most cases. Outdoor play gives excellent opportunity for vigorous physical play (see above).

Bruce (1991) suggests that double provision on such items as sand trays or pretend play areas can facilitate learning by allowing children to play at different levels

Scenario 2.7

A nursery has well-developed and well-resourced indoor play areas. The outdoor area is seldom used and poorly equipped. It has an area of grass and large trees and an area of tarmac.

(a) Design an outdoor play area that would promote the children's play and development.
(b) Describe how this area would extend indoor provision.
(c) State how you would ensure that the outdoor area could be used all the year round.
(d) Identify how your design would promote various areas of play and development.
(e) List the equipment required for the outdoor area and work out how much it would cost.

through varying the provision. Outdoor play can provide a form of double provision and is a good means of extending play, e.g. providing water play both indoors and outdoors. Play should move smoothly from indoors to outdoors, and the environment should be planned for continuity whilst allowing for the different levels of play in which the children may wish to engage; e.g. if the theme is 'the seaside' there can be a water tray indoors with water, pretend fish, boats, nets, and seaweed made from coloured paper. Outdoors the theme may be continued by creating a 'beach' with sand and water, buckets and spades, rock pools and pebbles.

Stages of experience with new materials or objects for play

When children explore new materials or objects they first investigate using their senses. This applies to every type of play material and situation including the use of their own bodies and other people or children. Babies will look at, listen to, handle and mouth any new object. They will throw it to the ground and watch what happens and repeat/practise the activities over and over again. Through trial and error, much repetition, further exploration and experimentation, children will achieve mastery in the use of various materials, activities and equipment. As they understand the properties of new materials and objects and master the basics in their play, the materials are used in a more controlled manner. Children will elaborate the activity and use it creatively as it becomes a commonplace everyday part of their experience. With a cardboard box, for example, a toddler will explore it by looking, touching and watching what others do with it. It may then push the box around, pour juice over it, turn it upside-down and on its side, and push its fingers though a small hole in the side. The toddler may climb inside many times until this can be done without difficulty, and then might use the box as a receptacle for toys which could go in and out of it all day long. After all these uses have been mastered and elaborated upon in play, the box might then become a vehicle for pushing other children around or a bed for a much-loved teddy.

Play tutoring

One of the main features of play is said to be its spontaneity, particularly in pretend play; but it is always important to note who initiates and develops the play. Adults need to be sensitive to children's interests and to build on these. Sometimes adults have to initiate particular areas of play because of needs amongst the children or when developing a theme. Some children seem much more able to enter into a rich variety of dramatic sequences than others, some of whom need help and encouragement. Pretend play is thought to be a vital part of children's experience which has many benefits (see list above). There have been studies which suggest that adult

interaction and sensitive intervention in this stimulates, deepens and improves the play (Smith and Sydall, 1978; Sylva *et al.*, 1980). This intervention is often called play tutoring. Some research (e.g. Smilansky, 1968) suggests that there may be social class differences in the quality of pretend play, or that it could be linked with improved creativity, symbolic thought or intelligence (Lieberman, 1977; Singer, 1973). Singer categorized children into those with high fantasy (HF) disposition and those with low fantasy (LF) disposition and found those who were HF were more creative or imaginative. Some of these studies have been criticized as leaving out important factors or being methodologically suspect. Nevertheless it is important for workers with young children to be aware of the central importance of pretend play.

Play tutoring enables adults to assist children in moving on in their play, and modern practice is to intervene sensitively. Workers should develop the ability to 'tune into' the play and expand the activities or concepts through discussion as well as providing a varied and rich range of materials and equipment. This can take the form of offering advice or support outside the play (outside intervention), or involve taking on a role within the play (inside intervention).

Scenario 2.8

There is a mixed-gender group of four children, aged 3 and 4 years, playing in the home corner. They have played at serving sandwiches and cakes to each other, clearing the table, and then offering tea. The conversation is sparse and dominated by one girl being a 'Mummy' and saying over and over again 'It's time for dinner.' This same group often plays together in the home corner enacting similar events and seems to have got 'stuck' in their play.

(a) How could the worker enrich and extend this play?
(b) What new props could be introduced?
(c) How could this play be used to extend mathematical concepts?
(d) How could this play be used to develop a multi-cultural perspective?

Equal opportunities in play

The full range of play experiences should be available to all children and not constrained by stereotyped attitudes towards race, culture, health status, gender or disability. Workers should be sensitive to children's backgrounds and cultures in their play provision.

When providing for play it is important to ensure that the provision reflects an antidiscriminatory, anti-bias approach. Play materials should reflect positive images of all

and should not assume all children come from a two-parent family. Families from different ethnic groups need reassurance that their children will be well cared for and that play provision is appropriate and not Eurocentric.

Often workers note that it is boys who engage in boisterous activities and monopolize the bikes or large construction and girls may predominate in other areas. Adults need to intervene to ensure that all children get access to the whole range of equipment and play choices.

Disabled children and those with particular needs should be given access to the same level of play opportunities as all children. Disabled children have the same needs and rights to play. Workers need to make sure that provision is made for disabled children and should understand that these children are in fact disabled by the society they live in when it does not provide for them (social model of disability). Chapter 5 describes in detail the inclusion of children with special needs and Chapter 8 covers the 'Code of Practice on the Identification and Assessment of Special Educational Needs'.

Scenario 2.9

Adam who is HIV-positive has been admitted to the nursery. Parents have heard about this through the local grapevine and have complained that they do not wish their children to share a room with Adam.

How could nursery staff deal with this to ensure that Adam and his family are not disadvantaged?

Scenario 2.10

You are a newly-appointed nursery manager and have inherited a situation where there is poorly developed play provision for children with a disability or sensory impairment.

How would you ensure that play opportunities were available for all children, including those

- with severe hearing loss
- in a wheelchair
- with learning difficulties.

Write a leaflet for parents explaining your nursery's policy on play provision for children with particular needs.

Play environments

Play and the wider environment

Early years workers sometimes say they are restricted in what they can provide for children in terms of a balanced range of experiences. Within individual settings the range of possible experience will vary, e.g. where there is space and a large garden with a wild area, more experiences are possible. However where children spend the majority of their waking hours in the setting, access to the wider world is essential. Children at home will usually go shopping, use public transport, attend clinics, visit friends and relatives, meet older people and through this learn about the society in which they live. Children in full-time provision should not be excluded from these experiences.

Children also require safe play space both within and outside the setting. *Health of the Nation* (DoH, 1992) talks of the 'active promotion of physical environments conducive to health' and the play environment is no exception. Children require protection and safe play space and parents and workers often have to work together to protect such areas. Play areas should be accessible, affordable, well-maintained, and clean and safe, so that children can play freely and unhindered; e.g. areas for children to play safely should be free of dogs and dog excrement, yet dogs still roam the streets fouling pavements and parks. Children in urban environments need natural wild areas to explore and climb as well as manufactured equipment. Children in rural areas can be very isolated and live in a dangerous environment with such hazards as agricultural equipment and chemical pesticides and are often poorly served with very little safe land for play purposes. However, Titman (1993) found that the most restricted children of all were found in suburban environments. It is clear therefore that in every part of the country children need opportunities in the wider environment to play and explore in safety.

Play in the early years setting

The play environment should be carefully planned, safe, age/stage appropriate, encouraging, stimulating and interesting with a variety of equipment and activity available, at different skill and conceptual levels to offer a challenge. Out of sight is often out of mind with young children, and they will need to be able to see and reach the equipment. Equipment should not be frequently moved or stored in different places as children need to know where to look for things to continue their play from day to day. This is difficult in certain situations where everything has to be packed up after each session, but the general principles can be adhered to.

It is important that young children should be able to use a balanced range of play materials each day as part of the overall curriculum plan. Sand and water play should always be available.

Thought should be given to carpeting areas where children will be on the floor or where noise needs to be minimized. Other children or adults should not use play areas as passageways. Small play spaces and dens should be encouraged within the bounds of safety. It is important to concentrate activity or equipment in general areas within a given space, e.g.

- *Quiet areas*
- *Book areas*
- *Graphics areas*
- *Messy areas*
- *Science areas*
- *Pretend play areas*
- *Construction areas*
- *Table areas for construction, puzzles and creative activity.*

All space and room features should be exploited to their best advantage, with adjacent corridors used where possible. Walls, windows, ceiling beams and partitions can be used for display purposes. Children should have a coat hanger, drawer or storage space which is exclusively theirs and where they can store their creative work or other precious objects in safety.

The environment should provide a link between the care/education settings and the child's home. Large, open spaces are threatening at first, as are groups of noisy children. Young children should have places to escape from the hubbub, and here there should be items that provide a link with home. A home corner, therefore, should contain dressing-up clothes or cooking equipment which reflect the home cultures of all the children and with which they can identify as well as those which extend their immediate experience.

A workshop-style provision where children are independent and help themselves to materials will facilitate children's choice, rather than adults deciding on what should be available. Where there is an overall curriculum plan, a variety of play materials supporting the plan should be available. Clearing away and storing equipment should be an extension of play, and the children should be clear where things are kept and learn how to keep their environment clean and tidy.

Equipment should be adapted as necessary to enable children with special needs to participate as fully as possible. Sometimes specialist equipment is necessary and available but often a simple adjustment is all that is required, e.g. to stabilize table equipment and stop it rolling away when children cannot grasp or reach effectively.

The adult's role in promoting play

In order to promote high quality play the adult should:

- ensure children's safety and well-being at all times.

- build on children's interests or initiate new areas of play.
- ensure that age/stage-appropriate play experiences, resources and activities are provided.
- ensure that play is recognized as a powerful medium for learning when planning provision.
- model or demonstrate how to play.
- support, extend and 'scaffold' play (see Chs 1 and 3).
- assess children's play and development and sensitively intervene in order to further the play.
- supervise and sort out disputes.
- ensure all children have access to the full range of play facilities regardless of race, gender, disability, cultural or religious factors.
- provide a safe and healthy play environment.
- provide a stimulating play environment where children have genuine play choices.
- maintain the play environment to an acceptable standard.
- maintain equipment to an acceptable standard.
- maintain stocks of consumables and note where and when new equipment will be needed.
- communicate with parents and other workers concerning children's play and development as appropriate.
- ensure continuity between indoor and outdoor play.
- enjoy playing with the children.

Assignments

Assignment I

Observe and assess the use of play space and equipment
1. Draw a rough plan of the play area (indoors and/or outdoors).
2. Observe several children (one at a time) and 'map' their movements on the plan, noting what they are doing and how long they spend at each play activity. Choose the same time of day and a time of 'free choice play'.
3. Draw on the plan the route the child takes and how long it spends at each activity.
4. Compare your results from different children/ages.

Questions to ask yourself:
(a) Are there certain areas that few children use or cannot easily access?
(b) Are certain children 'flitting' around and not spending time profitably anywhere?

(c) What are popular play areas and why?
(d) Which materials encourage long spells of concentrated play?
(e) How could the equipment and materials be changed to allow more elaborate play?
(f) Can you tell what made each child stop and play?
(g) How could the room layout be improved?
(h) Did the presence of an adult in a particular area cause it to be used more frequently?

Assignment 2

You are training to work with young children in a community pre-school and have in your care the following children:

1. 3-year-old Jason who has difficulty in fine manipulative tasks.
2. 4-year-old Anna who finds difficulty settling to any play activity and dislikes getting her hands dirty.
3. 3½-year-old Samuel who shows exceptional ability in creative activity.

Questions to ask yourself:

(a) How would you assess each child's skills?
(b) How would you identify goals for the children?

Devise a play-based programme for each child to encourage learning and development through play.

Assignment 3

Developing and extending children's pretend play

In consultation with your supervisor and preferably following the interest of the children, look for a way of developing and extending children's pretend play. Building on what is already taking place or introducing a new theme, help to create an environment where children can enjoy exploring new roles and playing together in an exciting and imaginative way.

Questions to ask yourself:

(a) How would you introduce the new materials and link them with previous or ongoing experience?
(b) What are your objectives for individual children and/or the group?
(c) How might the activity be developed and extended into other areas of play?

Carefully observe the children's reactions, language, interactions and behaviour. Review and evaluate the overall results.

Assignment 4

To promote learning through sensory play

Bearing in mind health and safety, make a toy or devise a game or activity which will extend a young child's sensory play experience. Provide a description of its potential use, the rationale for your choice and how the toy/game was made.

Where possible, discuss the reaction of children with whom you have used the item.

Assignment 5

To promote development of a baby under 1 year

Bearing in mind health and safety, create a 'treasure basket' to use with a small group of babies.

Describe and discuss the basket's contents. Where possible, use with a baby and note the baby's reactions. Discuss if development was promoted. Discuss how you would adapt and change the contents.

Assignment 6

To develop heuristic play with a group of babies from 10 to 24 months

Describe how you would set up and introduce heuristic play. Write a leaflet for parents explaining the value of this type of play and how it promotes the babies' development.

References and further reading

Abbott, L. (1994) 'Play is Ace!' Developing play in schools and classrooms. *In* Moyles J. (Ed.) *The Excellence of Play*. Milton Keynes: Open University Press.

Barbarash, L. (1997) *Multicultural Games*. Champaign, Illinois: Human Kinetics.

Bruce, T. (1991) *Time to Play in Early Childhood Education*. Sevenoaks: Hodder and Stoughton.

Bruce, T. (1996) *Helping Children to Play*. London: Hodder and Stoughton.

Bruner, J. (1980) *Under Five in Britain: The Oxford Pre-School Research Project*. Oxford: Grant McIntyre/Blackwell.

Cohen, A. and Cohen, L. (Eds) (1988) *Early Education: The Pre-School Years*. London: Paul Chapman.

Community Playthings 1990 *Criteria for Play Equipment*. Robertsbridge, East Sussex, England: Community Playthings.

Czerniewska, P. (1997) Girls and boys come out to learn. *Co-ordinate* (November) London: National Early Years Network.

Department for Education and Employment (1994) *Code of Practice on the Identification and Assessment of Special Educational Needs*. London: Department for Education and Employment.

Department of Health. (1992) *Health of the Nation*. London: HMSO.

Donaldson, M. (1978) *Children's Minds*. London: Collins/Fontana.

Economic and Social Research Council. (1997) *Children 5–16: Growing into the 21st Century*. Swindon: University of Hull.

Garvey, C. (1977) *Play*. London: Collins/Fontana Open Books.

Goldschmeid, E. (1989) Play and learning in the nursery. *In* Williams, V. (Ed.) *Babies in Day Care*. London: Day Care Trust.

Goldstein, J. (1997) *Understanding Toy Trends*. London: National Toy Council.

Gura, P. (Ed.) (1992) *Exploring Learning: Young Children and Block Play*. London: Paul Chapman.

Heal, S. (1997) All over the shop. *London Nursery World* **97** (3587).

Heald, C. (1997) *Construction Play*. Leamington Spa: Scholastic.

Hutt, J., Tyler S, Hutt C, *et al.* (1989) *Play, Exploration and Learning*. London: Routledge.

Isaacs, S. (1950) *Intellectual Growth in Young Children*. London: Routledge and Kegan Paul.

Lieberman, J. N. (1977) *Playfulness: Its Relationship to Imagination and Creativity*. New York: Academic Press.

Lieberman, L.J. and Cowart, J.F. (1996) *Games for People with Sensory Impairment: Strategies for Including Individuals of All Ages*. Champaign, Illinois: Human Kinetics.

Mane, N. (1997) *Challenging Racism through Play*. Bromley: NCMA Who Minds.

Matterson, E. (1989) *Play with a Purpose for Under Sevens*. Harmondsworth: Penguin.

Moyles, J. (1989) *Just Playing? The Role and Status of Play in Early Childhood Education*. Milton Keynes: Open University Press.

Moyles, J. (1995) *The Excellence of Play*. Milton Keynes: Open University Press.

Newsom, J. and Newsom, E. (1970) *Four Years Old in an Urban Community*. Harmondsworth: Pelican.

OMEP (Organisation Mondiale pour L'Education Préscolaire) 1966 *Play in Hospital*. Report by the World Organisation for Early Childhood Education.

Opie, I. and Opie, P. (1997) *Children's Games with Things*. Oxford: Oxford University Press.

Piaget, J. (1962) *Play, Dreams and Imitation*

in Childhood. London: Routledge and Kegan Paul.

Rouse, D. and Griffin, S. (1992) Quality for the under threes. *In* Pugh, G. (Ed.) *Contemporary Issues in the Early Years*. London: Paul Chapman with the National Children's Bureau.

Sanger, J. *et al.* (1997) *Young Children, Videos, and Computer Games: Issues for Teachers and Parents*. London: Falmer Press.

Save the Children. (1996) *Children's Participation Pack*. London: Save the Children.

Singer, J.L. (1973) *The Child's World of Make Believe*. New York: Academic Press.

Singer, D.G. and Singer, J.L. (1990) *The House of Make Believe*. London: Harvard University Press.

Smilansky, S. (1968) *The Effects of Socio-dramatic Play on Disadvantaged Pre-school Children*. New York: Wiley.

Smith, P.K. and Sydall, S. (1978) Play and non-play tutoring in pre-school children: *Child Development* **48**: 315–329.

Sylva, K., Roy, C. and Painter, M. (1980) *Childwatching at Playgroup and Nursery School*. Oxford Pre-school Research Project. Oxford: Grant McIntyre/Blackwell.

Titman, W. (1993) Special Places: *Special People Learning through Landscapes*. Winchester: Southgate.

Winnicott, D.W. (1971) *Playing and Reality*. London: Tavistock (reprinted 1974 Harmondsworth: Penguin).

3: CURRICULUM AND EARLY LEARNING

Objectives

- Introduction and definitions
- Influences on the early years curriculum
- The QCA desirable learning outcomes (early learning goals)
- Baseline assessment
- Anti-bias approaches
- Characteristics of the early years curriculum
- Contemporary views of the child as a learner

- The adult's role
- Curriculum for babies and toddlers 0–3 years
- Curriculum for 3- to 5-year-olds
- The National Curriculum
- Organization and environment
- Curriculum planning
- The planning cycle
- Planning routines

Links

This chapter has links with:
- NVQ (EYCE) Units: C10, C11, C14, C24, C25; E3; M7, M8.
- CACHE Diploma Modules B, H.

Introduction and definitions

The Qualifications and Curriculum Authority (QCA) (1998) defines a curriculum as 'the experiences, opportunities and activities that you offer in your educational programme to help children learn and develop'. In this chapter we broaden that definition by stating that the early years 'curriculum' includes all the above together with the informal everyday interactions and routines that take place within the home or the wide range of settings where children receive care and education until they commence the National Curriculum which is usually in Year 1 of Primary School. Every aspect of a young child's experience has some learning component and the learning curriculum is not just that which is structured, formalized and written down or planned. With such a wide definition of 'curriculum' this chapter can only provide a brief overview of the ideas behind the provision, and the likely interpretation by practitioners. References and ideas for further reading are provided at the end of the chapter.

There are many different viewpoints that have contributed over the years to a particular view of children and their learning and development. During the 1960s and 1970s the main function of nursery education was thought to be the prevention of later educational failure, especially on the part of working-class and ethnic-minority children. Programmes such as Headstart (see High/Scope later in this chapter) were devised to address this by giving children enriched early experiences which it was thought they were unlikely to receive at home. Today it is generally felt that good practice will provide a curriculum, which incorporates and uses in a positive way the children's own cultural and educational experiences from their homes and community.

The learning curriculum must be closely related to a child's sequence and stage of development and should be viewed in a holistic manner as young children do not perceive the world in separate chunks based on traditional subjects such as mathematics or science; e.g. counting and sorting the dessert spoons and making sure each person has one includes several concepts: one-to-one correspondence, shape and size recognition, classification and counting. In the context of setting the table for lunch there is a recognizable, informal, mathematics learning experience, but this is also likely to include language development through mathematics talk and social development through sharing the task and working with other children or adults.

Figure 3.1
Starting a movement
session in school.

Although the child's chronological age may not match its stage of development, it is frequently the former that dictates the types of activities, experiences and environment offered by those giving care and education. It is important to recognize that children do vary widely in their development and individual needs. Careful observation and assessment using a variety of sources of information and which consider children's differences and prior experiences should always form the basis of curriculum planning for individual and groups of children.

On the basis of convenience, this chapter looks at curriculum at three broad stages concentrating on the age range 0 to 5 years:

- *Babies and toddlers 0 to 3 years*
- *Children 3 to 5 years (desirable outcomes)*
- *Children 5 to 16 years (National Curriculum).*

Influences on the early years curriculum in mainstream settings

1. Historical

Many well-known historical figures in the world of philosophy and education have influenced the curriculum offered in mainstream settings in the UK today, e.g. Margaret McMillan, Friedrich Froebel, Rudolph Steiner and Maria Montessori. The influential work of Piaget on children's development was discussed in Chapter 1 and can be seen as directly applicable to early learning as can the work of other psychologists and researchers such as Bruner and Vygotsky. This chapter will consider the thinking and influence of some of these theorists as well as research from developmental psychologists and others.

2. Social and political

The curriculum has also had to respond to political and social pressures, with governments and politicians varying in their approaches to the teaching of parts of the curriculum such as reading and mathematics and attempting to influence how these are taught; e.g. the emphasis on basic skills in primary schools reflects the government's concern to ensure that the UK has a literate and numerate workforce better equipped to develop new ideas and technologies appropriate for the 21st century. This recent emphasis on basic skills has led to a slimming down of the National Curriculum requirements and for example, the introduction of the National Literacy Strategy (DfEE, 1998). In the past, workers with young children have stood out against so-called reforms or pressures which are designed to over-formalize the curriculum and which do not take into account the development of the child and the importance of learning through play. However, current trends in education in the UK appear to be encouraging a much more formal approach to pre-school learning in contrast to much of the rest of the world where formal school often does not start until 6 or 7 years of age.

Very young children in school

In recent years there has been a tendency to admit children into the reception class soon after their fourth birthday. This was partly as a result of falling school rolls, partly a cheap alternative to nursery education where the ratio of staff to children is higher, and partly reflects the concern that summer-born children have been shown to perform less well academically than those born during the rest of the year who were receiving a longer infant education. Recently, funding mechanisms have changed and many more schools are taking in very young children in some cases as young as 3 years of age. At present, schools are not subject to the Children Act 1989 inspection requirements and do not have to meet the staff ratios which are required in other settings such as pre-schools although they do have to conform to the requirements laid down in the various Education Acts. This has led to considerable concern because in some cases children have been plunged into a highly formal and structured environment with inadequate staff ratios which is quite unsuitable for their needs.

The consequences for early learning of very young children being admitted to school are serious. In response to the concentration on 'desirable outcomes' and the National Curriculum, some settings will provide over-formalized approaches which can damage children's attitudes to learning so that their experience of school will be one of boredom and failure. In addition where 4-year-olds in a neighbourhood are all in school this reduces the overall amount of provision as pre-schools or private nurseries fail to compete against schools and may have to close down.

The views of parents and other professionals

Often there is a lack of understanding of the aims and goals of a play-based early years curriculum. It is important to recognize that, for some, including parents and sometimes teachers, nursery education is 'just playing' or worse 'minding children' so it is vital to ensure that the curriculum content and method of delivery which is closely linked to the development of the child are clearly understood by practitioners, parents and other professionals. This in turn requires all workers with young children to be able to understand and justify the curriculum they offer in both educational and developmental terms.

3. Educational theorists

Jerome Bruner

An important part of Bruner's influence on the learning curriculum offered in early childhood has been through his insights on learning. Although his thinking and research span many years and have changed and developed, the concepts of 'scaffolding learning' and 'the spiral curriculum' are still useful.

Scaffolding learning. Bruner (1977) adopted the image of a scaffold erected by adults to support a child's learning, which occurs little by little. Bruner found that most of this learning took place in informal interactions and routines such as bathtimes and games such as 'round and round the garden'. These routines, with their repetitive nature, allow children to learn and to talk about regular events that make up their lives, and parents gradually extend this behaviour as they see the child making progress. Eventually the scaffold can be removed and the child has achieved competence.

The implications for early learning are to ensure that staff and parents use everyday informal opportunities for learning, stressing adult support and 'scaffolding' of the child's learning until mastery is achieved.

Spiral curriculum. At the heart of the concept of the spiral curriculum (Bruner, 1977) is the idea that 'any subject can be taught to any child at any age in some form that is honest.' This means that the basic themes at the centre of mathematics, science, literature etc. can be within the reach of any child at an appropriate level for their stage of development. Bruner has further developed these ideas to say that if what we offer children does not have within it possibilities for future learning, it should be considered to be unhelpful 'clutter'. In assessing the early years curriculum, it is an interesting exercise to view the activities and experiences traditionally offered to children at this stage and to assess whether or not they are laying the foundations for future learning. It is not always obvious that children cooking are laying foundations for understanding physics and chemistry, or that classifying through sorting and matching objects is a prerequisite for higher-order mathematical thinking. Equally, there are traditions in care and education which may not meet Bruner's criteria, e.g. adult-centred 'creative' activity, designed and presented to please adults, by adults and where the children play a peripheral role such as repetitively sticking one pre-cut shape on to another.

The implications for early learning are important, as every aspect of the learning curriculum in order to be valuable for the child should lead on to and form the basis for future learning.

Leon Vygotsky

The work of Vygotsky (1978) has also been influential in the development of the early years curriculum. Vygotsky's view is that learning takes place in part through social relationships. Vygotsky describes:

- *the zone of actual development – what the child can actually do unaided*
- *the zone of proximal development – what the child can do with help from adults and other children (see Ch. 1)*
- *the zone of future development – what the child will be able to do unaided.*

Vygotsky emphasized the need for the adult to support the child through these stages through instruction and involvement concentrating on what the child can do or can do with help. He also emphasizes the role of play in helping a child to progress, noting that in play the child often functions at a higher level.

The implications for early learning are an increased emphasis on the adult's role as 'teacher', a supportive adult/child partnership and the importance of learning through play.

Schemas (after Piaget)

Schemas are basically repeated patterns of behaviour which are thought to be brought about as a result of a child's experiences interacting with genetic (inborn) influences. Athey (1990) suggests that children who displayed often unconnected behaviour in the nursery situation were in fact working on a closely defined series of schemas. Schemas are patterns of repeated actions using objects, people or events and draw on Piaget's original ideas and descriptions. Athey has identified many schemas and named them according to their characteristics (about 36 different schemas in all). These activities or patterns of behaviour are repeated over and over again by children using different equipment and materials but with the same underlying theme. Children are motivated to develop their schemas which move from 'doing' to become internalized thought. Examples of schemas are:

- *Transportation – when the child constantly moves objects from place to place*
- *Enclosure – the child builds enclosures with Lego or bricks, or in paintings*
- *Rotation – the child is absorbed by things which turn such as cogs and wheels.*

Examples of a developing schema may often be observed, e.g. toddlers may often be seen walking to and fro between a pile of toys and a box. The toddler picks up a toy each time and then dumps it in the box. This is an early 'back and forth' schema

Scenario 3.1

Marianne, aged 4 years 1 month, spends a good deal of time climbing up the climbing frame by different routes and coming down the slide. She enjoys jumping up and down on the ground or climbing up various equipment and jumping down again. Her drawings and paintings often consist of lines up to the sky or ladders and tall trees and her language and play often relate to movements up and down. Staff have identified that Marianne is demonstrating a 'dynamic vertical schema' and have planned a programme for her and other children to extend her learning and build on her interests.

Marianne's parents have seen the nursery records of her development and have asked what the references to 'schema' mean.

Prepare an information leaflet for parents explaining how the nursery uses 'schemas' to help plan its provision.

that may provide the basis for later learning such as concepts of 'here' and 'there' or starting and finishing.

This understanding of schema in children's cognitive development is beginning to influence the nursery curriculum in mainstream settings. Athey suggests that children have particular schematic interests at different times and that the curriculum should reflect the children's current interests. If this is the case, workers will have to observe, identify, assess and extend schematic experience and make provision accordingly. Nutbrown (1994) suggests that children will follow their schemas regardless of what adults provide but that planning should include broad themes and topics that cover several schemas in different ways which allow for the needs of groups of children to be met.

Bruce (1997) states that schemas are best used as an observation tool and should not be seen as a curriculum method or model. When observing children it is important to use a variety of techniques and approaches as schemas are not the only method of observation. Schemas do, however, inform good curriculum practice which should draw on a wide range of theory and method.

Theory into practice: Penn Green.   Parents of children at the Penn Green Centre (Whalley, 1994) were each given a booklet introducing them to schemas and were also given a 'Parents' Observation' booklet. Parents were encouraged to record their observations about their child's schemas. This project was very successful and both parents and staff gained a wealth of information about the children's learning and patterns of behaviour. This information led to a change in the way Penn Green planned its provision which began to focus on children's 'burning interests', i.e. their schemas. Figure 3.2 is an example of planning using schemas to inform the planning process for individuals and groups of children.

4. The Qualifications and Curriculum Authority 'Desirable Outcomes for Children's Learning on entering compulsory education' (early learning goals)

The QCA 'Desirable Outcomes for Children's Learning on entering compulsory education' 1996 (referred to in this chapter as 'desirable outcomes' and discussed in more detail later in the chapter) represent a move towards learning outcomes rather than specifying curriculum input. The 'desirable outcomes' are designed for use by all early years settings with 4-year-olds who receive public funding. This educational provision offered to enable children to achieve the desirable outcomes is inspected by OFSTED and covers a variety of early childhood settings such as pre-schools and childminder networks as well as nursery and reception classes. The desirable outcomes are being revised and will be known as 'early learning goals' to be used with young children at a 'foundation stage', i.e. aged 3 to the end of the reception year. Desirable outcomes are not the same in the four countries of the UK.

Figure 3.2
Example of planning
using schemas.
Reproduced from
Whalley M. (1994)
Learning to be strong.
London: Hodder &
Stoughton, with
permission.

Weekly plan – 23/11

Area	Plan	Children	
Corridor	Add three hollow blocks Soft music Games on low table	Daniel, Zach, Nicolas Joanne, Stephen	Infilling Sequencing
Wet area	Long tray with sand and water Diggers and cars and container (bucket) all on floor Painting powder mixed water-colours liquid	Alex Chloe	Trajectory Infilling
Workshop	Glue Sellotape	Joely, John K. Zoe, Natalie S.	On top
Café	Drinks with ice cubes	Chloe	Change of state
Home-corner	Dried fruit and cereal	Robert, John M. Kerry	Transporting Trajectory
Drawing	Puzzles on different levels Flip chart (or easel for drawing)	James C. Alex R.	Tipping out Flight
Low ceiling area	Add small wooden blocks to hollow blocks and maple blocks	Daniel Zach	Infilling Trajectory
Writing	Well-resourced Letters to Santa	Chloe, Stephen C. Alex R., Kimberley	Trajectory Infilling
Outside	Musical instruments suspended for targeting Sand with containers, wheelbarrows and trailers Long tray with cube and ramps Ridealongs and pulleys	Stephen C., Enzo Craig, John K., Nicholas, John M., Stephen, John Mi. Natalie S. Craig	Targeting Trajectory Transporting Trajectory (Ramps)
Outings	Rutland Water, Tuesday morning	Staff: Lindsey, Becky, Carrie Children: Stacy D., Michael, Keith, Steven C., Zach	

The 'desirable outcomes' have influenced the curriculum offered in early years settings where there are 4-year-olds and although currently under review the areas of learning covered are used in this chapter as a basis for looking at the curriculum for 3- to 5-year-olds.

5. Baseline assessment

Baseline assessment is being piloted and phased into schools throughout England, Wales, Northern Ireland and Scotland although the schemes are different in each country. From September 1998 schools in England will have to assess children within their first 7 weeks of starting state provision and schools have a range of different schemes from which to select. In practice, however, schools often have to accept the local education authority's choice of scheme. Baseline assessment schemes act as a diagnostic tool to identify the stage of learning a child has reached and the child's subsequent progress is measured against this baseline. The schemes are designed to assist in the planning of individual programmes for children and to assist in measuring their progress. Some baseline assessment schemes can also be used as 'entry to nursery' assessments and record progress from entry to nursery through baseline at age 4 or 5 and can be used again as the children leave key stage 1.

There are many concerns about baseline assessment being expressed at the current time. It is thought that children might be 'labelled' at a very early stage in their education and that this label may influence their chances. Also the fact that children enter school at different ages and stages of development means that they are being assessed at different ages and stages and this does not always give a helpful picture. Some educationalists are suggesting that all children should be assessed either at pre-school or at the beginning of year 1 but the QCA Under Fives Unit suggests that 'teachers will have to take account of children's ages when using the baseline assessment scores for planning' (*Nursery World* 16 July 1998).

Baseline assessment schemes can also form the basis for measuring schools' performance. By comparing baseline scores with those achieved by the children at age 7 and 11, it will be possible to calculate how well schools have performed. Concerns have been expressed that there may be pressure to 'under assess' children's baseline scores in order to demonstrate that schools are performing well.

6. Anti-bias approaches

Children learn attitudes and values very early as part of their socialization. This early learning of attitudes and values is related to the child's experience within the family, the day care setting, the school, the peer group, the media and, indeed, any aspect of a child's life that exerts influence and has been known as the 'hidden curriculum'. These are messages that children receive concerning themselves and others that indicate a value is put on certain attributes, e.g. that white skin is more acceptable or that being a girl means you will not be good at maths or that coming from a lone parent family means you are more likely to become delinquent. There are discriminatory voices all around that children hear and absorb. These relate to race, gender, social class, religion, sexual preference, culture disability and appearance. In view of this there is no guarantee that an anti-bias approach in the early years setting will eliminate discrimination or change attitudes and values amongst children, families or staff. However, settings delivering an anti-bias curriculum are ensuring that all the children and families receive positive messages about themselves and this will help to counteract the negative stereotypes that may be present already in even the youngest children.

An anti-bias approach affects every aspect of provision from advertising the setting, admissions policy, staff recruitment selection and training, resources, equipment, the curriculum and routines and the various policies and procedures of the setting; e.g. an anti-bias approach might lead to a behaviour policy which emphasizes zero tolerance of name-calling or abusive discriminatory verbal behaviour. If an anti-bias approach is not taken seriously, discrimination may block children's full access to the formal early years curriculum. Although there are still many parts of the country where there may not be representatives of different ethnic groups, recognition that we live in a multi-cultural, multi-lingual, pluralist society and the need to promote a positive world-view should be integrated throughout the curriculum, and efforts should be made to ensure that all children receive positive images of themselves.

The following are examples of ways in which workers can check whether or not they are providing a non-sexist curriculum or whether aspects of sexism creep in under a 'hidden' curriculum.

- *Do you use gender-specific descriptions of people's jobs such as 'fireman', 'waitress', 'policeman', 'postman'?*
- *Do you have story books that depict people in non-stereotypical jobs?*
- *Do you encourage both boys and girls to use the bicycles and outdoor equipment?*
- *Do you discourage boys from activities such as dressing-up or playing in the home corner?*
- *Do you intervene if boys are dominating the wheeled toys in the outdoor area?*
- *What is your reaction if you find a boy playing with a doll?*
- *What is your reaction to boys when they are crying?*
- *What is your reaction when a boy dresses up in female clothes from the dressing-up corner?*

Browne and France (1986) offer practical ways of dispelling the myths attached to some areas of play; e.g. the idea that boys do not like playing in the home corner and that it is really a female domain is usually a result of staff discouraging boys from this type of play.

It has been argued by feminists that the very existence of a home corner only succeeds in reinforcing gender roles at an early stage, but this could be said about other activities such as riding bicycles, cooking and hospital corners. It is not the activity that is at fault but the attitudes of adults who label activities as 'for boys' or 'for girls'. In many instances adults need to encourage girls and boys to try out new activities in order that they may broaden their experience and develop new skills.

When children start in playgroup or nursery they are likely to be entrenched in the role that goes with their gender from their early experiences at home. In our society we still associate blue with boys and pink with girls and buy toys and clothes according to gender. This prevents children developing according to the individual interests and personal strengths, which may contrast sharply with their gender stereotype. Although staff should not be in open conflict with the child's family, opportunities will occur for children to participate in activities which might normally be denied them. This will extend and develop their learning.

The implications on early learning of an anti-bias approach have been positive, leading to the raising of awareness of the damaging effect of discrimination on young children's development and learning. It has also encouraged sensitivity to bias and the development of strategies opposing bias through every aspect of the work of the setting.

Figure 3.3
Girl at the
woodwork bench.

Scenario 3.2

A new, day nursery worker in a predominantly white, middle-class, suburban area becomes concerned because the nursery provides no material, equipment or activities which portray children from other ethnic or linguistic groups in a positive manner. She has noticed that many of the children's books are both sexist and racist.

(a) Why should she be concerned?
(b) What are the possible reasons for this situation?
(c) Devise a strategy she might use to mention her concerns to her supervisor.
(d) What practical changes might be introduced to remedy the situation in three areas of provision? Provide a rationale for your suggested changes.

Scenario 3.3

In a nursery school home corner, two 4-year-old boys have dressed up in a variety of hats, scarves, skirts and waistcoats. One is busy filling up a handbag with small items from the kitchen. A small group of boys of the same age dressed as 'super-heroes' approach and start to comment and whisper together. As they move away, a parting comment from one is 'You're a girl', spoken with the intention of offering an insult.

(a) Would you intervene in this situation?
(b) If you do intervene, how would you deal with each set of boys?
(c) What do you think is the underlying learning influencing the attitudes of the 'super-heroes'?
(d) What messages are the boys playing in the home corner receiving?

Other approaches to the early years curriculum

The High/Scope Curriculum

The High/Scope Curriculum is derived from work with deprived children and families which took place in the USA during the 1960s and 1970s (Hohmann *et al.*, 1979). These programmes involved work with parents and were designed to prepare children for school and to maximize future school success. The results of these programmes have been monitored and it is thought that they are effective in the long term in improving children's performance and life chances.

The High/Scope Curriculum involves a highly structured approach to children's learning and reflects much good nursery practice. Working on the premise that children are active learners who learn best from activities they plan and carry out themselves, the session is organized so that children engage in a plan–do–review sequence. The children are notified in advance if the routine is going to vary.

Through careful assessment of the children, developmental programmes based on 'key experiences' are devised for each child. These incorporate adult–child communication and teaching strategies, parental partnership and detailed record keeping.

Criticism of the High/Scope Curriculum is partly centred around the tight structure. Also Sylva, Smith and Moore (1986 – Nuffield Foundation Report) state that 'there is little evidence that the method meets one of its objectives which is to support and extend children's play.

The implications of the High/Scope Curriculum on early learning have been generally beneficial. Children are encouraged to be autonomous learners and are actively involved in planning their own programmes. Many mainstream settings use elements of the High/Scope programme.

Maria Montessori (1869–1952)

Maria Montessori was a doctor who worked in Italy during the early part of the 20th century. She viewed the development of children as a biological programme and believed that children go through sensitive periods in their development when they are more receptive to learning various skills and concepts.

The method involved providing a series of activities, carefully graded from simple to complex and within a planned environment, through which every child must proceed. Children were thought to learn from their own spontaneous activities and, within this highly structured environment, they were encouraged to work alone with the materials presented to them. Although Montessori did consider the whole child, she approached learning and development by concentrating on encouraging separate sensory experiences, and when the relevant learning had taken place she considered that it could be generalized to cover other situations.

There has been much criticism of the Montessori approach with its emphasis on formal work. It is thought to stifle creativity and as there is so little interaction, it does not encourage language development and social skills. Major criticisms are that the child is encouraged to work individually, there is little direct parental involvement and the role of the adult (directress) is limited as the child has a 'teacher within himself'. However, there are variants on the traditional Montessori approach which place emphasis in slightly different ways. In spite of this, aspects of her work are still useful today. The equipment she developed to encourage children's intellectual and sensory development has been modified and is widely used today, and her view of the child as an active, autonomous thinker is also encouraged, although not necessarily by the methods she used.

The Montessori approach tends to be restricted to Montessori schools and nurseries. Aspects of the method such as learning materials and activities are valuable and used in mainstream settings.

Structured programmes

Other highly structured programmes usually follow particular theories of how children develop, and consist of structured, sequential education activities which are thought to stimulate the child's cognitive and language development. The programmes do seem to have achieved a measure of success in that limited area, and are usually taught in specialist centres and privately funded through fees paid by parents, although they can take the form of postal lessons. Attitudes behind such programmes can be elitist and build on parents' anxieties to give their child the best possible start by providing sometimes misleading or biased information about how children learn.

Criticism of these types of programmes will vary accordingly but often centres around their apparent concentration on intellectual development rather than considering the whole child. Also, the tight structure gives little opportunity for creativity, social interaction, decision-making and problem-solving.

Te Whaariki

Te Whaariki is a curriculum framework offered in New Zealand. Its name is a Maori term meaning 'woven mat'. Within the Te Whaariki document, the principles, strands and goals provide a curriculum framework which weaves together the different perspectives on early childhood. The aim of the Te Whaariki curriculum is 'for children to grow up as competent and confident learners and communicators, healthy in mind, body and spirit, secure in their sense of belonging and in the knowledge that they make a valuable contribution to society' (New Zealand Ministry of Education, 1996).

Te Whaariki has four foundation principles that are: empowerment, holistic development, family and community, and relationships. The principles, although developed in New Zealand, have attracted interest across the world.

The Te Whaariki document indicates that the early childhood programme in all settings should include experiences which are:

- Humanly appropriate – equitable opportunities for full participation and access, with dignity and respect for the individual

- Educationally appropriate – building on best practice
- Individually appropriate – recognizing that children are individuals who develop at different rates and have different needs
- Nationally appropriate – to reflect in the case of New Zealand its democratic dual culture
- Culturally appropriate – supporting different cultures' child-rearing practices, values and beliefs.

Te Whaariki provides goals for settings on learning outcomes for children, questions for adults to encourage reflective practice, and examples of experiences designed to help children to meet the learning outcomes.

Characteristics of the early years curriculum

The curriculum should:

- start from the individual child's needs and stage of development whilst recognizing that many children share similar cognitive concerns and staff can plan the curriculum for groups as well as individual children.

Teachers who have taught 6-year-olds for instance, will know that it is not unusual for over half the class to have reading to an adult as top of their agenda.

Athey, 1990

- be differentiated in such a way that allows for the learning and developmental needs of most children but is flexible enough to cover the specific needs of individual children. This means that there has to be careful planning within an overall strategy. Where children show aptitude or interest that is outside the formal plan, there is sufficient flexibility to incorporate change and include further challenge.
- be broad and balanced. The Educational Reform Act 1988 emphasizes the need for a curriculum which 'promotes the spiritual, moral, cultural, mental and physical development of pupils at the school and of society, and prepares such pupils for the opportunities, responsibilities and experiences of adult life.'
- take into account the 'desirable outcomes' (early learning goals).
- take into account how children learn and the developmental needs of young children and should avoid too much formal learning before young children are able to cope. Comment has been made (HMI, 1989) that 'there is often insufficient exploratory and practical work to support the children's developing understanding of ideas and language before they start out on the formal work more appropriate to later stages of learning.'

- recognize that play is the best way to integrate and facilitate a young child's learning.
- emphasize the process of learning, whether skills, concepts or knowledge, rather than the products of learning such as paintings or models.
- be integrated where possible and not presented as separate subjects all of the time. Learning in the early years often involves working with projects or themes which integrate many aspects of the curriculum.
- use daily care routines such as bath- or meal-times, visits to the clinic or hairdresser as these can all be considered part of the curriculum, presenting important learning opportunities.
- ensure equality of opportunity for all children regardless of social, cultural, linguistic or ethnic origin, gender or disability and reflect this in all aspects of provision.
- include parents and significant people in a child's life in the delivery and planning of the curriculum. The child's experiences within the curriculum should complement, extend and involve the child's home and community life.
- offer continuity and progression between classes, schools, nurseries and playgroups.
- recognize and treat children as valued individuals within their own social context.

Contemporary views of the child as learner

- There are stages in children's development when they are more sensitive to certain types of skill or concept acquisition, and the curriculum offered should match these stages.
- Children's learning does not 'just happen'. Methods such as discovery learning have their place but modern research indicates a need for adults to be concerned about how children construct their own knowledge and then to structure the learning environment, to extend and to 'scaffold' the learning, where necessary, to teach and to provide for direct learning experience and to act as positive role models.
- Children learn and integrate learning and experience through play.
- Children learn best through direct experience, handling, exploring through their senses, solving problems, practising skills rather than through 'being told'.
- Children's learning is facilitated by their use of language which should be a central aspect of the curriculum.

- Children's learning should be founded on what is familiar to them and build on their individual experience and social and cultural context.
- Children need time to explore and consider in order to produce work of quality, and the time taken will vary amongst individuals. Time is necessary to practise and refine skills; children should not be rushed.
- Children's predisposition to learn and to explore their environment should be harnessed and utilized by early years workers when planning and implementing the curriculum, not stifled through a rigid and unimaginative regime.
- Children learn best in a secure environment where adults make clear the boundaries for acceptable behaviour and are consistent in their handling of the various conflict situations which arise, and where praise and encouragement are freely and appropriately given. Self-discipline is the goal for children rather than a rigidly imposed set of rules and regulations with which the child has to conform without any basic understanding of why.
- Children who do not have their basic needs met or who have suffered loss of self-esteem through poverty, abuse, disadvantage or discrimination will find it more difficult to learn and take advantage of opportunities offered to them.

The adult's role in the delivery of the curriculum

- The adult should provide a safe, stimulating and caring environment. This environment should be carefully planned and organized in order to provide for learning and to make the most of learning opportunities.
- The adult should adopt an active role in promoting learning, creativity and development and in the provision of suitable resources and environment both indoors and outdoors.
- The day-to-day routines and activities should encourage a child's independence of thought and action. The adult should enable the child to take ownership of the environment and feel confident in everyday activity. Through their increasing autonomy and sense of control, children will develop confidence, self-control and enhanced self-esteem.
- The interactions, both non-verbal and verbal, between adult and child are vital and should be of high quality, extending the child's language and thinking.
- Provision for children's learning should be based on careful observation and assessment of their progress.

- Detailed individual records should be kept based on observations of children and assessment of their future needs.
- Adults start where the child is and with what they can do, and build on this rather than concentrating on what the child cannot do.
- Adults need a deep knowledge of child development in order to observe and identify children's needs and special needs. They also require a wide range of skills and knowledge including interpersonal skills.

Scenario 3.4

Imagine a typical class of 4-year-olds some 30 or 40 years ago. Young children are admitted into a large class of perhaps 40 other children with one teacher. The day starts at 9 a.m. and parents are not allowed into the school. The desks are arranged in rows; there are few, if any, toys or playthings although there are crayons and pencils for drawing, and occasionally paints or modelling materials are allowed.

The morning begins with a formal assembly, followed by a strict timetable of subjects, e.g. writing followed by number work where the children are expected to count on their fingers or in their head and then to write down when they are able.

After play-time they might have PE followed by nature study. This might involve planting bulbs and putting them in a dark cupboard, or drawing flowers and trees.

After dinner some of the younger children are given a bed to rest on, whether or not they feel tired. Every day they are given vitamin capsules and made to drink their milk.

Afternoon school consists of further subject periods such as reading, history or geography before finishing at 3.45 or 4 p.m.

In the light of the information given in this chapter, the desirable outcomes and your own reading and experience, give a short critique of this type of provision. Allowing for lack of resources in those days but utilizing modern views on children's learning, discuss in outline what measures could have been taken immediately to improve the situation?

The curriculum for babies and toddlers 0 to 3 years

The curriculum for babies and toddlers in early years settings should be as carefully planned as at any other stage. This age group has particular needs and these should be reflected in what is offered. Learning starts at birth (and before!) and almost everything that happens to a baby or toddler is a learning opportunity. At this stage babies and toddlers are learning about themselves and the world. To make the most of this learning and interaction with the world babies and toddlers need to have their basic needs met. Babies who are hungry, cold, uncomfortable or unloved will not develop to their full potential. In particular, babies and toddlers in day care must have their attachment needs met (see Ch. 1 for details of attachment and development of babies and toddlers). Settings must provide consistent care from a small number of workers (key worker/s) for individual babies. Emotional involvement with young babies is a two-way process and can be difficult for workers who will need a supportive environment to be able to do this. It is however a major feature of providing quality care for the very youngest and most vulnerable. Babies who are content and well attached to their key worker will benefit most from the learning curriculum offered.

Babies and toddlers show a need to be competent and to master their own world. This gives them confidence and high self-esteem. They need to link their interaction with the environment to a change or response in that environment. In other words, they learn that what they do is effective and can change things for them in a positive way. This can range from crying because they are hungry or uncomfortable and being attended to promptly, to swiping at a pram toy and hearing it rattle or seeing it swing at their command. If their attempts to interact or communicate bring little or no response from people or objects, they receive the message that they are helpless and powerless and that response is pointless. This has important long-term effects on their feelings about themselves and about learning. Babies who receive little attention or care become passive and may lie for hours making meaningless repetitive movements or head banging. Their crying has been ignored and they have learned that it makes no difference.

Learning through play supported by language is a key feature of this stage and adult interactions with babies and toddlers can almost all be made fun for the baby and opportunities to play and communicate (see Ch. 2 for treasure basket and heuristic play for babies and toddlers). Talking and listening games should be used from the first days of a baby's life with time given to gain eye contact and allow the baby to respond. Songs, rhymes, stories, laughter and lively and expressive conversation should feature strongly during these early months and years, with one-to-one interaction being the most important feature. The most important resource is the adult who gives the young child time and undivided, one-to-one attention.

The present government is currently introducing a support programme for families with children under 3 years to be known as 'Sure Start'. This programme will give additional support to parents and is likely to emphasize parenting skills including how babies learn and how to promote development.

A nursery has started to take in babies from 6 months. Staff are not experienced with crawling babies and concerned that their determined exploration is unhygienic, and dangerous. Babies once mobile are placed for long periods in a playpen or a walker for 'safety' reasons.

You are a new nursery officer with responsibility for the babies in the nursery and have to make sure that other staff give them the best possible all-round care. Write a short booklet to help staff and parents understand the nursery's approach to:

- Preventing cross infection in the nursery
- Activities and experiences for babies
- Dealing with crying and demanding babies
- Parents' concerns at leaving their babies.

Toys and equipment should be available which promote all areas of development through play and exploration. They should be safe for the age range, e.g. large enough for tiny fingers to pick up and not to swallow or to choke on. Very young children should have regular access to basic materials to play, e.g. water, sand, dough (with adult supervision at all times to ensure safety). Large mirrors for babies to look at reflections of themselves and others assist with establishing a sense of self and provide a great deal of fun. Babies should have solid furniture or ballet bars attached to the wall to pull themselves up from the floor. Babies and toddlers will already be learning language and concepts that cover the whole range of experience including mathematics and science and need to hear maths language just as much as older children. Adults should use such language naturally taking every opportunity, e.g. 'teddy is bigger than …', 'up and down', 'in and out'.

To provide a learning curriculum for babies and toddlers, workers should:

- *meet attachment needs through key working.*
- *understand the stages and sequence of development and what to provide at each stage.*
- *learn to recognize early schemas.*
- *provide a balanced routine to ensure healthy growth and development.*
- *know how to observe and assess development and readiness to move on.*
- *understand the 'zone of proximal development' (Vygotsky, 1978).*
- *understand and provide for sensory stimulation.*
- *provide a learning curriculum embedded in everyday routines.*

- *ensure a safe and non-restrictive environment.*
- *encourage curiosity, exploration and discovery.*
- *provide physical comfort and contact.*
- *recognize when babies are bored as opposed to tired or uncomfortable.*
- *provide equipment and activities to keep the babies' interest, e.g. treasure basket.*
- *give the individual baby or toddler their full attention for parts of the day.*
- *never rush babies and toddlers but give them time to explore and to communicate.*
- *not keep the radio or TV on in the nursery except for short periods.*
- *allow for quiet and silent periods.*

A learning curriculum embedded in everyday routines

Parents or carers of babies and toddlers often find it difficult to recognize that they are in fact providing a learning curriculum for them in everything they do. The curriculum is embedded into the routines, activities, interactions, equipment and materials used and the opportunities for learning which are given in everyday situations. The curriculum offered to the under 3s should utilize everyday activities and routines to support learning. The importance of the interaction with the adult cannot be stressed enough, and every opportunity should be used sensitively; careful assessment of the child should reveal when they are ready to move on.

Bruner (1975) found three important features of parents/carers' interactions with their babies and young children in everyday situations:

1. *Parents are sensitive to their children's needs as learners.*
2. *Parents provide a flexible framework or 'scaffold' where children can learn.*
3. *Parents follow the conversational initiatives of their children in a meaningful way.*

Early years workers should ensure that they use these findings to improve their service to young babies and their parents, especially in the care routines described below.

Using care routines

Dressing, nappy changing, bathing and washing give opportunities for physical contact and for sensory exploration. Make eye contact and bathe the baby in language as well as water. Allow baby to kick without its nappy to enjoy the freedom. This type of activity can provide many types of learning, e.g. about the properties of water or the baby's own body awareness.

Feeding and meal-times should be happy times without pressure to eat everything. Meal-times are social occasions when babies learn to sit with others and enjoy food and begin to learn social skills.

Learning can take place in sleep and quiet times as babies and toddlers relax. Gentle songs, lullabies, stroking or light massage can encourage sleep and rest.

Using the environment

Ensure that the baby has space to crawl, to shuffle, to explore, to touch and to feel a variety of objects in safety, to go outdoors, to the shops and the park. Encourage the baby to learn about the environment, the properties of materials, object permanence, different sights, smells, sounds by constantly labelling, 'discussing', possibly singing, e.g. 'here is big red bus...like in your book...granny comes to see us in a bus...see the wheels of the bus...the wheels of the bus go round and round, round and round.'

The curriculum for 3- to 5-year-olds

Many children between 3 and 5 years begin to enter some type of early years provision. A large proportion will enter primary schools shortly after their fourth birthday. Wherever children of 4 years of age are placed in pre-schools or reception or nursery classes they are likely to be working towards the 'desirable outcomes' most of which can be achieved through structured (guided) play experiences. Different settings will provide different programmes designed to meet the same goal, i.e. the desirable outcomes (see below); e.g. a community pre-school may emphasize informal approaches through play, whereas a primary school in a middle-class area may be pressured by parents to deliver a more formal approach. However, good practice in all settings and stages will involve careful planning and structuring of the early years curriculum which should be broad and balanced and incorporate the 'Characteristics' outlined above. It should be noted that extensive government consultation is currently taking place on the education of this age group, the outcomes of which may change the early years curriculum; e.g. introduction of the early learning goals and the foundation stage from 3 years to the end of reception.

Implementing the desirable outcomes for children's learning on entering compulsory education

The desirable outcomes are goals for children's learning by the time they enter compulsory education which is in the term after their fifth birthday. They are presented as the six areas of learning providing a foundation for later achievement. Each area of learning relates to the National Curriculum.

The desirable outcomes documentation:

- *identifies common features of good practice.*
- *recognizes parents as partners.*

- *forms the basis of OFSTED inspection of early years settings.*

Effects on the early years curriculum

There have been a range of effects on the curriculum, including:

- There is a common language across settings.
- Planning and record keeping is more focused.
- There is a greater emphasis on education in early years settings.
- Much of the learning for 4-year-olds is directed towards these areas of learning, therefore some of the breadth of provision has been lost.
- Providing evidence of the children's achievements can lead to over-formalizing the curriculum.
- The curriculum offered to 3-year-olds and younger children has in some cases been affected and lost its breadth and integration.

Desirable outcomes for personal and social development (QCA, 1996)

These outcomes focus on children learning how to work, play, co-operate with others and function in a group beyond the family. They cover important aspects of personal, social, moral and spiritual development including the development of personal values and an understanding of self and of others. They should be interpreted in the context of the values agreed by the adults, including the parents, involved with each setting.

Children are confident, show appropriate self-respect and are able to establish effective relationships with other children and with adults. They work as part of a group and independently, are able to concentrate and persevere in their learning and to seek help where needed. They are eager to explore new learning, and show the ability to initiate ideas and to solve simple practical problems. They demonstrate independence in selecting an activity or resources and in dressing and personal hygiene.

Children are sensitive to the needs and feelings of others and show respect for people of other cultures and beliefs. They take turns and share fairly. They express their feelings and behave in appropriate ways, developing an understanding of what is right, what is wrong and why. They treat living things, property and their environment with care and concern. They respond to relevant cultural and religious events and show a range of feelings, such as wonder, joy or sorrow, in response to their experiences of the world.

To many early years workers personal and social development is perhaps the most important area of learning. Confident, well-adjusted children with good self-esteem learn well and take advantage of opportunities offered to them. Encouraging this outcome should be an integral part of every activity and routine. Personal and social development should run like a thread through every area of the curriculum and early childhood routines and curriculum plans should be checked to ensure that this developmental area is covered.

Adults should support children's growing sense of awe and wonder in the world around them. Using all their senses children should be encouraged to marvel at the living world and to respect life and each other. Children's spiritual development and sense of personal morality and concern for others are vitally important areas and adults should encourage positive attitudes to the world and its peoples. Differences in culture, religion, race, gender, abilities and social class should be celebrated by staff through recognition of the value of each. The worker's own values and attitudes are very important as children will soon see through prejudice and cynicism and may copy what they see.

Desirable outcomes for language and literacy (QCA, 1996)

> These outcomes cover important aspects of language development and provide the foundation for literacy. Children must be helped to acquire competence in English as soon as possible, making use, where appropriate, of their developing understanding and skills in other languages. The outcomes focus on children's developing competence in taking and listening and in becoming readers and writers. Other areas of learning also make a vital contribution to the successful development of literacy.
>
> In small and large groups, children listen attentively and talk about their experiences. They use a growing vocabulary with increasing fluency to express thoughts and convey meaning to the listener. They listen and respond to stories, songs, nursery rhymes and poems. They make up their own stories and take part in role play with confidence.
>
> Children enjoy books and handle them carefully, understanding how they are organised. They know that words and pictures carry meaning and that, in English, print is read from left to right and from top to bottom. They begin to associate sounds with patterns in rhymes, with syllables, and with words and letters. They recognise their own names and some familiar words. They recognise letters of the alphabet by shape and sound. In their writing they use pictures, symbols, familiar words and letters, to communicate meaning, showing awareness of some of the different purposes of writing. They write their names with appropriate use of upper and lower case letters.

Language and literacy are very important areas of children's learning as they underpin so much other learning but children's communication skills will go beyond language, e.g. non-verbal communication, or communication through the expressive arts. The learning curriculum will encompass the four modes of language, i.e. speaking, listening, reading and writing. In the early years children's ability to read and write develops from and builds on their speaking and listening skills so children must be given time to develop these skills.

Speaking

Children should be encouraged to talk and to express themselves verbally. Although most young children can talk fluently, not all can or will; however, given the oppor-

Figure 3.4
A story-telling
session by Beulah
Candappa at Cherry
Orchard School.

tunity, most will communicate, question, solve problems, debate, argue, listen and wonder. To encourage children to talk and interact, the environment should have quiet and busy areas, interest tables and displays and a wide range of activities. The most effective learning opportunities are those where the language and communication have a purpose such as planning for a visit. A crucial area of learning and experience is the use of stories and rhymes that help to introduce children to the world of symbols and ideas which underpin much future learning.

Listening

Workers should practise active listening in order to understand properly what children are attempting to say and to encourage children to listen themselves. Too much background noise can hold back children's language development. Children with dyslexia (difficulty with words) find developing listening skills particularly helpful. Listening games should be used but with sensitivity where children have difficulties with hearing or speech. All nurseries should have periods of quiet.

Reading

The National Literacy Strategy (1998) 'Framework for Teaching' sets out targets for children's literacy from reception class through to year 6 and suggests that every primary school should have a formal literacy hour each day preferably using whole class teaching methods although the strategy recognizes that support staff could be used to create smaller groups. Early years specialists emphasize the importance of ensuring that nursery and reception class children are not pressurized into an over-formal literacy curriculum.

Reading is helped by encouraging children to understand that print has meaning. This can be done in many ways, e.g. labelling in the nursery or looking at the print in the environment when outside the nursery or through books and stories, especially real-life, 'home-made' books that feature the children or perhaps their own stories written down. 'Big books' that can be home-made but allow a group of children to 'read' together are particularly helpful. Children often enjoy pretend 'reading' to each other and this should be encouraged. Success in reading is linked to being read to or told stories, and this is an important part of the curriculum. In many nurseries parents are encouraged to borrow books to take home to read to their children.

More formal reading skills should be encouraged as the individual child is ready but will certainly be introduced in the reception year under the National Literacy Strategy. There will continue to be different ways in which children are taught to read and teachers will use a variety of methods but there is likely to be less variation and a greater use of phonics as staff will have to follow the teaching framework in the strategy.

Children (4 to 5-year-olds) are to be taught in their reception year:

- *Phonological awareness, phonics and spelling*
- *Word recognition, graphic knowledge and spelling*
- *Vocabulary extension*
- *Handwriting*
- *Grammatical awareness*
- *Understanding of print (reading)*
- *Reading comprehension*
- *Understanding of print (writing)*
- *Composition.*

The above topics are developed and extended through to year 6.

Phonemes is the term used widely in the National Literacy Strategy to refer to sounds and associated symbols which children need to be able to identify. There are 44 phonemes in the English language consisting of short vowel sounds such as 'a', (cat), long vowel sounds such as 'ay' (day), other vowel sounds such as 'oy' (toy), consonant sounds such as 'p' (pet) and other consonant sounds such as 'ch' (chip).

Children need to learn both 'top down' skills in reading which is where the child has to understand the meaning and context and 'bottom up' or decoding skills which relate to the child distinguishing the sounds that make up words. Adults supporting children's reading will give opportunity for children to learn 'top down' skills by asking questions about the meaning in a story such as 'What word fits in here?' or 'What is she going to say next?' and 'What makes sense here?', i.e. predicting what the rules of language might allow. As well as this they will need to draw children's attention to the 'bottom up' skills, by sharing picture books and drawing attention to the text, perhaps by pointing to words as they read and ensuring that there is abundance of meaningful print in the nursery to which they can refer naturally, e.g. 'Jane's name begins with the sound "J". Here is the letter "J". "J" is for jumping.' In addition, games using phonics and sounds can be fun and it is the skill of the adult in ensuring that children enjoy their games and activities with print that will encourage children to become readers.

Writing

In order to develop writing skills children need to have developed hand–eye co-ordination and fine motor skills through their early play experiences. Children benefit by using pens, crayons or paint to explore the circles, lines and spirals that form the shapes of the letters of the alphabet. Tracing letter shapes in the air, talking about the shapes and sounds of letters, making shapes in dough or finger paints all assist, especially if they are accompanied by verbalizing the movements involved, e.g. 'top to bottom all the way', 'round and down the hill'. Writing can be encouraged through the provision of a writing workshop or graphics area where tools and materials are left for the children to explore and/or use with adult helpers who should demonstrate how to hold the pens and assist children sensitively. Other opportunities for the children to 'write' could be shopping pads in the home corner and telephone message pads. Painting, creative work and the development of manipulative skills and hand–eye co-ordination through a whole range of activities help with the development of writing. Children's early attempts at mark-making should be explored and discussed with them, and as they develop greater skill they will use familiar shapes, symbols, words and letters. Writing their own books with adult support or sitting with the adults who write the book at the child's dictation is excellent.

By the time the child enters formal school the desirable outcomes state that children should be able to write their names with appropriate use of upper and lower case letters. The National Literacy Strategy sets out what the children should be taught in the reception class.

Desirable outcomes for mathematics (QCA, 1996)

These outcomes cover important aspects of mathematical understanding and provide the foundation for numeracy. They focus on achievement through practical activities and on using and understanding language in the development of simple mathematical ideas.

Children use mathematical language, such as circle, in front of, bigger than and more, to describe shape, position, size and quantity. They recognise and recreate patterns. They are familiar with number rhymes, songs, stories, counting games and activities. They compare, sort, match, order, sequence and count using everyday objects. They recognise and use numbers to 10 and are familiar with larger numbers from their everyday lives. They begin to use their developing mathematical understanding to solve practical problems. Through practical activities children understand and record numbers, begin to show awareness of number operations, such as addition and subtraction, and begin to use the language involved.

Mathematics learning is not just about numbers and counting, but about comparison, shape and size, length, volume and capacity, area, weight, sorting and grouping, spatial relationships, patterns, problem-solving, time, and understanding that words and symbols convey ideas of quantity. The child is surrounded by mathematical ideas and relationships in the everyday world and adults should take every opportunity to develop these concepts, particularly through practical activities, discussion and the use of mathematical language. Children learn concepts such as up/down, across, in/out, over/under, around/surrounding in practical situations before they can learn more abstract concepts such as shape. The desirable outcomes expect children to use maths language such as circle, triangle, in front of, bigger than, and words to describe shape, position, size and quantity. Terms such as 'how much', 'none', 'lots', or 'how many' in practical situations convey ideas of number or volume from the earliest years. The language of mathematics and conceptual development will become more sophisticated as the children are ready and many young children will, for example, weigh out flour for cooking very precisely and understand the need for accuracy before being able to formally understand or record number symbols. In the pre-school/reception stage, children will be learning through practical activities about weight and volume as well as classifying materials by colour, shape or other features. They may also learn to understand and record numbers.

The desirable outcomes require children to recognize and use numbers up to 10 and acquire familiarity with larger numbers through everyday experience. Counting the plates at meal-times or the number of steps to the front door are valuable routine experiences for children which reinforce numeracy. There are many number songs, finger plays and rhymes which teach children about numbers in an informal and pleasurable way.

Many of the practical activities in the nursery will develop mathematics concepts and help with practical problem-solving and it is important that these are recognized and used, e.g. the home corner will provide opportunities for children to estimate the size of dolls' clothes; the construction area will allow children to explore size, shape and spatial relations; water play and sand play develop ideas concerning volume and density; creative activities will help children to recognize and create patterns. Adults should point out mathematical patterns in the environment.

The desirable outcomes state that children should show awareness of number operations such as addition and subtraction and begin to use the language involved. Care should be taken in introducing these concepts as young children are tied to the concrete world of their own experience and early learning and will only move on to deal with more abstract and symbolic numbers as and when they are ready. It is not appropriate for children to be given formal written mathematics work until they have

Table 3.1
An example of
planning for language
and literacy from
Cambridgeshire LEA
(1996).

Table 3.1 Language and literacy

	Music and dance	Toys, games, puzzles	Creative and construction	Communication (books, writing and IT)	Imaginative and role play
Talking and listening	Nursery rhymes, songs, number rhymes Music – listen and talk about feelings Rhythms – body percussion Circle games 'Music talk' – speed, rhythm	Sequence puzzles, group and floor puzzles Sound lotto Group games Ordering games Observations of weather, seasons Large outdoor play equipment Farm/shop visits	Printing – hands, vegetables, shapes, tracks Drawing/painting – close observation, imaginary Colour mixing Experiments with paint – bubbles, marbles	Develop book language — cover, page, title, front back, word — share and discuss books with friend/adult — relaxed comfortable area – reading area — stimulating/exciting books — dual-language books — books in different scripts — listen to taped stories	Role play area — office, hairdresser, shop, cafe, travel agent, picnic, doctors, hospital, home Outdoor role play — bus, train, spaceship — puppet play
Reading	'Music' area – play instruments, sort and label Songs, finger play, ring games to develop narrative	Follow instructions Match word/letter/picture Alphabet games/puzzles Lotto/matching games Look for print in environment on walks and visits Sequence events/stories	Design and make own books/cards Follow recipes Label and display painting and models Plant seeds – seed packet	Book area – listen to, read, re-tell stories Participate in repetitive areas Books as a source of information Groups share Big Books Parents as partners 'Listening area' – taped stories in English and home languages	Dramatize stories — Three Bears, Three Little Pigs Reading in role play — menu in cafe — orders in cafe — bills/catalogue in shop — messages in office — phone numbers/names
Writing	Music as stimulus to painting/writing	Draw maps of journeys Picture and captions of outside places and events	'Writing' on sand/clay with paint, crayon, felt pen Adults 'scribe' for children's narrative Make plans/drawings Printing 'Water painting'	Write letters – grandparents, visitors, thank you's, invitations Make own books/group Picture stories 'Rewrite' stories Word processing Writing in different scripts	Role play area — lists, bills, messages — cafe orders, menus — price labels — prescriptions — letters Writing area — clipboards, paper, cards — felt pens, crayons, pencils, scissors, rulers, stamps

grasped many basic concepts and staff should be sensitive to the individual child's stage of development. In this way children can be encouraged to deal competently with mathematics.

Teachers and other early years workers use a variety of techniques to teach numeracy skills and concepts. It is likely that mathematical concepts will be integrated in a carefully structured way throughout all the curriculum activities as well as having an area of the room devoted to mathematics learning. At this stage formal workbooks or worksheets should not be the primary way of teaching or encouraging mathematics.

There is now a strategy for numeracy similar to that of literacy which will require staff in schools to spend about 45 minutes to 1 hour per day in mathematical activities. The strategy recommends that a proportion of the teaching is interactive and done with the whole class. There will be a strong emphasis on mental arithmetic and learning times tables and a limitation on the use of calculators especially for the under 8s. It is uncertain at present what implications the numeracy strategy will have on nursery and reception classes.

Scenario 3.6

Parents are asking questions about their children's learning of number and counting. You have been asked to prepare a leaflet for parents about mathematics in the nursery in order to introduce them to how the nursery approaches the full range of maths learning.

Prepare the leaflet showing clearly:

- what the term 'mathematics' covers in the nursery settings
- how children develop mathematical concepts
- what activities and planning the nursery provides to encourage mathematical learning
- how parents can support mathematical learning at home.

Desirable outcomes for knowledge and understanding of the world (QCA, 1996)

These outcomes focus on children's developing knowledge and understanding of their environment, other people and features of the natural and made world. They provide a foundation for historical, geographical, scientific and technological learning.

Children talk about where they live, their environment, their families and past and present events in their own lives. They explore and recognise features of living things, objects and events in the natural and made world and look closely at similarities, differences, patterns and change. They show an awareness of the purposes of some features of the area in which they live. They talk about their observations, sometimes recording them and ask questions to gain information about why things happen and how things work. They explore and select materials and equipment and use skills such as cutting, joining, folding and building for a variety of purposes. They use technology, where appropriate, to support their learning.

Knowledge and understanding of the world is a wide ranging area which can be included in almost all aspects of nursery life. It covers:

- *Science (including e.g. minibeasts, animals, plants, reptiles, fish, weather, properties of materials and matter, electricity, magnetism, gravity, sound, light)*
- *Technology (including e.g. flight, cutting, sticking, video, computers)*
- *History (including e.g. people, families, grandparents, houses, transport)*
- *Geography (including e.g. rivers, mountains, counties, towns, natural resources).*

Figure 3.5
Games with magnets.

Children are interested in the natural world and how things around them work from a very young age. They enjoy experimenting and exploring, e.g. mixing earth and water or playing with insects and worms. They are fascinated with the technological world around them and can be very sophisticated in their use of computers and calculators. The simple use of magnets, mirrors or batteries and circuits lay important foundations for understanding the physical world.

The science curriculum should build on children's experiences and interests in the everyday world. As well as using these events, experiments can be carefully set up by adults to stimulate interest, and children should be encouraged to observe closely, discuss and perhaps draw or paint what they see. The introduction or changing of one element in an activity, such as the addition of cocoa powder to colour a cake mixture in a simple cooking activity, introduces another variable and this forms the basis of scientific investigation (what will happen if ...?). Planting seeds or bulbs can teach children about the sequence of events in nature and the cycles of growth and development.

Good practice with young children has for many years involved activities which are basically scientific, but which have not been recognized or called science. All work which contains elements of observation, investigation, experimentation, and eliciting ideas and hypotheses from children is likely to have a substantial science component. Workers with young children need to develop confidence in their own ability to understand and to provide for children's scientific learning which covers many of the everyday activities undertaken in the nursery and not to be put off by the terminology sometimes used.

Scenario 3.7

You are working as a nursery nurse in a reception class with a group of 4-year-olds, many of whom are lively and anxious to learn and explore. The children are offered a full and interesting curriculum, and the class is well-resourced and well-staffed. The parent of a bright 4-year-old complains to you that all her child ever does is play, he never brings home any paintings or creative work, his home reading books are too easy and he is just wasting his time. She wants him to get on with some 'real' work such as maths or writing, for which she thinks he is more than ready. You are concerned about this and discuss it with the class teacher.

(a) Does the parent have a point?
(b) What would be an appropriate form of action to take?
(c) How could you explain to this parent that her child was gaining valuable experience and developing skills in these areas of learning?
(d) Justify three areas of provision which assist in the development of reading and writing.

Knowledge and understanding of the world also covers technology. This can range from simple forms of technology such as windmills and the use of scissors to more complex forms such as developing electronic circuits using batteries, cooking activities, sound and light, magnetism, and heat and cold. Information technology such as using computers or telephones is also included.

A growing understanding of history and geography can also be encouraged, e.g. talking about their own families, photographs before and after, talking to older people, and looking at artefacts or clothes from long ago. Visits to the seaside or other types of holiday help children to begin to understand geographical concepts.

Desirable outcomes for physical development (QCA, 1996)

> These outcomes focus on children's developing physical control, mobility, awareness of space and manipulative skills in indoor and outdoor environments. They include establishing positive attitudes towards a healthy and active way of life.
>
> Children move confidently and imaginatively with increasing control and co-ordination and an awareness of space and others. They use a range of small and large equipment and balancing and climbing apparatus, with increasing skill. They handle appropriate tools, objects, construction and malleable materials safely and with increasing control.

It is important that children have opportunity to develop physically. Ideally they need space and time to develop physical skills (see Vigorous physical play in Ch. 2). Physical development is encouraged in many ways and in enjoyable activities such as swimming, using small and large apparatus, dancing and games such as football.

Desirable outcomes for creative development (QCA, 1996)

> These outcomes focus on the development of children's imagination and their ability to communicate and to express ideas and feelings in creative ways.
>
> Children explore sound and colour, texture, shape, form and space in two and three dimensions. They respond in a variety of ways to what they see, hear, smell, touch and feel. Through art, music, dance, stories and imaginative play, they show an increasing ability to use their imagination, to listen and to observe. They use a widening range of materials, suitable tools, instruments and other resources to express ideas and to communicate their feelings.

Children's creativity should be encouraged in all the range described in the outcomes (see Creative play in Ch. 2)

The National Curriculum for 5- to 16-year-olds

The National Curriculum applies to all pupils of compulsory school age in maintained schools. Although early years workers will not generally be responsible for planning the teaching of the National Curriculum, which is undertaken by qualified teachers, they will in some settings be required to work alongside the teacher in its implementation. It is important that staff working with young children have knowledge of the National Curriculum and in particular how to support literacy and numeracy

There are four stages for different age groups known as 'key stages' (KS):

- *Key stage 1 from age 5 to 7　　Year groups 1–2*
- *Key stage 2 from age 7 to 11　 Year groups 3–6*
- *Key stage 3 from age 11 to 14 Year groups 7–9*
- *Key stage 4 from age 14 to 16 Year groups 10–11.*

At KS 1 and 2, primary schools are required to teach a broad and balanced curriculum, including the 10 National Curriculum subjects and religious education. The 10 subjects are:

English*
Mathematics*
Science*
Information technology*
Design and technology*
History
Geography
Art
Music
Physical education.

* The full National Curriculum requirements for English, mathematics, science, information technology and religious education have to be covered but there is now greater flexibility for schools to decide what is taught in design and technology, history, geography, art, music, and physical education (with the exception of swimming which remains a statutory requirement).

For each subject and each KS, programmes of study set out what pupils should be taught and **attainment targets** set out the expected standard of pupils' performance. Pupils are assessed at set points throughout their schooling against these attainment targets. The tests are called Standard Assessment Tasks (SATs).

At the end of KS 1, 2 and 3 for all subjects except art, music and physical education, the standards of pupils' performance are set out in eight-level descriptions of increasing difficulty with an additional description above level 8 for exceptional performance, e.g. most pupils at KS 1 will achieve in the range of levels 1–3 and in KS 2 most pupils will achieve at levels 2–5. For art, music and physical education there are 'end of key stage' descriptions which indicate the standard of performance that most pupils are likely to achieve.

Public examinations such as GCSE are the main means of assessing attainment at KS4.

The National Curriculum in Wales includes Welsh as an additional core subject where it is the pupil's first language or the school is Welsh-speaking. In Scotland and Northern Ireland there are other differences. In Scotland, there are different areas of learning than those offered in England and teachers assess children when they feel they are ready to move to the next level rather than using SATs. In Northern Ireland, children follow a similar programme to Scotland but are tested in a similar way to England.

Organization and environment

This will depend to some extent on the individual setting where children receive care and education. Some situations will be well-staffed and well-resourced, whereas others will be chronically under-funded and in difficult physical circumstances; e.g. some inner city or, by contrast, isolated rural pre-schools do fine work under very difficult circumstances which often involves removing displays after every session and packing up all the play equipment after usage when using a multipurpose hall. For workers such as childminders or nannies offering full-day care and education there are constraints on the usage of the environment. It is not always possible to have messy play areas available every day or regular access to high quality outdoor experiences. However, good organization underpins good practice and frees adults and children to concentrate on the activity or experience without distraction. There are certain basic principles (outlined below) which should, wherever possible, govern provision:

- Health and safety are always the first considerations.
- The environment should foster the all-round development of the child.
- Children should be given maximum space and freedom to explore and to discover.
- For very young children rooms should be divided where possible into areas, well-defined by screens, shelves or walls but with doors or openings for children and adults to see within. This encourages children to concentrate and to talk to each other as well as reducing noise. Separate areas may be for messy play, sand and water, quiet areas for using books or puzzles, science and exploration, garden, construction, domestic play, music and imaginative play.
- For older children there should be a classroom layout where whole class teaching can take place but this should be a flexible arrangement which can be reversed into areas for smaller groups.
- In the nursery the provision of a workshop-style environment where adults actively structure and facilitate rather than instruct will encourage learning and should be adopted wherever appropriate. There will, of course, be times when it is necessary to adopt a more formal approach, and sufficient flexibility should allow for this.
- Separate areas should be carefully sited in a logical manner, designed to integrate learning and to facilitate easy access. It is also important to discourage through-traffic (other children or adults

going from one place to another) and to make the best use of basic facilities such as sinks and other fixtures.

- Double provision where possible, i.e. providing more than one of a particular activity, to allow children to play at different levels, e.g. sand play and painting provided indoors and outdoors using different materials and equipment.
- Flooring should be appropriate for the type of area usage.
- Work areas should have adequate numbers of child-sized tables and chairs so that children are encouraged not to crowd in.
- Wherever possible, indoor and outdoor areas should be planned together so that children's activity continues naturally from one to the other. Access to outdoors should not be restricted to certain times and seasons.
- Displays should be at child height as far as possible and involve items that can be handled and explored.
- Children should have their own storage space, coat hanger, table mat, flannel, toothbrush and towel.
- Presentation and preparation of the environment should be attractive to all the children, equipment well-cared for, and items such as junk carefully sorted and stored.
- Animals should be fed and cleaned regularly and shown respect and care.
- The environment should consider children with special needs and provide for physical or sensory impairment and children with learning difficulties.
- Good organization derives from good planning, and written plans should be available for adults to use.
- Organization should allow the child time for reflection, prioritizing, forward-planning and predicting.
- Children should be encouraged to work collaboratively.
- Clearing-up routines should be used as learning events.

Materials and equipment

- A wide and balanced range of materials should be available and be easily seen and within reach of the child.
- Materials and equipment to promote all types of learning and development should always be available; this applies particularly to basic materials such as sand and water.
- Materials, activities and equipment reflect positive images to all children and actively promote and use cultural and linguistic diversity.
- Material and equipment allow for extension and progression of children's learning.
- Equipment and materials are arranged so that children are encouraged to help themselves and do not have continually to depend on adults.

- Tools, equipment and context should be 'real' wherever possible.
- Sets of sized items such as dolls' clothes are hung up or displayed in ways which demonstrate size differences.
- Equipment and materials are labelled and stored in the same place so that children know where to find and replace them and wherever possible kept where they are used. This can be facilitated by providing templates on the storage surfaces for children to match, photographs or colour coding of item. Identical or similar items are best stored close together.

Planning the curriculum

Planning the curriculum should involve parents, children, staff and volunteers. Even in schools where teachers take overall responsibility for planning, best practice is achieved through a team approach where nursery nurses, other support staff, volunteers and parents are included. Meetings to plan the curriculum should be held at a time that everyone can attend and should take place well in advance of implementation. Team planning means that everyone is involved, ensures a consistent approach and can identify areas of staff development that are required. Students on placement often have relevant ideas to contribute and are required to understand curriculum planning as part of their training.

Plans should be available for all parents and adults to see and to work from. Good plans will clearly indicate the learning outcomes expected and where relevant will make formal links with the 'desirable outcomes' (early learning goals). Individual education plans for children with special needs need to be incorporated into the plans whilst allowing for individual differences as necessary.

Areas of learning

There is continuity between the desirable learning outcomes and the National Curriculum KS 1. Staff working with young children should be broadly familiar with the attainment targets for National Curriculum KS 1 and very familiar with the desirable outcomes in order to provide appropriate learning experiences that will ensure that wherever possible children achieve the desirable outcomes by the time they enter compulsory education. Children will generally be able to meet the desirable outcomes via a curriculum based on structured or guided play. Children under compulsory school age should be offered a developmentally appropriate curriculum and should never be forced into a formalized curriculum until they are ready.

Elements of learning

It is useful when planning a curriculum to use the four elements of learning identified below as they provide a broad framework within which the needs of the whole child may be met.

1. *Knowledge*
2. *Concepts or ideas*
3. *Skills*
4. *Attitudes.*

In practice, planning a curriculum is done in many different ways, with different emphasis. Nurseries may offer a curriculum which is skills-based, whereas children in the second year of formal school may work more in the realms of ideas and concepts. The important thing is that the curriculum has breadth and balance. This means that nursery children need not concentrate wholly on, say, using tools or developing physical skills but should also be given the opportunity to develop concepts such as shape, time, spatial awareness or skills associated with early reading and writing. Equally, older children need to continue with the skills curriculum. In planning a curriculum, it is important to make sure that the four elements of learning are considered together with the desirable outcomes and that workers make sure that there is sufficient breadth and balance overall. To develop and provide an appropriate curriculum, adults need a knowledge and understanding of child development and how children learn most effectively. This enables the curriculum on offer to be meaningful to children and to motivate them to learn.

Long-term planning

As the curriculum extends to all aspects of the life of the setting, long-term planning provides a permanent framework that informs all the other aspects of the work which only needs to be reviewed from time to time. Long-term plans should not be overly detailed or prescriptive but should allow some flexibility to respond to the changing needs of children. Plans should cover issues such as:

- *admissions/settling in*
- *pattern of attendance, e.g. sessional, full-time*
- *age at starting or leaving*
- *organization of the learning environment both indoors and outdoors*
- *an outline of the curriculum, learning objectives, themes or learning priorities for the whole setting*
- *the types of medium-and short-term plans to be used and the basis of these plans*
- *links with OFSTED or Children Act reports and action plans*
- *how equality of opportunity will be addressed*
- *how children with English as an additional language will be supported*

- *inclusion of parents as partners*
- *how children will be encouraged in their learning*
- *how adults will support learning*
- *planning, assessment and record keeping*
- *meeting all the children's needs including those with special educational needs and disability or sensory impairment*
- *ensuring all children receive their full entitlement to all areas of learning*
- *behaviour policies and issues*
- *resourcing the plan*
- *reviewing the plan's effectiveness.*

Medium-term planning

Medium-term plans help staff to focus on how they will develop the curriculum within the long-term plan and can be termly, monthly or weekly depending on the setting. Medium-term planning usually involves a series of carefully identified and linked activities and experiences and should be informed by the observations and assessments staff have made of the children over the previous weeks or on entry to the setting. Plans should also relate to the child's interests and enthusiasms and their ages and abilities. Many settings will review children's progress monthly or termly and will identify specific learning priorities for each child and group of children.

Planning may need to concentrate on specific aspects of the curriculum which support the overall policy of the school, nursery or pre-school or where assessment of the children reveals a specific need; e.g. where there has been much good work done in the area of language and literacy, but little on technology, obviously this should feature strongly in forward planning.

Short-term planning

Short-term planning follows on from long- and medium-term and is usually a working document which is focused and detailed. Short-term plans usually focus on:

- *specific learning intentions for the day or week*
- *particular children needing support*
- *specific activities or experiences*
- *teaching and learning strategies*
- *which staff will be where and what they will be doing*
- *resources required.*

All adults involved will need to be very clear about the learning intentions, how topics will be introduced, the language on which to focus and the balance between adult- and child-initiated activity and how to deal with unplanned learning, e.g. when a child arrives with something unexpected and wishes to share it. Best practice involves

Figure 3.6
Example of
medium-term
planning for a
cross-curricular
topic.

Knowledge and understanding of the world

- Visit seaside including lifeboat and fish market
- Use all senses – sight, smell, touch, taste and hearing
- Understanding fish for eating have to be stored in ice or in tins and why
- Collect stones, rocks, shells, seaweed, driftwood – make rock pool
- Illuminate lighthouse with batteries and circuits
- Create underwater scene in large tank
- Floating and sinking experiment
- Postcards / pictures / posters of seascapes / fish / sea mammals
- Books on whales and dolphins
- Discuss tides and moon
- Pretend play-corner as fish shop

Personal and social

- Planning outing involving parents
- Making tuna sandwiches, eating together and with parents
- Make a platter of different seafoods
- Working in pairs
- Work of lifeboats
- Visitor to school from lifeboat association
- Girls on lifeboats
- Story of Grace Darling
- Appreciation of beauty of sea and sea life. Understanding of power of waves, rough seas and tidal waves

Sea and coast project

Physical development

- Dance and movement – like waves, fish, crabs. Hauling in nets
- Fine motor skills using scissors, folding and sticking
- Climbing frame 'cliff' Paddling and splashing in sea

Language and literacy

- Sea and coast vocabulary, labelling all displays and items
- Rhymes and tongue twisters – she sells seashells
- Songs – I do like to be beside the seaside. Shoals of herring
- Listen to sea shanties
- Listen to tape of sea noises. Practise noises of waves – loud and soft
- Listen to tape of whale and dolphin sounds
- Video of life boat
- Books to support themes – factual and stories around them of sea and coast
- Make a 'big book' of the visit In 'fish shop': price labels, names of fish
- Home corner – shopping list pad

Creative development

- Table top display using large net and fine net
- Model fishes, crabs, jellyfish, lobsters and starfish
- Make models of pier and lighthouse (with year 1 and 2) use small world people to make scene
- Seaside collage – use sand, paper fish, silver paint, seabird shapes
- Bird prints in sand Drawing, painting and modelling for collage

Mathematics

- Models of star fish, crabs
- Maths language, how many arms / legs, deep / shallow
- Make sun hats. Folding and measuring paper, using scissors, staplers or glue. Estimating size
- Making paper boats Looking at fish scales – pattern and symmetry
- Patterns in sand
- Sets of shells by size and colour
- Number rhymes – 12345, once I caught a fish alive
- Fish shop – weighing, pricing, estimating, counting, pretend money
- Barometer and pressure

frequent (usually short!) meetings where issues are clarified and some evaluation of progress takes place and where changes can be made if needed.

Curriculum policies

Many settings will have a curriculum policy from which it derives its curriculum plans, e.g. High/Scope or Montessori nurseries will base their curriculum policy on particular philosophies and approaches. Curriculum policies should be clear and explain the educational basis of the programme offered and how learning is evaluated and recorded. Best practice indicates how parents can support the learning taking place in the nursery. A clear policy will assist parents in making decisions with and for their children.

Types of curriculum plan

Cross-curricular themes and topics
Cross-curricular topics or themes are commonly used as means of delivering the curriculum in an integrated way. These themes can be developed in a variety of ways using the children's own interests, stories or nursery rhymes, and many other subjects or situations. The example of a theme in Figure 3.6 is just one way of planning for some work in the nursery related to the desirable outcomes.

Planning around different types of learning experience
Some types of learning activity such as learning to use particular tools are not so easily integrated, and may need to be taught as individual components of the curriculum. Other types of plan will be drawn up according to different needs or if it is felt the children lack experience in particular skills which need some work; e.g. the centre of a planning web might be 'manipulative skills' and the planning may focus on how these can be developed. It is important to remember that there is no right way of planning, and it should always be flexible and responsive to the children and circumstances.

Customizing planning for individual needs
There will always be a requirement for plans to be differentiated to meet the needs of individual children. Short-term, and sometimes medium-term, plans must be flexible enough to accommodate differing needs; e.g. a child who is aggressive to others and will not settle may require specific adult time and attention and may need an individual programme at certain times of day. Activities within the plan may need to be adapted for children who have particular needs but can still remain in the overall theme.

Figure 3.7
Example of a daily plan (QCA, 1998).

Adult-focused activities

Adult/group	What do we want children to learn?	What will children do?	Resources	What have children learned? What next?
Kate with Charlene, Ben, Triston, Arzu, Sean, Clarissa, Joshua, Amina	To increase understanding of '*under*', '*behind*', '*in*'.	Read/talk about *Three Billy Goats Gruff.* Use role-play to act out story.	*Three Billy Goats Gruff.* Crates and plank.	Most children used language accurately. Sean still uncertain about '*under*'. Needs more practice.
Paramjeet with Simon, Mehmet, Grace, Nazrul, Ellene, Alex	To develop an understanding of '*under*', '*behind*', '*in*'.	Make *Where's Spot?* type books with themselves as the character.	*Where's Spot?* Paper, pencils, crayons, stapler, hole punch, sticky tape.	Mehmet and Ellene unsure about the use of English but able to describe in preferred language. Need to practise in range of situations.
Simon with Christie	To have practical experience of '*under*', '*behind*', '*in*'.	Participate in obstacle course created outside.	Crates, planks, blankets, hoops.	Christie successfully followed completed course. Encourage to describe where she is next time.

Experiences and activities – Water

Resources	**Resources**	**Resources** Plastic bottles, sieves, funnels, jugs	**Resources**	**Resources**
Key questions	**Key questions**	**Key questions** Can you pour water through the funnel to fill the bottle? How many jugs of water are there in the bottle? Can you see the water coming out of the sieve?	**Key questions**	**Key questions**

The planning cycle

The planning cycle will be used for all levels of plan, i.e. long–medium–short-term. The cycle involves:

- *the goals of the initial plan linked to assessment of need and the overall strategy as discussed above*
- *the implementation of the plan*
- *the monitoring of the plan*
- *the assessment and evaluation of the plan.*

Figure 3.8
The planning cycle.

The planning cycle is ongoing and should flow seamlessly from one cycle to another. There will be planning cycles going on for individuals and groups of children within the overall plan.

Implementation (putting the plan into practice)
After the initial planning comes the implementation phase which in the early years is always flexible and responsive to changing needs and circumstances.

Monitoring and recording
Ongoing monitoring of the plan is important. Observing, assessing and recording children's achievements against the identified learning requirements are needed to ensure that the plan is fit for its purpose. Monitoring may not lead to immediate change of plans but could lead to some modifications.

Review and evaluation (How did it go? What needs changing?)
The review and evaluation phase is a vital part of the cycle and will inform future planning. Evaluation should consider whether the aims and goals were fulfilled both for the group and individual child. If they were, how could the activity or experience be extended or improved? If not, the evaluation considers why and how things could be changed. Self-evaluation of performance is a useful exercise.

Planning routines

The planning of routines is an essential skill for many early years workers. Routines are the daily (or 24-hour) programmes of activities and experiences offered to young children that include the curriculum described above. Children thrive with regular, consistent, high quality routines, which they know and anticipate. Where children do not have routines or where the routines are always changing, they are generally less settled and less able to take advantage of the opportunities offered.

Routines will vary enormously from family to family and setting to setting and there are no 'right' or 'wrong' routines as long as they meet the children's needs. Routines must be flexible and start with the basic needs of the individual child or groups of children. When planning a routine, the individual's needs, the age/stage of the child and the parents' wishes should be taken into account and the following areas considered:

- *Waking, sleeping and resting*
- *Bathing, washing, teeth cleaning, toileting, care of skin and hair*
- *Outings*
- *Fresh air and physical activity*
- *Indoor activities*
- *Activities to promote overall development*
- *Social opportunities*
- *Opportunities to give and to receive love and care*
- *Interaction with carers on a one-to-one basis*
- *Self-help activities*
- *Learning to help others*
- *Stimulating curiosity*
- *Play opportunities*
- *Food and drink*
- *Regular commitments*
- *The competing needs of several children in a family or early years setting.*

Scenario 3.8

A family with four young children has moved into the area; two of the children are in primary school and one has a part-time place at the local family centre. The children are often away from school and very rarely arrive on time. You are a family support worker who has been asked to work with this family to help them settle and to develop manageable routines for the children and parents.

How could you support this family in developing a routine?
Write a report for your supervisor detailing the routine you are proposing.

A routine for a baby under 3 months will be very different from a child of 4 years but in both cases the areas listed above should be met, considered and included in the routine at the appropriate level.

As with curriculum plans and activities, routines should be reviewed and evaluated regularly to ensure that they are meeting the changing needs of the children involved.

Assignments

Assignment 1

Identify several activities taking place in your work-setting that might involve a variety of different ways of learning for the children
Observe the children closely as they engage in the activity and assess what they are doing and learning on an individual basis. After you have done this, write up the activity in the following way:

Example: Water play using funnels, sieves and measuring jugs of different sizes
1. Why was this activity provided?
2. How was it presented and introduced?
3. How did it link with other ongoing activity?
4. What previous experience did the children have using this equipment or similar?
5. What were your expectations of how the equipment would be used?
6. What learning/development did you expect to take place (skills, concepts, knowledge and attitudes)?
7. What actually happened?

Questions to ask yourself:
(a) What aspects of development and learning were promoted by the experience?
(b) How could this activity be developed and extended?
(c) Is this activity providing a foundation for future learning?
(d) What would be the next learning steps?
(e) Projecting ahead as far as possible, identify those skills, concepts, knowledge and attitudes which might be linked with identifiable areas of knowledge such as science or technology.
(f) Is it possible to make those links in the areas you have chosen? If not, why not?
(g) Do your findings help you to understand the concept of a spiral curriculum?

Assignment 2

To plan, implement and evaluate one aspect of the curriculum in your work-setting

You are training to be a nursery nurse in an inner city nursery school. You have children from many different ethnic groups in your class: several have very little spoken English but converse freely in their home language when they have the opportunity.

After discussion with your supervisor, work on a small-scale plan for one aspect of the curriculum in your work-setting designed to promote language development. Set out your goals clearly and consider the feasibility of what you are doing and how it will fit in with the overall curriculum plan. Think of ways in which parents or other adults could be involved in the project. Implement and evaluate your plans.

Assignment 3

To develop and extend children's love of stories and books

In discussion with your supervisor or tutor and the children you work with, plan and make a short book suitable for young children. The book may be written by you and the children working together or just by you; it should be relevant to your situation and provide fun for and possibilities for discussion with the children. It may include photographs or be a group book containing drawings and individual stories by the children. Other ideas may be:

- a book for counting
- a book for colours or shapes
- a book about the locality
- a book about a difficult or challenging real situation
- a simple story
- a rhyme book
- a 'big' book.

Evaluate the experience and say how the children responded.

Assignment 4

To extend and expand children's scientific understanding

In discussion with your supervisor, set up an area where children can explore and experiment with natural or created materials. Wherever possible, choose new or unfamiliar items for them to explore. Structure the activity so that children can test their ideas in a non-threatening manner.

Questions to ask yourself:

(a) How might you best introduce the activity/experience?
(b) What are your learning objectives?

Carefully observe the reactions of the children.

Note how the activity might be developed and extended.

Assignment 5

To devise a routine for a baby room and ensure that staff deliver a learning curriculum embedded into everyday routines

A nursery worker has oversight of a room containing two babies under 6 months and four between 6 months and 1 year. Devise a daily routine which would work for this room. When the routine is devised, justify each activity in terms of the learning and development for each baby. Include:

- the staffing needs
- how staff training and NVQ assessment could be incorporated
- how the staffing is organized
- how staff are monitored
- how staff are supported.

Discuss your proposal with staff in a baby room. What are their views?

If possible, ask parents what they would like for their babies.

If possible, implement your routine and evaluate its effectiveness.

Assignment 6

To devise a curriculum plan for home-based care and education
Develop a medium-term curriculum plan for a 4-year-old who is with you part-time after a morning session at nursery and full-time in school holidays. Base your plan on the desirable outcomes. Discuss your plan with a colleague or parent or NVQ assessor.

Questions to ask yourself:
(a) What did you consider in your planning?
(b) What outcomes were difficult to cover?
(c) What were the strengths/difficulties for home-based care?

Assignment 7

To observe a young child's schema based on repeated patterns of behaviour and to identify ways of enriching and extending provision for the child based on your findings.
It is recommended that before undertaking these observations you familiarize yourself with 'schema' through reading the work of Athey (1990), Nutbrown (1994) or Bruce (1997) and you discuss the topic with colleagues, tutors or supervisors.)

Observe a child under 5 over a period of several days who you feel is demonstrating repeated patterns in play, e.g. over and under, back and forth, side to side, circular direction or containing and enveloping. Choose a manageable method of observing and recording such as a time sampling.

From your observation, note if you can identify any repeated patterns of behaviour which demonstrate the child's major interests.

Based on your findings, plan a programme of work which will extend and develop the child's schema and assist in learning.

REFERENCES AND FURTHER READING

Abbott, L. and Moylett, H. (Eds) (1997) *Working with the Under-3s: Responding to Children's Needs*. Milton Keynes: Open University Press.

Abbott, L. and Moylett, H. (Eds) (1997) *Working with the Under-3s: Training and Professional Development*. Milton Keynes: Open University Press.

Althouse, R. (1998) *Investigating Science with Young Children*. London: Cassell.

Athey, C. (1990) *Extending Thought in Young Children. A Parent Teacher Partnership*. London: Paul Chapman.

Baker, C. (1988) *Reading through Play*. London: MacDonald.

Blenkin, G. and Kelly, V. (Eds) (1997) *Principles into Practice in Early Childhood Education*. London: Paul Chapman.

Botham, J. *Enjoying the Outdoors in the Early Years*. London: BAECE.

Brown, B. (1990) *All Our Children*. London: BBC Educational.

Browne, A. (1993) *Helping Children to Write*. London: Paul Chapman.

Browne, A. (1996) *Developing Language and Literacy 3–8*. London: Paul Chapman.

Browne, N. and France, P. (1986) *Untying the Apron Strings: Anti-sexist Provision for the Under Fives*. Milton Keynes. Open University Press.

Bruce, T. (1997) *Early Childhood Education*. Sevenoaks: Hodder and Stoughton.

Bruner, J. (1975) The ontogenesis of speech acts. *Journal of Child Language* 2.

Bruner, J. (1977) *The Process of Education*. Cambridge, Mass.: Harvard University Press.

Bruner, J. (1980) *Under Five in Britain. The Oxford Pre-school Research Project*. Oxford: Grant McIntyre/Blackwell.

Cambridgeshire County Council. (1996) *A Framework for a Foundation Curriculum for Under Fives*. Cambridgeshire: Cambridgeshire County Council Education, Libraries and Heritage Department.

Clarke, M. (1988) *Children Under Five: Final Report to the Department of Education and Science*. London: Gordon and Breach.

Commission for Racial Equality. (1989) *From Cradle to School*. London: CRE.

Concern No. 68. (1989) *Creating a Learning Environment: What's Special About Under Fives?* Spring 1989.

Curtis, A. (1986) *A Curriculum for the Pre-school Child*. Windsor: NFER/Nelson.

David, T. (1990) *Under Five – Under-Educated?* Milton Keynes: Open University Press.

Denman-Sparks, L. (1989) *Anti-bias Curriculum, Tools for Empowering Young Children*. Washington DC: National Association for the Education of Young Children.

Department of Education and Science. (1975) *The Bullock Report: A Language for Life*. London: HMSO.

Department of Education and Science. (1978) *The Warnock Report: Special Educational Needs*. London: HMSO.

Department of Education and Science. (1990) *The Rumbold Report: Starting with Quality*, part 2. London: HMSO.

Dowling, M. (1988) *Education 3–5*. London: Paul Chapman.

Dowling, M. (1995) *Starting School at Four*. London: Paul Chapman.

Drummond, M., Lally, M. and Pugh, G. (Eds) (1989) *Working with Young Children: Developing a Curriculum for the Early Years*. National Children's Bureau/Nottingham Educational Supplies.

Early Years Curriculum Group. (1989) *Early Childhood Education: The Early Years Curriculum and the National*

Curriculum. Stoke on Trent: Trentham Books.

Edwards, S. (1998) *Managing Effective Teaching of Mathematics 3–8*, London: Paul Chapman.

Equal Opportunities Commission. *An Equal Start: Guidelines for those Working with the Under Fives*. Manchester: EOC.

Goldschmeid, E. (1989) Play and learning in the nursery. *In* Williams, V. (Ed.) *Babies in Daycare*. Daycare Trust.

Griffiths, R. (1988) *Maths through Play*. London: MacDonald.

Haylock, D. and Cockburn, A. (1997) *Understanding Mathematics in the Lower Primary Years*. London: Paul Chapman.

Hazareesingh, S., Simms, K., Anderson, P. et al. (1989) *Educating the Whole Child: A Holistic Approach to Education in the Early Years*. London: Building Blocks Educational.

Henderson, A. and Benjamin, T. (1992) *Play and Learning for the Under Threes*. London. Pre-School Learning Alliance.

Her Majesty's Inspectorate. (1989) *The Education of Children Under Five*. London: HMSO.

HMSO. (1985) *Curriculum Matters 2: The Curriculum from 5 to 16*. London: HMSO

Hohmann, M., Banet, B. and Wiekart, D. (1979) *Young Children in Action*. High/Scope Press.

Hurst, V. (1997) *Planning for Early Learning*. London: Paul Chapman.

Jones, C. and Kitson, P. (1990) *Setting the Pace – Physical Activities with Children in the Early Years*. Newcastle upon Tyne: University of Newcastle.

Kasser, S. (1997) *Inclusive Games*. Champaign, Illinois: Human Kinetics.

Lancashire County Council. (1986) *Science in the Early Years*.

Leach, B.J. (1997) *Small World Play*. Leamington Spa: Scholastic.

McGuiness, D. (1998) *Why Children Can't Read*. Harmondsworth: Penguin.

Miller, L. (1996) *Towards Reading*. Milton Keynes: Open University Press.

Minns, H. (1990) *Read it to Me Now*. London: Virago.

Moss, P. and Penn, H. (1996) *Transforming Nursery Education*. London: Paul Chapman.

National Children's Bureau. (1989) *Highlights*, nos 88 and 89. London: Nelson.

National Literacy Strategy. (1998) London: DfEE.

National Writing Project. (1989) *Becoming a Writer*. London: Nelson.

Ministry of Education. (1996) *Te Whaariki*. Wellington: New Zealand Learning Media.

NFER/SCDC. (1987) *Four Year Olds in Schools*. Windsor: NFER/SCDC.

Nutbrown, C. (1994) *Threads of Thinking*. London: Paul Chapman.

Nutbrown, C. (1996) *Respectful Educators – Capable Learners*. London: Paul Chapman.

Nutbrown, C. (1997) *Recognising Early Literacy Development*. London: Paul Chapman.

Qualifications and Curriculum Authority. (1996) *Nursery Education: Desirable Outcomes for Children's Learning on Entering Compulsory Education*. London: DfEE.

Qualifications and Curriculum Authority. (1998) *An Introduction to Curriculum Planning for Under Fives*. Middlesex: QCA.

Riley, J. (1996) *The Teaching of Reading*. London: Paul Chapman.

Rouse, D. (Ed.) (1991) *Babies and Toddlers, Carers and Educators. Quality for the Under Threes*. London: National Children's Bureau.

SCAA. (1997) The National Framework for Baseline Assessment (free booklets), Middlesex: QCA.

Smith, J. and Elley, W. (1998) *How Children Learn to Write*. London: Paul Chapman.

Sylva, K., Smith, T. and Moore, E. (1986) *Monitoring the High/Scope Training Program 1984–5. Final Report*. Oxford: Department of Social and Administrative Studies, University of Oxford.

Vygotsky, L.S. (1978) *Mind in Society*. Cambridge, Mass.: Harvard University Press.

Whalley, M. (1994) *Learning to be Strong*. Sevenoaks: Hodder and Stoughton.

Whitehead, (1997) *Language and Literacy in the Early Years*, 2nd edn. London: Paul Chapman.

Wolfendale, S. (1991) *All About Me*. Nottingham: NES/Arnold.

Wood, A. and Attfield, J. (1998) *Play, Learning and the Early Childhood Curriculum*. London: Paul Chapman.

Wray, D. (1989) *Bright Ideas – Writing*. Leamington Spa: Scholastic.

Yates, I. (1990) *Bright Ideas – Language Activities*. Leamington Spa: Scholastic.

4: WORKING WITH PARENTS

Objectives

- Setting the scene
- Parents as customers and service users
- Parents and the education service
- Parents and social services
- Parents and voluntary, private and independent settings
- Early Excellence centres

- Principles of work with parents
- Involving fathers
- Practical ways of encouraging positive interactions with parents
- Roles and functions that parents undertake
- Evaluating the effectiveness of work with parents

Links

This chapter has links with:
- NVQ (EYCE) Units: P1, P2, P4, P5, P7, P8, P9.
- CACHE Diploma Module S.

Setting the scene

Although it is often the natural parents who care for their young children, especially the mother, in this chapter the term 'parents' refers to the principal carers of children, whoever they may be and includes those who have 'parental responsibility' under the Children Act 1989. The carer may have any one of a variety of different relationships with the child, such as grandparent, childminder, foster parent, step-parent or older sibling, but, for the purposes of this chapter, it is understood that the carer usually has the main care of the child.

In the UK today the family is seen as the basic unit of society. Although we may see this as a social construction rather than a 'natural' one, it is the unit that most of us come from and identify with. Within this umbrella term a wide variety of kin relationships exist, and in all our involvement with parents we need to recognize and

Figure 4.1
Extended family.

accept this. Many families today struggle under huge pressures and this requires sensitivity from all staff involved with them. Also many family and cultural patterns exist with which workers may not be familiar and this requires them to examine their own values and attitudes in order not to make unfair judgements. According to the Government Household survey 1994 only one in four children in UK classrooms come from the traditional, long-term, two-parent households. Therefore many children are affected by a range of family circumstances such as:

- *multi-generational or single-parent families*
- *pressures on working parents*
- *effects of separation, divorce and re-marriage*
- *non-custodial parents losing touch*
- *step-parenting*
- *families on benefits or long-term unemployment*
- *being from ethnic minority families or having recently entered the country*
- *being long- or short-term fostered.*

Parents are the people who have primary responsibility for caring and are the main educators of their young children (e.g. up to 85% of language used by adults is in place by age 5 years) and staff must work in partnership with parents rather than creating a 'them' and 'us' situation. Parental partnerships are beneficial both to the family and to the institution as both parties will then be working to the same goals.

Many professionals involved in early years care and education have seen the need to include parents as fully as possible and will have developed parental partnership policies to make this transparent to all. Some parents come to the partnership relatively powerless, perhaps as a result of a referral from social services where a child has been identified as in need. In these cases staff have to work hard to overcome the barriers and encourage a true partnership. Staff in successful partnerships with parents have learned how to listen sensitively and how to interpret parents' needs and aspirations and to modify their own approach to the parent accordingly. Many parents lack confidence in their parenting skills and may have both positive and negative views of their children. These parents need staff who will support them in the parenting role in a non-judgemental manner and staff who will accept that it is sometimes difficult to feel positive about children when the circumstances of life seem hard. Staff must be careful not to promise more than they or the setting can deliver and will find that keeping to hand a range of information about local support services is very useful.

Parental or family partnerships will mean different things according to the setting and the ethos of the setting. A psychologist may use the term to refer to planned activities involving parents in therapeutic activities with their children. Social workers may see parental involvement with their child in a group setting as a positive indicator in the rehabilitation of a family. A teacher may see it as referring to the practical help offered in a classroom. Others may feel that involving parents should be restricted to fund-raising, whilst other groups see it as being linked with management and decision-making within a school or other organization. It is important to recognize that there can be many ways in which this term is interpreted, each with its own philosophical and ideological basis.

Scenario 4.1

Sarah is the mother of twin children aged 3 years, and has recently moved into the area as part of re-housing following an abusive relationship where both she and the twins were physically and verbally abused. Social services have recommended that the family is given support at the local family centre and that the twins receive day care for lengthy periods during the week to give the mother some space to recover.

The staff have found that although the twins are generally well cared for, the mother's behaviour is erratic and changeable. Sarah feels guilty about leaving, 'depriving the twins of their father' and putting her own needs first and feels she is unable to give her children the love and care they need. Sarah will only talk about her feelings to the twins' key worker who is about to go on maternity leave and feels that the other staff and parents think she is a bad mother.

What plan of action could the centre make for this family?
What skills and support strategies will the staff require?
How might Sarah react when the key worker leaves?

Involvement by parents has not always been encouraged, and there are still examples today where workers do not encourage such partnerships. However, parents today of all backgrounds tend to be well-informed and in possession of a good deal of knowledge about the education, health and other services open to them and most will wish to be closely involved with the care and education of their child.

Parents as customers and service users

Parents and families are users of the services provided and in many cases directly purchase the service offered often within a competitive marketplace. The relationship between purchaser and provider is one where the purchaser usually holds the balance of power as the purchaser may choose between the range of services on offer. In the past this balance of power has often been the other way round and parents have felt excluded and powerless against state bureaucracy. Over the last few years the formal inclusion of parents in the governance of schools and the development of charters for parents and consumers who use other services which is sometimes supported by legislation or codes of practice is leading to a changing emphasis which has empowered parents.

As well as partnerships with parents, early years workers now have to offer good customer service to parents who are purchasing their services. Early years settings are accountable to parents for the quality of the service they offer.

Parents and the education service

Background

Traditionally, home and school were seen as separate, and parents were often physically excluded except on occasions such as special open evenings. Signs saying 'No Parents' or similar were not uncommon until the 1960s, and in some cases the underlying attitudes still exist. The exclusion of parents from the area of their young child's education reflected the prevailing attitude that teacher knew best and that parents were better kept outside. When they were invited in there was not likely to be an assumption of mutual support and understanding, but a one-sided attempt to influence parental values and behaviour.

The exception to this rule could be found in the work of Margaret McMillan, who could be termed the founder of modern nursery education. In the early years of this century her voice was heard arguing for the right of mothers to participate in their child's education and in the management of the nursery schools they attended. Some of her ideas emerged in the 1960s and 1970s, particularly the notion that mothers should be able to enter the school when they wished and that their views were to be respected.

Equality of opportunity

It was during the 1960s and 1970s in a period of greater political interest in issues of educational disadvantage and deprivation that the importance of parental influence on a child's overall attainment at school came to the fore. In one particular study, a group of children born during a week in March 1958 was studied. Amongst many variables examined over a period of years the effect of social class and disadvantage on children's educational attainments was considered. The findings, along with other research of the period, were that children from working-class homes did not succeed as well in the education system as children from the middle classes. The Plowden Report (1967) discussed the importance of parental attitudes to their child's education as being a crucial factor in the child's success or failure. As a result, greater levels of parental participation were recommended, although the idea that the school was accountable to parents did not emerge until many years later.

Scenario 4.2

Some years ago this would not have been an unusual set of circumstances and in places these attitudes persist.

A family in a rural community is isolated and has very limited neighbourhood networks. The middle child, Jane, is aged 4 years; she has a sister of 7 and a brother of 2. The mother has great difficulty in getting Jane and her sister to school on time as the children are often unco-operative, and she is frequently late collecting them.

The school's policy is to keep parents outside as far as possible. There is no opportunity for the mother to explain her practical difficulties to the teacher, or to discuss the children's difficult behaviour. The mother finds great difficulty in communicating through the school secretary and headteacher. She is becoming increasingly alienated from the school as getting the children there is such a burden and she feels the school would not be sympathetic to her problems. If the toddler is sick, or there is tension at home, or extremely bad weather, often the mother will keep the children at home.

What practical measures could this school take:

(a) For this particular mother?
(b) For this rural community?

The influence of child development theory

In the past many working with young children took the view that intelligence was inborn and that this was the most important factor in deciding how well children would perform in the education system. However, in the post-war period and beyond, theories were emerging which stressed the importance of early environment in enabling children to reach their educational potential.

Early mother/child relationships and their link with other aspects of development, cognitive as well as emotional and character development, were stressed by workers such as John Bowlby (see Ch. 1). Projects such as Headstart in the USA were set up with the aim of encouraging parents to work through an educational programme with their children. The short-term benefits of these seemed to be inconclusive, but longer-term studies of the children at 15 and 16 years showed that this type of intervention did have benefits (see High/Scope in Ch. 3).

The development of language was seen as a crucial area of importance for working-class children who were thought to be linguistically deprived at home, and therefore disadvantaged in the middle-class school culture. These attitudes are demonstrated to some extent in the Bullock Report (DES, 1975). At this time parent education concentrated on demonstrating the importance of talking and reading to children, but at the same time parents were not encouraged to involve themselves in teaching their child to read which was a job for the 'professionals'. It is much less likely that researchers and educationalists today will see working-class children as a group linguistically deprived. The responsibility is placed firmly on the school to build on children's differing cultures and early experiences and not to blame 'inadequate' homes.

Parental pressure

Pressure for more involvement in schools has not come just from political groups. Parents themselves have formed consumer groups that press for more information and influence in their children's schooling. The Advisory Centre for Education (ACE) provides parents of children in State Education with free information and advice. It also acts as a national watchdog body. The National Confederation of Parent – Teacher Associations which represent the various parent groups and PTAs also act as a pressure group.

Legislation

Much recent education legislation has supported parental partnerships, e.g. the Nursery Education and Grant Maintained Schools Act 1996 which gives the Secretary of State power to fund nursery education in the private, voluntary and independent sector. This funded provision is inspected by OFSTED and one of the areas within the inspection framework for nursery education is partnerships with parents and carers. OFSTED inspectors are required to make judgements on the extent to which the involvement of parents or carers contributed to the early learning goals for young children (see Ch. 3).

Parents in education settings

It is important that parents are welcome in schools and are as involved as possible in their child's education, not just at the nursery/infant stage, but beyond. They are, after all, the prime educators of their children. It is widely recognized that such involvement brings great benefits to children and parents alike. The advantages for the institution are also considerable. As well as perhaps raising money for much-needed material resources, parents are themselves invaluable human resources and their involvement in schools and increased understanding of child development and the educational process have many benefits. Children learn best when there is continuity in their experience, and parents can inform and help plan the curriculum in all areas, especially regarding the child's social and cultural context. Teachers do not generally receive training for working with parents, but are often asked for their advice on a wide range of social and welfare issues, as well as child care and educational development. Clear lines of communication are needed to avoid misunderstanding and to ensure common goals. Staff are sometimes concerned that their roles as educators are being diluted as their time is taken up with issues not directly concerning the education of children. Genuine parental partnerships do however mean a change of emphasis for workers with young children calling for further professional development and training.

Parents themselves often report a growth in confidence and self-esteem as they work alongside professionals and feel their contribution is equal and valued. As the above legislation indicates, this is a view increasingly held by government, as well as professionals involved in education. The quality of parental involvement is crucial. Although attitudes vary, it is important that parents are involved not merely on the periphery but in the central issues affecting their children. Research has shown how the use of schemes such as PACT (home and school reading) and IMPACT (home and school mathematics) in which parents were involved in the curriculum, brought about higher levels of achievement in children. With the slimming down of the National Curriculum in primary schools and the greater emphasis on literacy and numeracy, the role of parents in supporting these areas of learning will continue. There are many examples of local initiatives throughout the UK to link school and community and to promote parent education and involvement, e.g. the 'Early Literacy Education with Parents' project (Nutbrown and Hannon, 1997) in Sheffield. There is also the Family Literacy Programme provided by the Basic Skills Agency which supports both large and small scale development programmes to help parents and children overcome literacy difficulties by working together. However, there is no coherent nationwide strategy and it is unclear if it will be seen as a priority in the near future.

Parents and social services

Background

Historically, the provision of welfare services had its origins in the Poor Law of 1834. The rationale was simple: people became poor largely through their own fault. The workhouse system was harsh and families were often split up. Services improved with the coming of the post-1945 welfare state, which aimed to eradicate poverty and ignorance, but prior to the Social Services Act 1970, care for children and parents was likely to be undertaken by different local government departments often with very little liaison between them. Every local authority is now obliged by law to provide a social services department that provides some services for young children. However, many social service departments contract out services to private providers and use sponsored childminding places. With the introduction of Childcare Partnerships, the local education authority has in some places taken over many of the services to young children and their families with the exception generally of child protection.

Under the Children Act 1989 (see Ch. 8) local authorities have a statutory responsibility to register and monitor the variety of establishments and individuals such as childminders who offer care or education to pre-school children. Local authorities also have a clear responsibility for child protection, and are closely involved with families where children are deemed to be at risk. This can and often does lead to a certain tension in relationships between social services and their clients.

Traditionally, the involvement of social workers with families has led to a deficit view of those families, although staff today usually work hard to avoid this situation. This means families can be seen as in need of help and support, and implies that their parenting skills are likely to be deficient. As a result of these attitudes, decisions concerning children have often been taken out of parents' hands although it is thought that the Children Act 1989 has improved the situation. All this has profound implications for work with parents and the delicate relationship that exists between client and worker demands high levels of interpersonal skill and empathy.

Family centres and day nurseries

Some social services departments provide family centres and/or day nurseries or contract out provision to private providers, although many of these cater only for children and families in particular need. In some areas (although this is rare) parents are offered subsidized day nursery places to enable them to work or study, and this provides for a more representative mix of children in the nursery. In family centres children are less likely to be cared for on a full-time basis, but hours offered are, where possible, tailored to the needs of the child and family within the constraints of the setting. Here parents are encouraged to be actively involved with their children, parenting skills are modelled and high quality interaction with the child is encouraged. This is an important role for family centres where a central aim is likely to be the creation of a safe and facilitating environment for children within stable homes.

Most social services establishments will operate a key worker system, where a designated worker will take the primary responsibility of working with an individual family.

Scenario 4.3

You are a newly-appointed senior nursery officer in a family centre situated in a council estate in the inner city. You have a brief to develop work with parents who are very suspicious of the role of the family centre. The family centre has no policy for work with parents and lacks direction.

1. Devise a policy or policies for work with parents.
2. Devise a series of training days for existing staff on work with parents.

Parents in social service settings

It is easy to assume that parents with involvement in social services day care will have little to give back to the institution, and will somehow be recipients only, but the emphasis today is away from the parent as somehow 'lacking' towards the parent as partner. Although it would be foolish to say that this is always an easy relationship, the establishment of family centres and the move towards greater parental participation does indicate a changing emphasis. The basis of this is a move towards empowering parents to take control of their own lives through encouraging decision-making and building up self-esteem. In this way it is postulated they will become better parents and more positive and whole people.

Much of the work with families involved with social services is likely to be with some of the most stressed, vulnerable and disadvantaged individuals in society. Some parents will be at the nursery or centre as part of family rehabilitation when children are being returned home 'on trial' after being in care. They are often confused and angry, and the children can exhibit difficult and testing behaviour. Parents can often be depressed and feel unable to cope, their self-esteem will be low and they feel powerless. Work with this type of client group, although potentially very rewarding, is demanding upon staff at all levels. Parents need skilled help and parenting for themselves in some cases, before they feel able to become involved with their child or others in the institution.

Whilst recognizing this, it is also important that parents are encouraged to become involved and to begin to take control over their own lives. It is often difficult for staff to work positively with parents who perhaps have not cared for their children and who seem to have little motivation to do so.

Legislation

The Seebohm Report (1968) indicated a need for clients to be much more closely involved with decision-making and delivery of service. The Children Act 1989, which is dealt with in Chapter 8, was influential in forming attitudes towards parents as partners. The emphasis has changed from parental rights to parental responsibilities.

Scenario 4.4

Teenage parents of a 2½-year-old child are anxious to have the child returned to them after a brief spell in care. At 2 years, the child was found to be seriously underweight, and the health visitor had discovered he was left alone during the evenings when his parents went out. The parents are very anxious about their son and want to try again; they have been visiting him at the foster parents regularly where he was seen to be thriving.

A recent case conference has been held and, although invited, the parents arrived too late to participate. Since then a contract has been drawn up whereby the parents have to attend the local family centre with their son at a regular time each day.

The aim is to spend a major part of that time in direct interaction with their son and other times to participate in a group with other young parents. However, when the worker tries to involve them in play activities with their son, they are unable to participate, seem stiff and awkward and soon get bored. They are very quiet in the group and seem overwhelmed and intimidated by the set-up.

(a) The parents really want their child back with them: how might they be feeling in this situation?
(b) How might staff in the family centre be feeling?
(c) What practical steps could be taken to encourage the parents' involvement?
(d) What are the main concerns for the staff?

Parents and the voluntary, private and independent sectors

Background

In the voluntary sector there are many groups both large and small providing care and education for young children. There are many different types of organization in this sector with varying functions. Organizations such as Home Start provide trained volunteers to support families under stress; often these volunteers are parents themselves with a deep understanding of what their clients are experiencing. The Pre-school Learning Alliance (PLA) was started by a parent, and relies heavily on parental partnerships to exist. It provides for an enormous number of children and families and is typical of the move towards self-help and community initiative which has characterized the past 20 to 30 years.

Many of these initiatives have arisen out of a lack of statutory provision, and although self-help groups are often criticized as possibly preventing real social change, in general they are an invaluable additional resource. There is a considerable difference between large organizations employing staff, and small self-help groups run by parents. However, the voluntary and charitable status of large institutions such as the National Children's Homes can assist in their relationship with parents and carers, as there is less stigma associated with them than with social services. Parents are more likely to be involved in the management and day-to-day organization of voluntary groups. As such they may be clients and consumers as well as managers with varying but often substantial degrees of involvement.

In the private and independent sectors that cover childminding, workplace crèches and private group day care, the relationship is not always as straightforward as consumer and provider; e.g. sponsored childminding through a local authority is using what was traditionally an independent sector resource to care for young children, and sometimes to monitor the parenting. There are variants of this type of scheme throughout the UK, e.g. day fostering.

For social, demographic and other reasons, the numbers of women in paid work seeking day care for their children have risen in recent years and this has led to an increase in private sector provision, e.g. in the provision of workplace crèches. Many of these are run as business ventures.

Parents in voluntary, private and independent settings

In the voluntary sector it is expected in general that there will be a high level of parental involvement, which will, of course, vary with the purpose of the organization. Often the organization is set up for parents by other parents who participate

Scenario 4.5

A recently-divorced mother of two pre-school children is trying to overcome the difficulties of the past year or so and make a new life for herself. The elder child has joined the local pre-school but the mother is finding great difficulty in coping with other parents and staff members who are attempting to draw her in to help. She is not working outside the home at present and although there are money problems, they are not overwhelming. She has a few friends but no family locally.

(a) How might the mother be feeling at this point?
(b) What advice and help could the play leader offer to her, and what community resources might be available?
(c) Discuss this parent's needs and consider what advantages or disadvantages the involvement in a voluntary sector playgroup has over other forms of pre-school provision.

together in the management and the day-to-day running of the service. Often parents can be more involved as they work within informal neighbourhood care networks, which are flexible in terms of hours and access. As parents work together, with help from professionals where necessary, they can gain more confidence and be empowered to move on. Small voluntary groups are more flexible to local needs and attract local people as resources.

Funding is often a great problem, and these difficulties can restrict the scope of the various projects and make it difficult for all but the most dedicated. Lack of training for staff and poor or non-existent salaries also affect relations with parents. Sometimes there can be difficulties in ensuring common goals, and young parents may not always have the time and support networks to be involved in voluntary organizations, even those designed specifically for them.

In the private and independent sectors young children are often there to allow their parents to work. Involving working parents is difficult in itself as they are usually

Scenario 4.6

You are a qualified nursery nurse in a private day nursery where the majority of children stay long hours in the nursery as their parents work. There is very little time for in-depth contact between staff and parents and you are concerned that the parents are missing out on their children's development.

Devise a system for ensuring that parents are kept informed on their child's progress. Prepare an information sheet on the importance of parents spending quality time with their children.

pressed for time and tired after work. They may also live some distance from the crèche. Good relationships between staff and parents continue to be very important as parents must know they can trust the quality of care and education offered and will wish to be fully informed of their child's progress.

Early Excellence centres

In March 1998 the new government commenced its programme of announcing the first of an anticipated 25 Early Excellence centres. These centres are education-led, and usually have well-designed premises, regular attendance, a local catchment area, give their staff innovative job descriptions, provide regular staff time for training and planning, provide a means-tested subsidy for all children, act as a resource base, listen to children's views and provide a parents' charter. The centres are designated by the current government to demonstrate and disseminate best early years practice and are combined centres often with several functions, e.g. they may provide:

- *day care*
- *nursery education*
- *support for families*
- *support for children in need*
- *accommodation for a voluntary sector pre-school playgroup*
- *support for childminder networks*
- *crèches for meetings*
- *training*
- *community work and outreach*
- *parent education*
- *demonstrating good parenting.*

The inclusion of a parents' charter in the Early Excellence centres will emphasize the partnerships with parents which are now so fundamental to best practice in early years service provision.

Principles of work with parents

Parents vary in their levels of confidence and in their parenting skills, but it is important that workers recognize the central role that parents play in the life of the child. A key principle of all work with parents is in ensuring that all the informal, everyday interactions between staff and parents reflect a positive acceptance and valuing of them and their culture. Below are some general principles and attitudes which assist effective work with parents.

Workers should recognize that parents:

- *usually know more than anyone else about their child.*
- *are equal partners.*
- *have rights as citizens and tax-payers.*
- *can be effective policy-makers for the setting.*
- *have a right to be consulted on changes affecting their children.*
- *have a right either to participate in management or to be represented.*
- *are consumers and expect good customer service.*
- *can offer effective care and education to their child.*
- *have a right to negotiate with staff over issues affecting their children.*
- *should understand and participate in the formulation of aims and goals for their child.*
- *have a right to regular and relevant information.*
- *can be learners with their child and with staff.*
- *have useful skills and personal strengths.*
- *sometimes need a break from their children.*
- *may feel negative about their children.*
- *sometimes lack confidence.*
- *may feel upset or guilty about leaving their child with others.*

Best practice in work with parents indicates that workers should:

- *contribute positively and actively to welcoming parents.*
- *know the parents' correct names and preferred modes of address.*
- *be sensitive to parents' differing views.*
- *interact positively and professionally with parents at all times.*
- *recognize the personal and environmental stresses affecting parents.*
- *recognize the need for confidentiality in dealing with parents.*
- *recognize that some parents will not agree with the goals of the setting for a variety of reasons.*

Best practice in early years provision indicates that workers in settings:

- *should recognize and value the parent, parental culture, heritage and language.*
- *have a responsibility to inform and work with parents.*
- *have a responsibility to give parents every opportunity to understand what is going on in the setting and the rationale behind it, e.g. different types of play activity.*
- *should give parents the opportunity to participate in observing and assessing their children.*
- *should encourage parents in their parenting role.*
- *should encourage mutual trust between parents and workers.*
- *have clear policies to deal with incidents of stereotypical parental attitudes and prejudices.*

- *have a clear settling-in policy which is flexible enough to cover individual circumstances without compromising the basic principles.*

If these principles and attitudes are generally understood, it is likely that parents will feel much more able to participate and that they will have something valuable to contribute. However, there are parents who, for whatever reason, either do not wish to become involved in the care and education of their child outside the home, despite every encouragement, or may prefer to be visited at home. This should be respected generally, but there are some situations, such as in child protection cases, where the setting has made a contract with the parent in order to achieve a particular goal. Not attending the centre may mean the parent is breaking the contract and steps will be taken to deal with the situation.

Settling-in policies are very important to ensure that the child is supported during this potentially difficult transition. Parents should understand right from the outset the settling-in policy which will often require them to spend some time in the nursery supporting their child. Settling-in policies vary but settling in a child should not be rushed; parents should stay as long as the child needs them and as long as they themselves need so that the separation takes place with a feeling of confidence. Very young children should not be left to struggle with feelings of loss and grief. Long periods of distress and crying are not generally acceptable.

It should be acknowledged that involving parents is not always easy: it takes effort, commitment and time. Not all parents will share the goals of the institution, and some will seem to sabotage efforts made to involve them. Demands on staff can seem very heavy at times, and recognition of this and adequate support systems should always be available.

Involving fathers

It has often been difficult to involve fathers or male carers in the work of early years settings. Whalley (1994) describes how Penn Green Centre attempted to make the setting more friendly to men. As well as providing positive images of men in non-stereotyped roles, Penn Green employed male workers, ran a men's group and developed strategies for encouraging men's participation. Involving fathers and male carers has been slow and many useful lessons have been learned at Penn Green such as the need to ensure that trust is built up and that all staff are appropriately recruited, have undergone police checks and are closely supervised irrespective of gender.

Practical ways of encouraging positive interactions with parents

Ways in which parents are involved will depend largely on the setting and the ethos of the setting. Some factors to bear in mind are:

- Wherever possible, parents should be given their own room where they can sit and talk with other adults, make coffee and relax without undue pressure.
- Mother and toddler groups, toy libraries, parent education classes, specialist home–school liaison staff, bilingual staff contacts, voluntary sector groups and other inter-agency facilities should be provided under one roof.
- Parents should have open access to staff, headteachers, officers in charge and key workers.
- Initial home visits should be encouraged.
- Joint nursery records which are open for parents and staff to add their own notes or suggestions.
- Physical access should be as straightforward as possible and the environment friendly and encouraging.
- Storage for buggies and prams should be available.
- Toilets and nappy-changing areas should be clearly marked.
- Information should be available in all community languages and readily accessible.
- At the initial interview, parents should be given information on session times, and the settling-in policy should be explained together with its rationale.
- Information on community resources and persons to contact in particular situations should be readily available.
- The rules, policies and programmes of the setting, including policy on equal opportunities and early years curriculum programmes, should be available for all parents with details of complaints and appeals procedures.
- It should be made very clear to parents that their presence is welcomed and open discussion should take place about the type of involvement where appropriate.
- Provision of a crèche may be vitally important to some parents to enable them to participate in activities.

Roles and functions that parents undertake

Parents can be involved in many different ways which utilize their individual skills and where they feel confident. Where parents cannot offer a particular service, their contribution should be valued, no matter how small. The list below is not exhaustive and there are many other ways to work with parents.

- *As governors, policy-makers and in management roles.*
- *In curriculum planning.*
- *In fund-raising.*
- *In the classroom or nursery, offering general support to the staff, or more specific help such as listening to children read, or cooking with small groups.*
- *Playing with children or providing general supervisory help.*
- *Help with basic care and management.*
- *Repairing and maintaining equipment.*
- *Maintaining the environment.*
- *Running libraries for books or toys.*
- *Helping with outings.*
- *Helping to run groups or support other parents.*
- *Helping with parent/parent–teacher association.*
- *Helping with swimming or sports.*
- *Visiting as part of their occupational role, e.g. fire-fighter.*
- *Providing specific skills and services.*
- *Helping with cultural events and festivals.*
- *Helping where there may be a language difficulty.*
- *Helping with social events and open days.*

Figure 4.2
Parental involvement.

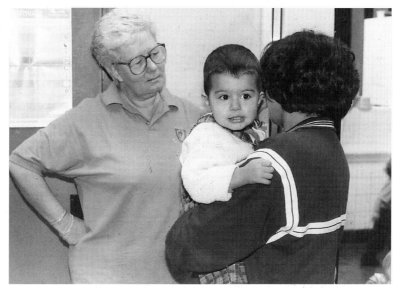

Evaluating the effectiveness of work with parents

Many informal and formal arrangements for work with parents exist but in order for these to be meaningful settings must be prepared to draw up criteria for evaluation. Braun (1992) suggested the following criteria for evaluating the effectiveness of work with parents in nurseries:

1. *How many parents are we on first-name terms with? How representative are these of all the parents?*
2. *What proportion of parents raises questions and makes comments about their child?*
3. *What proportion of parents makes suggestions about how the nursery operates?*
4. *What proportion of parents requests specific provisions?*
5. *Who makes use of the provisions we develop?*
6. *What have we changed as a result of working with parents?*

Questions such as these should form part of the formal evaluation of the work of the early years setting and will help this important area of work to become of central importance in the life of the setting.

Assignments

Assignment 1

Encouraging family involvement
You are working in a community nursery where one-third of the families represented are from Afro-Caribbean or Asian backgrounds and several children have English as a second language. You are conscious that the nursery still presents a very 'white', mono-cultural image, and that there are racist elements in the local community.

Devise an activity or theme to use with the children which includes definite possibilities for involving all the children and families. Discuss how you would use this theme/activity to involve parents from all the ethnic groups in a manner that is likely to present a positive world view and to increase awareness.

Assignment 2

Encouraging partnerships

You are a childminder in an inner city area, and have been asked by social services to take two children, aged 1 and 3 years, from a family where the mother has a history of depressive illness. She is currently receiving treatment at a local hospital and day centre which takes up about half a day three times a week. You do not feel you really know much about this condition and are concerned to find out as much as possible before the children start with you.

Devise a plan of action which would help you to find out this information. Discuss the types of general information you would find helpful, as well as information specific to this problem.

Discuss strategies for ensuring clear lines of communication with the parent, designed to ensure that the parent does not feel excluded and that there is a real partnership between you both.

Assignment 3

Devising and producing a leaflet

Devise and produce a leaflet designed to introduce parents to a group, pre-school, or other child care/education setting. Stress the aspects most likely to encourage parental partnership.

Assignment 4

To help parents feel more at home in the nursery

In discussion with your supervisor, look critically at the waiting area, hall or room where parents spend time. Devise a series of alterations/improvements to the area that might make it more welcoming; wherever possible implement these changes and discuss the outcomes.

Evaluate the outcome of your efforts, noting comments from parents and staff.

Assignment 5

To encourage parents to become more involved in a particular aspect of play or other child-centred activity
In discussion with your supervisor, work with a parent or group of parents in an activity with the child or children. Select your activity carefully, e.g. creative activity, role play, story telling or cooking. Encourage the parents to allow the children to explore and to express themselves. Where possible, demonstrate that the process of the activity is more important than the end product.

Discuss with parents their feelings about the session. Briefly record what you have learned and the value of the session to parents and children.

Assignment 6

Devise a questionnaire to use with parents to test the effectiveness of the setting's work with parents
Where possible use the questionnaire with parents.

Analyse your results drawing out the important points for the nursery. Where necessary suggest changes in practice to improve the setting's work with parents.

Assignment 7

Devise a series of role-plays for staff designed to develop communication skills with parents, children and other staff
Assess the effectiveness of levels of staff communication. What training needs are highlighted?

REFERENCES AND FURTHER READING

Central Advisory Council for Education (England). (1967) *The Plowden Report: Children and their Primary Schools*. London: HMSO.

Craft, M. *et al.* (Eds) (1980) *Linking Home and School*, 3rd edn. London: Harper and Row.

Cyster, R. Clift and Battle, (Eds) (1990) *Parental Involvement in Primary Schools*. Windsor: NFER.

Department of Education and Science. (1975) *The Bullock Report: A Language for Life*. London: HMSO.

Department of Education and Science. (1978) *The Warnock Report: Committee of Enquiry into the Education of Handicapped Children and Young People with Special Educational Needs*. London: HMSO.

Douglas, J.W.B. (1964) *The Home and the School*. London: MacGibbon and Kee.

Lynch, J. and Pimlot, J. (1976) *Parents and Teachers*. Basingstoke: Macmillan.

Miller, S., Robinson, J. and Sutton, E. (1997) *Starting Out*. Morpeth Northumberland: Education Development Centre.

Moss, P. and Petrie, P. (1997) *Children's Services: Time for a New Approach*. London: University of London Institute of Education Paper.

National Association of Toy and Leisure Libraries. (1997) *Playing and Learning at Home*. London: NATLL.

Nutbrown, C. and Hannon, P. (1997) *Early Literacy Education with Parents* (Manual and Video). Sheffield: Sheffield University Education Resources.

Pugh, G. (Ed) (1992) *Contemporary Issues in the Early Years*. London: Paul Chapman with the National Children's Bureau.

Pugh, G. and De'Ath, E. (1989) *Working Towards Partnership in the Early Years*. London: National Children's Bureau.

Seebohm, F. (1968) *Local Authority and Allied Personal Social Services*. London: HMSO.

Smith, N. Parental perspectives. *Social Work Today* **21**(47): 25.

Taylor, T. (1977) *A New Partnership for Our Schools*. London: HMSO.

Tizard, B., Mortimore, J. and Burchall, B. (1981) *Involving Parents in Nursery and Infant Schools*. Oxford: Grant McIntyre/Blackwell.

Whalley, M. (1994) *Learning to be Strong*. Sevenoaks, Kent: Hodder and Stoughton.

Wolfendale, S. (1983) *Parental Participation in Children's Development and Education*. London: Gordon and Breach.

Wolfendale, S. (Ed.) (1989) *Parental Involvement: Developing Networks between School, Home and Community*. London: Cassell.

5: THE INCLUSION OF CHILDREN WITH SPECIAL NEEDS

Objectives

- Debate on labelling
- Definitions of inclusion
- Historical perspectives
- The Warnock Report
- Present perspective
- Education Act 1993 (part 3)
- Code of Practice 1994
- Assessment of a child's educational needs
- Integration/inclusion
- Provision for under-5s
- Involving parents
- Bonding
- Conductive education
- Portage scheme
- Children with specific learning difficulties
- Children with dyslexia
- Children with dyspraxia
- High ability children
- Attention Deficit Hyperactivity Disorder
- Self-image of children with disabilities
- Advocacy and empowerment

Links

This chapter has links with:
- NVQ (EYCE) Units: C17, C18.
- CACHE Diploma Module R.

Introduction including labelling and inclusion

It could be argued that at some time in their lives all children have special needs which may require extra attention from the parent or carer: however, the children referred to in this chapter are those who have conditions which may handicap or partially handicap their all-round development. When referring to children with special needs it is important to be sensitive in the language that is used; e.g. it is probably better to refer to 'children with handicaps/disabilities' than to refer to 'handicapped/disabled children'. By using the former it makes it clear that the children come before the handicap, thus we talk about 'children with special needs', 'children with a hearing impairment', etc. However, there is a school of thought, led by people like Micheline Mason and Richard Rieser, who argue that:

> 'Special' needs is a euphemism for 'abnormal' needs and as such is still within the medical model of disability. Disabled to us is like the word Black. Once a negative term in people's minds, people who suffered racism decided that they had to reclaim the word and turn it into both a political identity, and a description of which to be proud. We have made a similar decision.
>
> *Micheline Mason 1993*

Descriptive labelling is a sensitive area and where possible should be avoided, although even the Warnock Committee realized that it was necessary to have some form of distinction between the types of special need in order to ensure that needs were met. The terminology relating to special needs has changed dramatically in recent years, mostly in response to legislation. However, not all textbooks that you read will be written in terms which reflect these changes. In recent years, people with disabilities have been enabled to state publicly their views on these matters and this has gone a long way towards changing the attitudes of society.

The major underlying philosophy relating to good practice in special needs is one of inclusion. This means that, wherever possible, children with special needs should be included within the mainstream provision, including the education and day care systems. The DfEE document 'Excellence for All Children. Meeting Special Educational Needs' (1997) makes it very clear that the underlying principle for children with special educational needs must be one of inclusion. The document lists seven practical steps which can be taken to promote greater inclusion of these children into mainstream education:

- Requiring local education authorities (LEAs) to submit plans for taking inclusion forward
- Priority should be given to securing inclusion for younger children or those with particular forms of special educational need (SEN)
- Requiring all children to be registered on the roll of a mainstream school
- Increase levels of capital support to extend the existing Schools Access Initiative
- Target specific grant measures which would enhance mainstream schools' ability to include pupils with SEN
- Seek ways of celebrating the success of those schools which improve their ability to provide for a wide range of special needs
- Give some priority for capital support where possible planned school reorganizations will enhance SEN provision in mainstream schools.

Inclusion does need to be carefully thought through so that the child benefits most from the process, for as Margaret Clark (1988) points out: 'to place some children with special needs in an ordinary unit may indeed not be to integrate but to deny their special needs.'

It is not the intention of this chapter to offer medical definitions and causes of handicap, although conditions may be mentioned as examples of certain types of special need which may benefit from specific types of care and education. What this chapter is doing is looking at the reports and legislation that have led to present-day attitudes and highlighting the good practice and role of pre-school education and care for children with special needs.

Historical perspectives

During the past 20 years the attitudes of society towards its members who have handicaps or impairments have changed dramatically. The UK was once a place which generated large institutions such as workhouses, psychiatric hospitals and hospitals for the mentally handicapped; it is only since the 1970s that the philosophy has changed and moved towards community care.

As recently as the 1960s, if a child was born with an obvious handicap such as Down's syndrome or cerebral palsy, it would probably have spent only the first few years of its life within the family before being admitted to a large mental handicap hospital where it might have spent the rest of its life. This was not due to callousness or lack of feeling on the part of the parents but what at the time was viewed as the best possible treatment for the child. Lack of facilities in the home, such as washing machines, bathrooms, inside toilets and central heating, made it impossible for the majority of parents to care for such a child within the home. (This was prior to the Court Report (1976) which looked at child health and the better co-ordination of health and social services and education in order to enable children with disabilities to remain in their own home.) At the time the large institution was the place where the child could live and have all the specialist care that it needed, including 24-hour nursing care; remember there were no respite or Crossroad schemes at that time. These institutions/hospitals were usually situated on the outskirts of large towns and cities, making it difficult for parents and family to visit regularly. As the child grew older and lost the bond with its immediate family, so visits were likely to decrease. It could be said that many of these children were abandoned to the institution.

The Education Act 1921 had recognized five categories of handicap: blindness, deafness, physical defectiveness, mental defectiveness and epilepsy. This did not necessarily mean that the state provided educational facilities for the children in all these categories, although it was not uncommon to find residential establishments for the blind or 'deaf and dumb'.

The Education Act 1944 made it the legal duty of the LEAs to provide education for children with disabilities, either in special schools or via some other arrangement. This Act defined eleven categories of handicap: blind, partially sighted, deaf, partially deaf, physically handicapped, delicate, diabetic, epileptic, maladjusted, educationally subnormal and speech-defective. Not all the children in these categories were educated or had special educational provision, for the Act clearly stated that the provision could be schools or other arrangements. In many cases the 'other arrangements' were within the large institutions, where schoolrooms were set up and the children sent to these for certain hours of the day. The teachers in these hospital schools were paid by the LEA (rather than by the health authority which ran the establishments), and so the authority claimed that it was carrying out its duty in accordance with the Act. The children never left the confines of the institution, and as teaching in such schools was not seen as a prestigious job, the schools did not always attract good teachers.

The Education Act 1970 made provision for those children with severe mental handicap and who prior to the Act were not provided for as they were seen as uneducable. Once again the LEAs were given the responsibility of making arrangements for the education of these children. The way most LEAs responded to this was, once again, to set up schoolrooms within existing institutions.

The Warnock Report

A major breakthrough for children with special needs came in 1974 when the Warnock Report was published. A committee under the Chairmanship of Mary Warnock was set up by the government to: 'review the educational provision in England, Scotland and Wales for children and young people handicapped by disabilities of body or mind.' The terms of reference were broad and this meant that the committee had a free rein to investigate most aspects relating to educational provision of children with handicaps. The Warnock Report made a number of recommendations:

- The abolition of the categorizing of children by the nature of their handicap.
- The introduction of the concept of special educational needs.
- Special educational needs were defined as mild, moderate or severe.
- The introduction of the term 'specific learning difficulties' for those children who had difficulty in just one area of the curriculum.
- The conclusion that one child in five is likely at some time to require some form of special education provision.
- A change of emphasis from where education took place to the type of education required.
- The notion of integration and the concept that where possible children should be educated with their peers.
- That there should be a partnership between parents and the school, and that parents should be kept fully informed of all facilities and support services available to them.

- Early identification of children's special needs by a five-stage model of assessment. Assessment could be undertaken at the parents' or local authority's request.
- Special emphasis on the needs of the pre-school child.

The Warnock Report provided the basis for the Education Act 1981 which totally changed the framework for special education. Following the Act the government published two circulars (8/81 and 1/83) which not only offered advice to local authorities in interpreting the Act but also made it clear that a child's special educational needs referred to its abilities as well as disabilities, and that assessment should be ongoing.

Other legislation brought in prior to and after the 1981 Act facilitated its implementation. Legislation brought in benefits for the families of children with handicaps, such as mobility allowances, attendance allowances, laundry allowances and money to carry out essential conversions on homes in order to enable access for wheelchairs, etc. Local authorities provided transport for children to and from school and facilities were available for holiday and respite care. All these things went a long way to encouraging parents of a child with special needs to care for that child within the family.

Around this time changes were also being made in the National Health Service which discouraged the continuation of large institutional hospitals for specialist care, viewing them as detrimental to the welfare of the patients and expensive to run. These hospitals were slowly being emptied and their clientele rehabilitated to live within the community. People whose only home had been the hospital were now finding that they were capable of living in sheltered hostel accommodation. Social services departments actively promoted foster care programmes for children with special needs who were unable to remain with their families or had previously been housed in one of the large hospitals.

The Education Reform Act 1988 makes scant reference to children with special needs except to state that all subjects and stages of the National Curriculum must be taught in special needs schools. This has led to a number of criticisms from educationalists who feel that time in these schools could be better spent than trying to get children of doubtful or little ability through the National Curriculum tests.

Present perspective

The present situation is one whereby most children with special needs are able to be accommodated within the family and those who are not are able to live with foster parents. Education for these children may be in mainstream school or in a special school which caters for their specific learning difficulties. Some mainstream schools

Figure 5.1
Children with
different types of
special need.

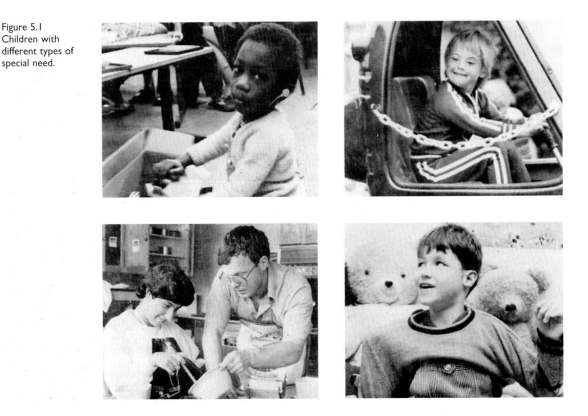

have special units attached to them such as a unit for the partially hearing. The children are educated in the special unit but at all other times they join the children from the main section of the school. In this way the special needs are met but the children do not miss out on the social inclusion aspects of their education. It is not uncommon to find pre-school children with special needs attending playgroups, opportunity groups, community nurseries, nursery schools and nursery classes. However, Clark (1988) makes the following point which questions whether a day nursery could be considered as appropriate mainstream provision:

> Many or indeed most children attending such units are already 'at risk' in many ways, to such an extent that it must be questioned as to how 'ordinary' such provision indeed is.

Whilst there is a major emphasis on inclusion, there is also an emphasis on avoiding the early labelling of children into special needs categories. Psychologists and other professionals are unwilling to assess children under the age of 5 years, although parents have the right to ask for an assessment. If pre-school children are allowed to integrate into mainstream provision it is far easier to ascertain what their abilities are and what they may be capable of in the future.

The Children Act 1989 makes social services departments responsible for providing for children 'in need'. Disability is one of the categories defined as 'in need' and means:

> a child is disabled if he is blind, deaf, or dumb or suffers from mental disorder of any kind or is substantially and permanently handicapped by illness, injury or congenital deformity or such other disability as may be prescribed.
> *The Children Act Guidance and Regulations. Vol. 6: Children with Disabilities*
> *(1991)*

The local authority social services departments are bound to provide services for children with a disability and such services should be of the appropriate range and level to 'safeguard and promote the welfare of children in need.' The Act charges local authorities to provide services which will enable children with disabilities to be cared for within the family. A requirement of the Act is that social services departments must keep a register of children with disabilities, but obtaining services is not dependent upon a child's name being on that register, and parents are not obliged to register their child. Unlike the local education department which may deal only with children of statutory school age, social services facilities are available to children from birth. The Guidelines to the Act mention 'packages of services' which may be provided through statutory and voluntary agencies. The NHS Community Care Act 1990 requires social services departments to assess the needs of those people who may need community care services; this assessment becomes part of the long-term 'care package' that is devised for each client. A contract is drawn up between the child's family and the service providers which clearly states what will be provided for the child.

The Children Act and the NHS Community Care Act place emphasis upon co-ordination of the services which are available to each family. In the past there have been numerous examples of families that have more than 20 people going into one household to give different caring services to one child. Inevitably such un-co-ordinated situations are expensive, lead to unnecessary overlap and instil confusion in the parents or carers.

The Education Act 1993 (Part 111) lays down the current policy for children who have special educational needs. The Act states:

> A child has special educational needs if he or she has a *learning difficulty* which calls for *special educational provision* to be made for him or her.

> A child has a *learning difficulty* if he or she:

> (a)   has a *significantly greater difficulty* in learning than the majority of children of the same age.

> (b)   has a disability which either *prevents or hinders* the child from making use of educational facilities of a kind provided for children of the same age in schools within the area of the local education authority.

(c)   is *under five* and falls within the definition at (a) or (b) above or would do if special education provision was not made for the child.

A child must not be regarded as having a learning difficulty solely because the language or form of language of the home is different from the language in which he or she will be taught. *Special educational provision* means:

(a)   for a child over two, educational provision which is additional to, or otherwise different from, the educational provision made generally for children of the child's age in maintained schools, other than special schools, in the area.

(b)   for a child under two, educational provision of any kind.

Education Act 1993 (Part 111) Section 156

The Code of Practice 1994 is a guidance document for local authorities and school governing bodies or other establishments responsible for children with special educational needs on how best to implement the 1993 Education Act. The implementation of the Code of Practice is to be monitored by OFSTED as part of the inspections which they routinely carry out. The fundamental principles of the Code of Practice are as follows:

- the needs of all pupils who may have special educational needs either throughout, or at any time during, their school careers must be addressed; the Code recognises that there is a continuum of needs and a continuum of provision, which may be made in a wide variety of different forms
- children with special educational needs require the greatest possible access to a broad and balanced education, including the National Curriculum
- the needs of most pupils will be met in the mainstream, and without a statutory assessment or statement of special educational needs. Children with special educational needs, including children with statements of special educational needs, should, where appropriate and taking into account the wishes of their parents, be educated alongside their peers in mainstream schools
- even before he or she reaches compulsory school age a child may have special educational needs requiring the intervention of the LEA as well as the health services
- the knowledge, views and experience of parents are vital. Effective assessment and provision will be secured where there is the greatest possible degree of partnership between parents and their children and schools, LEAs and other agencies.

DfEE 1994 *Code of Practice on the Identification and Assessment of Special Educational Needs P2*

Further details relating to the Code of Practice can be found in Chapter 8.

Assessment of a child's educational needs

Part of the assessment process requires a statement to be written on the child's specific learning needs. The aims of the statement are to identify the areas of need and define the treatment/educational requirements for such needs. The statement on the child must be updated regularly in conjunction with the programme of ongoing assessment. It is essential that any assessment process is carried out in partnership with the parents/carer. Parents must be informed of the local authority's intention to assess their child before any action can be taken and parents have a right to respond within 29 days. Most parents respond positively to the request as they realize that it is to the benefit of their child for the assessment to take place. Once the assessment has taken place and the statement drafted, it is usual to send a copy to the parents and the parents do have a right to appeal against the contents of the statement.

Section 5 of the Code of Practice relates to assessments and statements for children under 5 years of age. If a child is under 2 years of age and has special educational needs, an assessment may be made of the child's educational needs if a parent/guardian consents to this happening or requests it. It is rare for children under 2 years to have a statement and procedures for carrying out such an assessment are not laid down in the legislation. Most referrals of children of this age will come via the health visitor or general practitioner. A statement may be issued because of a child's complex needs or in order to ensure that the child is able to receive a particular service such as home-based teaching or a developmental play programme. Home-based voluntary sector programmes such as Portage are usually offered by the LEA without the necessity of a statement. Any assessment should be carried out in a place where the child and parents/carers feel comfortable.

For children aged 2 to 5 years who are in nursery school or class, the assessment procedures are the same as for those children of compulsory school age.

Children with special needs who attend mainstream educational establishments should have a statement which clearly lays out the extra resources they require. In the absence of such a statement the school is not able to obtain the money to fund such resources and therefore would be unlikely to be able to provide them. This is particularly pertinent to children with physical disabilities who may require a full-time carer to help them with their mobility, toileting or feeding. Special facilities such as speech therapy, physiotherapy or hydrotherapy need to be clearly documented in the statement if the local authority is to provide the services.

Some children have very minor special needs, particularly those with communication difficulties. In the past such children would have had access to the peripatetic speech therapists who worked in mainstream schools and would therefore not need to be statemented in order to obtain this facility. In recent years, as a result of economies in spending by local authorities, there has been a cutback in the numbers of speech therapists employed in mainstream schools and this has resulted in a number of

Michael is 3 years old and has Down's syndrome. Recently his mother, Mary, finds that the sounds he is making are beginning to form speech patterns. Mary is keen not to let the opportunity pass if Michael is now attempting to communicate using speech.

What would Mary need to do in order to ensure that Michael can get the speech therapy that he needs?

children not being supplied with the service. If a child has a statement which requires them to have regular speech therapy, then the local authority is bound to provide this, but without such a statement there is no guarantee that the child will receive the service. There is a requirement upon local authorities to review statements annually in order to ensure that the provision is relevant to the child's needs.

The Children Act 1989 very clearly lays down the responsibilities of the local authority in relation to children in need. However, a child will be required to be diagnosed and labelled as 'in need' before the local authority will respond. There are some obvious handicapping situations which would leave no element of doubt that a child was in need, e.g. cerebral palsy, Down's syndrome, deafness or blindness. There are other handicapping situations which are not so clear-cut and which may not be assessed until a child reaches school age, such as communication difficulties or emotional difficulties, and for which there are unlikely to be any special facilities available for children under 5.

Integration/inclusion

Section 2 of the 1981 Education Act sets out the requirements for integration of children with special needs into the mainstream school system. The philosophy for integration came from the Warnock Report and hinges upon the idea that teachers should be encouraged to look at the needs of all the children in their classes and adapt the curriculum accordingly. In 1987 a government Select Committee reported on the implementation of the 1981 Education Act. On the question of integration the Committee recommended that local authorities should have a clear policy statement on this matter and this should take into account the quality and appropriateness of the integrated provision. The Fish Committee 1985 stated:

> The concept of integration as a dynamic process is difficult to grasp. It is often confused with physical location and discussed in terms of specific situations rather than the whole life styles of children. Integration is about planned interaction between a child and his or her environment and is not about changing the concept of special educational needs but about its context.
>
> *Equal Opportunities for All? Report of the Committee Reviewing Provision to Meet*
> *Special Educational Needs. [Fish Report] 1985*

Most local authorities are developing their integration policies gradually as long-term commitments would require a significant input of resources, e.g. providing ramps, lifts, special toilet facilities, etc.

Scenario 5.2

Molly and Jim are bringing up their grandson Jason. He is 6 years old and has spina bifida. He is a bright little boy, who is a wheelchair-user and at present attends the local school for children with physical disabilities. All his friends are able-bodied and Jason is often sad that he cannot go to the same school as them.

Recently, Molly and Jim saw a programme on TV about integrating children with handicaps into mainstream education, and they feel that this would be the best approach for Jason.

(a) Using your LEA's policy, find out how Molly and Jim would go about enabling Jason to attend the local mainstream school.
(b) Are there likely to be any reasons as to why this might not be possible?

When the 1981 Education Act was published many people thought that the integration policy would lead to the closure of special schools and parents would inundate local authorities with requests to ensure that their children could be educated in a mainstream school. For a number of reasons this did not happen. Parents were sensible in their approach to integration and realized that it may not always be the best option for their child. Parents were very conscious of the good adult/child ratios and the wealth of equipment that is provided in the special schools and wanted their children to have the continued benefit of these things. For children with mobility difficulties, access to some mainstream schools was a problem, and the government did not offer schools extra resources in order to undertake structural adaptations.

Some special schools have closed down but it is difficult to determine whether this is as a result of integration or owing to other factors such as a fall in the birthrate, teenage vaccination for rubella, early detection of handicap by fetal scanning and easier access to abortion, which have all led to a decline in the number of children needing these particular facilities.

However, there was always a school of thought, particularly from parents of children with special needs and the Disability Rights Movement, that integration was another word for 'assimilation'. In other words, children with learning disabilities were welcome in mainstream school provided they managed to merge with the other children and did not demand too much attention. What these parents and others wanted was inclusion, i.e. children with special needs being included in all parts of education and school activities. This reasoning is reflected in the DfEE document, 'Excellence for All Children. Meeting Special Educational Needs' (1997) which also offers examples of good practice.

There is no doubt that inclusion does offer benefits for both the child with special needs and the other children in the class. Children who spend time with others who have special needs learn to understand that we are not all the same and that some people may need special help at certain times. Inclusion also goes a long way towards removing the stigma that society attaches to those with special needs. Children who have gone to school together often develop positive relationships that can continue throughout their lives.

Figure 5.2
Integration in
practice.

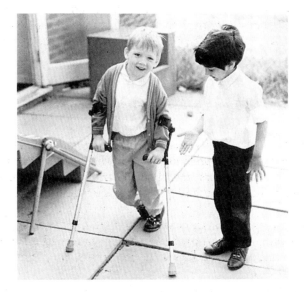

Provision for the under-5s

As previously stated, local authorities are not keen to statement children under the age of 5 unless a specific request is made by the parents. The first 5 years of life are an important period in a child's development and for this reason it is better not to label children at an early age. Some children are slower to develop than others but they may have caught up by the time they are 5.

The Children Act 1989 states:

> every local authority should provide services designed –
>
> (a) to minimise the effect on disabled children within their area of their disabilities; and
> (b) to give such children the opportunity to lead lives which are as normal as possible.
>
> *The Children Act 1989, Paragraph 6 of Schedule 2*

Thus once a need has been defined the local authority social services department must match that need to the available services. For pre-school children this may be a place in a day nursery, family centre, nursery school, pre-school playgroup, opportunity group, etc. It may also involve people working with the child within its own home, such as family aide worker or a Homestart visitor or Portage teacher.

Research has shown that families who have a child with a disability suffer more stress than other families. Services which enable the child to spend time outside the home not only benefit the child but offer respite periods for the family. Often people going into the home to work with the child find themselves having to act as family counsellors for they may be the only people that the family members feel they can talk to.

Involving parents

The Code of Practice (DfEE, 1944) is very clear that parents must be seen as 'partners in the educational process with unique knowledge and information to impart'. Parents are children's first carers and their contributions to debates around their child's needs must be listened to and respected. Clear lines of communication with parents need to be set up by all the professionals involved. Parents expect and deserve ongoing information and explanation as to how their child is being assessed and how their child is progressing. As part of the assessment process there needs to be a sharing of information and understanding between parents and professionals.

Many of the structured programmes devised for the child will require the confidence and involvement of parents if they are to be effective for the child. It is essential that such programmes are explained to the parents in a way which they understand and are therefore able to actively participate in with their child. Where there are communication problems for the child, parents need to be enabled to become familiar with the signing system which is being used with the child so they can confidently continue this in the home situation and communicate with their child. There must be respect and sensitivity for parents' needs, their culture, religion, living circumstances and other situations which might impinge on their daily lives. Parents need support from professionals and other parents who have children with special needs. Parent networks set up locally are a good method of bringing parents together.

The process of pre-school assessment

The procedures for assessment of children under 5 years has already been mentioned earlier in this chapter. However, once any child is a participant in some form of pre-school provision they will have their development assessed on a regular basis. Drummond and Nutbrown (1997) point out that

> Children's learning is so complex, rich, fascinating, varied and variable, surprising, enthusiastic and stimulating that to see it taking place every day of the week before one's very eyes, is one of the great rewards of the early years educator.

Thus by observing and assessing children each individual child's learning needs can be identified and catered for. Challen (1997) offers a model of pre-school assessment developed in one London borough. Initially children are monitored by the Health Authority, usually by special needs health visitors, and can be referred to a number of services prior to official notification of the child's special needs. These services include Portage, hearing and visually impaired services, physiotherapy, speech therapy, etc. Young children's progress is monitored at 6-monthly intervals at multi-disciplinary (health, education and social services) review meetings. Once formal notification of the child's special needs is made then an educational psychologist carries out an initial assessment based on a pre-school assessment schedule which focuses on collecting the child's developmental history, current skills and areas of concern. In this particular borough there are three nursery assessment bases, two integrated for children with general development delay and one special for children with profound and multiple developmental delay. At the nursery assessment base children's progress is monitored and reviewed on a regular basis. Specialist intervention programmes are devised, implemented and reviewed. The whole process is undertaken in partnership with the child's parents/carers. Many other local authori-

Scenario 5.3

Trevor and Janice have three children, Zoe who is 11 years old, Mark who is 8 years old and Daniel who is 3 years old. Daniel is autistic and exhibits very bizarre behaviour patterns, ranging from severe temper tantrums to prolonged repetition of one movement or activity. Recently, Zoe has been getting poor school reports and Mark has started to wet the bed at night. Trevor and Janice are nearing their wits' end as it seems that now all their children have developed problems.

You are Trevor and Janice's home visitor and are having little success in getting Janice to be interested in playing with Daniel as all she wants to do is talk about her problems.

(a) What can you do for Janice to help her through this difficult period?
(b) What facilities are available for Daniel?

ties have similar systems for dealing with provision for under-5s with special needs, e.g. Early Years Assessment Managers, designated assessment centres, child development centres, etc. The DfEE publication 'Excellence for All Children. Meeting Special Educational Needs' (1997) cites examples of good practice and suggestions as to how best children's special educational needs can be met.

Bonding

There are many examples of mothers rejecting their children because they have been born with an obvious disability. In some cases such rejection is temporary and in others it may be more long lasting with the mother needing help in order to overcome her feelings. Everyone wants a perfect baby and it can be a great shock to find that you have given birth to a less than perfect child. Feelings of rejection are often accompanied by feelings of guilt, that it was something that the mother did wrong during her pregnancy which led to her child being disabled. In most cases such guilt feelings are irrational as the reasons for many handicaps are still unknown.

Rejection may not always happen at birth but at a later date when the child may not be responding as it should, e.g. Fraiberg (1989) studying blind babies found that the mothers of these children withdrew from their babies because they were unresponsive and did not make eye contact. There are now special programmes to help mothers of blind babies bond with their children.

The bonding process does not happen over night but takes a number of months to become established. Early intervention can help the parents to bond with their disabled child and counselling can help them to overcome any feelings of guilt.

In some cases parents may bond too strongly with their child who has a disability and this may lead to other children in the family being neglected. There is an old adage that says, 'It is not just a handicapped child but a handicapped family', meaning that the whole family is affected when one of its members has a disability. Such strong bonding can also inhibit a child's development as the parents can become overprotective and unwilling to allow the child to develop its independence. In these situations it is most beneficial for the child to spend some hours of the day away from the home by attending some form of pre-school provision.

The policy of keeping children within the family helps the family to bond with the child and it is extremely rare to find a mother who never bonds with her child once she has recovered from the initial shock of finding that it has a disability.

Conductive education

The Peto Institute for Motor Disorders in Hungary is now world famous for its specially devised methods of conductive education. The clinic was founded in 1945 by Dr Andreas Peto and was loosely based on the theories of the Russian psychologists, Pavlov, Luria and Vygotsky. The aim of conductive education is to assess the child's potential in relation to the next progressive stage; it does not concentrate on the child's current abilities. Conductive education is only any use in cases of motor disorders and in all cases the first step is an assessment to decide whether the child will benefit from this treatment. Conductive education takes an holistic approach to the child and does not just concentrate on the area of the handicap, hence it requires staff who have multi-disciplinary skills. The Hungarian Peto staff have undergone a 4-year multi-disciplinary training which includes skills in teaching, nursing, physiotherapy, speech therapy and occupational therapy. The children's programme is intensive and requires them to be either resident at the Institute or to come in daily from 8 a.m. to 5 p.m. The programme is best started when the children are very young (under 2 years) and continued over a number of years. The children who appear to fare best from conductive education are those that suffer from cerebral palsy and it is with these children that the programme has had its greatest successes.

There has been criticism of conductive education, one of the main arguments being that the one-to-one intensive situation is responsible for the child's improvement rather than the education programme itself. Whatever the reason, conductive education does seem to work and it has become a sought-after treatment by the parents of those children who have cerebral palsy. There is now a centre for conductive education in Birmingham and it is possible that we shall see more of these centres opening in the UK in the future. Conductive education has the backing of SCOPE and other voluntary organizations and in recent years has had a high media profile.

The Portage programme

Portage is an idea that originated in America in the 1960s and consists of a home-teaching programme for pre-school children whose development is delayed owing to specific handicaps. A specially trained Portage teacher visits the home on a regular basis and shows the family members how they can work with the child. An activity sheet is drawn up and on this parents can register the child's progress.

Portage uses the six main child development areas: language, self-help, motor, socialization, cognitive skills and stimulation and devises a structured learning programme for specific tasks within these areas. Each task is broken down into small steps which are arranged in a developmental sequence. Parents and carers are then able to work with the children on these small steps; once one has been mastered they move to the next step until the whole task is achieved. A record is kept of the child's progress so that each achievement can be seen. Families are given a Portage Kit which contains record sheets and small cards on which the steps towards a task are written, one card for each step. The cards are colour-coded for developmental area and difficulty of the task.

Figure 5.3
Portage record chart.

Age Level	Card	Behaviour	Entry Behaviour	Date Achieved	Comments
0.1	1	Sucks and swallows liquid		/ /	
	2	Eats liquified foods, ie. baby cereal		/ /	
	3	Reaches for bottle		/ /	
	4	Eats strained foods fed by parent		/ /	
	5	Holds bottle without help while drinking		/ /	
	6	Directs bottle by guiding it toward mouth or by pushing it away		/ /	
	7	Eats mashed table foods fed by parent		/ /	
	8	Drinks from cup held by parent		/ /	
	9	Eats semi-solid foods fed by parent		/ /	
	10	Feeds self with fingers		/ /	
	11	Holds and drinks from cup using two hands		/ /	
	12	Takes spoon filled with food to mouth with help		/ /	
	13	Holds out arms and legs while being dressed		/ /	
1.2	14	Eats table food with spoon independently		/ /	
	15	Holds and drinks from cup with one hand		/ /	
	16	Puts hands in water and pats wet hands on face in imitation		/ /	
	17	Sits on potty or infant toilet seat for 5 minutes		/ /	
	18	Puts hand on head and takes it off		/ /	
	19	Pulls off socks		/ /	
	20	Pushes arms through sleeves, legs through pants		/ /	
	21	Takes off shoes when laces are untied and loosened		/ /	
	22	Takes off coat when unfastened		/ /	
	23	Takes off pants when unfastened		/ /	
	24	Zips and unzips large zipper without working catch		/ /	
	25	Uses words or gestures indicating need to go to bathroom		/ /	
2.3	26	Feeds self using spoon and cup with some spilling		/ /	
	27	Takes towel from parent and wipes hands and face		/ /	

The Portage scheme has been very successful as it involves all members of the family working with the child and achievements are shared by everyone. It also offers parents and carers a positive interaction with the child, enabling them to see even the smallest progress that the child is making. Portage can be used with children who have specific handicaps or with those who may only have minor developmental problems. Many of the tasks can be incorporated into play situations making it fun for the child and carer.

Children with specific learning difficulties

Specific learning difficulties was a term used by the Warnock Report to describe children who may have a disability in one particular area of their development. These children are likely to need a specific learning programme in order to overcome the disability.

Children with dyslexia

There is a long and hard debate surrounding the specific learning disability called dyslexia; part of this debate relates to the difficulty in diagnosing the condition and whether there is a distinct group of children with the condition. Recently scientists have found research evidence which suggests that there may be a genetic link associated with dyslexia and this may explain why it can affect more than one child in a family or be present in more than one generation in a family. Basically, dyslexia is a condition whereby children have difficulty in acquiring literacy skills; it may also affect the acquisition of language. Stow and Selfe (1989) refer to the following 'alerting signs' which children with this specific learning difficulty may have:

- *skills requiring sequential or spatial ordering of letters or numbers, e.g. children may muddle months of the year, or reverse numbers or letters*
- *rote or short-term memory for letters and numbers, e.g. children may have problems remembering their tables;*
- *laterality, e.g. knowing their right from their left, body awareness and direction*
- *sound blending*
- *systematic visual scanning.*

These children will undoubtedly underachieve unless they are given a special educational input. The Warnock Committee took the heat out of the dyslexia debate when it devised the category of 'specific learning difficulties' which was intended to cover a wide spectrum of areas which could result in a child underachieving.

Children with dyspraxia

Dyspraxia is the name used to refer to children who have co-ordination problems, motor difficulties and/or clumsiness. It is not necessarily accompanied by mental or intellectual impairment and in the past has often been referred to as 'the clumsy child syndrome'. Children with dyspraxia have difficulties with fine and large motor movements and appear clumsy and awkward. They may also have difficulty in organizing their thoughts, articulating clearly what they wish to say and may have a limited attention span. Whilst there is no cure for this condition, a lot can be done to help affected children improve their co-ordination by encouraging them to participate in balancing games, throwing and catching activities, dressing and undressing dolls, screwing and unscrewing activities, action rhymes and songs, etc. These children will need to be given more time to carry out routine tasks such as undressing and hand washing and may need additional help from the adult. Extra help for these children can be provided through the Code of Practice (see Ch. 8). The incidence of dyspraxia is thought to be rather high, possibly affecting up to 10% of the population. It affects four times as many boys as girls. As a result of this high incidence there is a lot of research being done on dyspraxia and the results of these are likely to be publicized in the near future.

High ability children

Children who have abnormally high ability or are, as they are sometimes called, 'fast learners', are often overlooked as coming into the category of children with special needs. The other term which is sometimes used to describe such children is 'gifted'; however, as Wyatt points out this term is a misnomer as often slow learners have isolated 'gifts'. Children with high ability may have accelerated learning in a specific area such as maths or music or may be all-round fast learners. Ogilvie (1973) offered six areas in which children are likely to show high ability:

1. *Physical talent*
2. *Mechanical ingenuity*
3. *Visual/performing abilities*
4. *Outstanding leadership/social awareness*
5. *Creativity*
6. *High intelligence.*

Parents are not always the best judges of whether their child is of a particularly high ability because they lack the experience of dealing with large numbers of children over long periods of time and are therefore not familiar with the normal ability range. High ability children often exhibit behavioural difficulties which may be the result of boredom or frustration. At the pre-school stage these children are best helped by attending play groups, nursery schools or nursery classes where they can be offered activities which will meet their needs.

Some children with high ability may have social or personality problems and find it difficult to mix with other children. Children who have high ability in selected skill areas may underachieve in other areas. This is often the case when parents have concentrated their efforts on developing the 'gift' of the child rather than on the all-round development of the child. The recent introduction of computers into nursery schools and playgroups has meant that these children are less frustrated as they can have an individual programme to work on and do not have to undertake the same activities as their classmates.

Attention deficit hyperactivity disorder

Between 1% and 2% of children in the UK have attention deficit hyperactivity disorder (ADHD) and it is more common in boys than in girls. Although there has been a lot of speculation that dietary/food allergies are connected with ADHD, scientists have found no evidence to support a causal link. There are three basic features associated with ADHD which are carefully monitored before a diagnosis is made:

1. *Attention deficit – including the inability of the child to concentrate on the task; they get bored easily, are easily distracted and find it difficult to play with anything for a significant length of time*
2. *Overactivity – restlessness, fidgeting, purposeless overactivity inappropriate to what is going on, activity during sleep*
3. *Impulsiveness – acting without reflecting which leads to dangerous behaviour, difficulty in taking turns, difficult to manage, more 'at risk' of accidents than the average child.*

Diagnosis is not made unless all the above factors have been observed in more than one situation, i.e. home and school. Teachers and parents are asked to fill out very detailed questionnaires relating to the child's behaviour and these are carefully examined by the educational psychologist before a diagnosis is made. Usually teachers are aware that the child's behaviour is more serious than just being naughty. Early recognition can bring early intervention and improve the chances of bringing about positive changes in the child's behaviour.

Other children with specific learning difficulties

Other groups of children may also be designated as having specific learning difficulties, such as children with behavioural or emotional difficulties or those with communication difficulties. The latter group may include children with speech impediments, or those with poor language development. Most of these children would benefit from nursery education in the pre-school years and, given the right opportunities to develop, may start school on a par with other children.

There is no doubt that children with special needs benefit from early attendance at nursery school or playgroup where they can socialize with mainstream children and participate in activities which will aid their development.

The self-image of children with disabilities

Many children with disabilities suffer from having a poor self-image and lack confidence to explore the world around them. Woolfson (1989) lists the likely behavioural signs exhibited by children with a poor self-image as:

- *Find difficulty in giving love to or receiving love from other children and adults including parents.*
- *Do not relate well to their peers and feel socially isolated from those around them.*
- *Tend to make derogatory remarks about anything they do even when these achievements are of a satisfactory standard.*
- *Are more likely to be ashamed of themselves, to have guilt feelings and even to be depressed.*
- *Have a high level of anxiety and therefore find every day experiences unusually stressful.*
- *Have difficulty in being honest in their relationships with other people because of lack of trust in themselves.*
- *Are defensive when relating to other children and adults and assume the worst of everyone.*
- *Take longer to settle down when they start school and have slower academic progress.*

A poor self-image can be a problem for any child whether the child has a disability or not. For the child with a disability, however, there is a strong likelihood that the child will need to be given help in order to develop a positive self-image. Children develop their self-image from the way adults and other children interact with them, by comparing themselves and their performance with that of other children and by becoming familiar with their own bodies/features and how these may be the same or different from the bodies/features of other children. It does not take a child with disabilities very long to realize that they are different from other children.

As a child care worker, you can do a great deal to help the child with disabilities to develop a positive image. In many cases you may be the first adult whom the child meets outside its own home and for this reason your reactions to the child are important. It is important that the child's privacy and dignity are maintained at all times.

- Always treat the child as an individual and ensure that you consider the child first and the disability second.

- Never address the person pushing the wheelchair, always address the occupant, even if it is a small child.
- Make an effort to ensure that the child mixes with the other children; do not leave the child isolated.
- Do not allow other children to poke fun at the child; the able-bodied children must be taught to respect the child with disabilities.
- Always praise and encourage the child even for the smallest achievement.
- Involve the child in all the activities that are going on and encourage exploration of the child's environment.
- Report the child's progress to the parents/carers on a regular basis and make sure they are aware of the child's achievements, however small.
- Do not make exceptions for the child's behaviour; the child must be encouraged to develop the same self-discipline as other children.
- Have realistic expectations of the child and the child's abilities.
- Provide the appropriate activities for the child's abilities so that there is a chance of achieving.
- Give opportunities for the child to make decisions and encourage the child to make choices.

As a child care worker it is important that you set an example of good practice for the other adults that come into contact with the child. It is also important to adopt a supportive attitude for the parents/carers of the child as this will encourage them in their efforts to help the child lead a lifestyle that is as normal as possible.

Advocacy and empowerment

The movement for child advocacy started in the USA in the 1960s. It was used initially to describe every type of action that was undertaken on behalf of children; however, it is a term which is becoming more frequently used in the UK to describe adults ensuring that the wishes of the child are heard and considered. This is a concept now enshrined in the Children Act 1989. Along with advocacy goes the concept of empowerment, where the child is enabled to make its wishes known to adults. Advocacy and empowerment are very strong concepts which need to be included in all work undertaken with children with special needs. These are the children who are least likely to have a spokesperson and least likely to have their wishes considered. It is an important aspect of the child's self-image that the child can have a voice and it is probably no coincidence that the National Children's Bureau uses as its motto: 'The Powerful Voice of the Child'. Child care workers must be alert to situations and not condone a child being treated in a way that is degrading or against its wishes. If the child cannot make itself heard, then the adult must act as advocate for that child. Listening to children and responding to their wishes is part of the Code of Practice and the Children Act. The carer should also undertake activities with the child which will empower the child to make its own wishes known by helping with communication, giving the child the choice and encouraging the child's decision-making skills. In order to do this effectively the adult needs to understand and respect the child's needs and ensure that there are very good channels of communication between the child and the adult. The UN Convention on the Rights of the Child, which the UK has ratified, has articles which refer to the basic rights of children throughout the world. Article 12 relates to the child's right to have its views heard, and Article 23 specifically relates to the rights of children with disabilities and learning difficulties.

Assignments

Assignment 1

You are a playgroup leader and in 1 week you will be admitting a new child, Tommy, who has spina bifida. How will you prepare the staff and children in the playgroup for Tommy's arrival?

Assignment 2

Your neighbour has an 18-month-old child who has Down's syndrome. You think that the family might benefit from participating in the Portage programme. How do you sensitively explain Portage to the family, particularly the benefits it would bring for the child and the parents. What advice would you give them as to how they could become involved in the scheme?

Assignment 3

Many recent policies on the care and education of children with special needs mention advocacy and empowerment. What do you understand by these terms? How would you integrate advocacy and empowerment experiences into the daily activities of children with special needs?

Assignment 4

A new child has been admitted to Year 1 class of the infant school where you work. The child is referred to as a 'statemented child'. What does this mean? What will the school need to provide for the child?

Assignment 5

Prepare a booklet for parents explaining the local facilities which are available for their child with learning disabilities, with particular emphasis on 'out of school' facilities.

References and further reading

Alcott, M. (1997) *An Introduction to Children with Special Educational Needs*. London: Hodder and Stoughton.

Challen, M. (1997) A pre-school assessment model. *In* Wolfendale, S. (Ed.) *Meeting Special Needs in the Early Years*, pp. 14–29. London: David Fulton.

Clark, M. (1988) *Children Under Five: Educational Research and Evidence*. London: Gordon and Breach.

Dare, A. and O'Donovan, M. (1997) *Good Practice in Caring for Young Children with Special Needs*. Cheltenham: Stanley Thornes.

Department for Education and Employment. (1994) *Code of Practice on the Identification and Assessment of Special Educational Needs*. London: DfEE.

Department for Education and Employment. (1994) *Special Educational Needs; a Guide for Parents*. London: DfEE.

Department for Education and Employment. (1997) *Excellence for All Children. Meeting Special Educational Needs*. London: The Stationery Office.

Department of Education and Science. (1978) *Special Educational Needs. Warnock Report*. London: HMSO.

Drummond, M.J. and Nutbrown, C. (1997) Observing and assessing young children. *In* Pugh, G. (Ed.) (1997) *Contemporary Issues in the Early Years, 2nd edn*, pp 102–118. London: Paul Chapman.

Fraiberg, S. (1989) Insights from the blind. *In* Bee, H. *The Developing Child*, 5th edn. Ch. 14. London: Harper and Row.

HMSO. (1985) *Equal Opportunities for All? Report of the Committee Reviewing Provision to Meet Special Educational Needs. [Fish Report]* London: HMSO.

HMSO. (1989) *Children Act*. London: HMSO.

HMSO. (1991) *The Children Act Guidance and Regulations, Volume 6: Children with Disabilities*. London: HMSO.

Mason, M. (1993) *Inclusion, the Way Forward: A guide to integration for young disabled children.* Starting Points Series No. 15. London: Voluntary Organisations Liaison Council for Under Fives (VOLCUF).

Newell, P. (1991) *The UN Convention and Children's Rights in the UK.* London: National Children's Bureau.

Ogilvie, E. (1973) *Gifted Children in Primary Schools.* Basingstoke: Macmillan.

Ramage, R. (1997) *Every Child is a Gifted Child.* Christchurch, New Zealand: Kea Press.

Rieser, R. and Mason, M. (1990) *Disability Equality in the Classroom: A Human Rights Issue.* London: ILEA.

Stow, L. and Selfe, L. (1989) *Understanding Children with Special Needs.* London: Unwin Hyman.

Woolfson, R. (1989) *Understanding your Child.* London: Faber and Faber.

Wyatt, S. *The Identification of Fast Learners.* Gifted Children's Information Centre (National Association for Gifted Children). (Undated)

6: RESPONDING TO ILLNESS IN CHILDREN

Objectives
- Responding to the sick child in the nursery or at home
- Hospitalization
- Separation theories – Bowlby and Robertson
- Prepared hospital admission
- Chronic or terminal illness
- Coping with death
- Supporting the child and the family
- Role of the hospital play specialist

Links

This chapter has links with:
- NVQ (EYCE) Units: C2, C5, C17.
- CACHE Diploma Module G.

Introduction

At some time during the early years of life a child is likely to become sick. The type of illness a child may contract can range from the common cold or an infectious disease such as chickenpox to a serious illness which requires hospitalization. Evidence from the study by Davie, Butler and Goldstein (1972) found that almost half of the children in the UK were likely to have been in hospital at least once by the time they were 7 years old. More recently, the Audit Commission Review (1993) found that children accounted for 10% of hospital and community health services expenditure.

This chapter concentrates on responding to the needs of children who are sick in the nursery, at home or in hospital. The chapter does not go into the signs and symptoms of childhood illnesses (details of these can be found in Chapter 2 of O'Hagan, M. (1997) *Geraghty's Caring for Children*, 3rd edn) but explores the needs of children when they are sick and how best to respond to them. The section dealing with children in hospital examines the effects of chronic and terminal illness on children. The chapter also looks at the roles of the multi-disciplinary care team and the support networks that are available for the child and its family.

Responding to a sick child in the nursery or home

Children can be taken ill with minor ailments and discomforts such as a high temperature or colic, or may have sudden acute illness such as a convulsion (fit) or gastro-enteritis. When a child is not feeling well it is the duty of the parent/carer to determine the seriousness of the situation. The child may have a cold and just be feeling miserable or there may be a rash, vomiting, diarrhoea or other symptoms which need to be taken seriously and advice sought from a doctor. Any symptoms which prevent or make it difficult for the child to breathe or if the child loses consciousness or has a convulsion (fit) require immediate medical attention.

Whatever is wrong with the child, the parent/carer must stay calm. Children will be worried about what is happening to them and will become distressed if they see the adults around them not being in control. Certain illnesses such as asthma are very frightening for the child and the symptoms are likely to get worse if the child starts to become distressed. If parents/carers are responsible for a child who is an asthmatic they should be familiar with inhalers and nebulizers and ensure that they understand how these work and how the child must use them in order to gain the maximum benefit from the drug they contain.

If a child is taken ill at the nursery, the carer must reassure the child, make the child as comfortable as possible and inform the nursery manager or other senior staff member. The child's symptoms, temperature, colour (i.e. flushed or a pallor) should be monitored. If the child is known to have a recurring condition such as asthma or sickle cell anaemia, then the drugs held by the nursery in the event of such an attack should be administered by a senior member of staff. When a nursery holds such drugs, there must be written parental consent to administer them if the child becomes ill and this should be obtained at the time that the parent leaves the drugs with the nursery. Under the Department of Health guidelines the nursery is required to keep up-to-date records on children's health and to have a system for accurately recording any drugs administered to a child by staff at the nursery. Any information about a child's health must be kept confidential and other staff informed on a 'need-to-know' basis. All nursery staff should be in possession of an up-to-date First Aid Certificate to enable them to deal with emergencies.

When a child is taken ill at the nursery, the child's parent/guardian must be contacted and informed of their child's illness and arrangements made for the child to be collected from the nursery. Until the parent arrives the child needs to be able to rest in a quiet place, given a comforter or favourite toy, be able to lie/sit in a comfortable position and a member of staff must stay with the child to give reassurance and to monitor the child's condition. All this needs to be done with the least amount of disruption to the routine of the other children in the nursery. However, it may be necessary to re-organize programmes and adapt routines in order to provide activities which can be safely carried out with one less member of staff.

Children attending the nursery who may have chronic illness conditions will have other professionals that may be dealing with the family such as health visitors, community nurses and physiotherapists. There need to be good lines of communication between the nursery staff and the other professionals working with the family to ensure that everyone is working towards the same goals for the child and to ensure that all the child's needs are being met.

When children are not feeling well, they may regress in their behaviour and require a lot of attention. It is best to give them activities that are meant for younger children so that they have the opportunity to achieve without needing to use a great deal of concentration. The child care worker will need patience and imagination when dealing with a sick child. Children who feel ill also lose their appetites so food needs to be given in small quantities and made to look attractive in order to tempt them to eat. Favourite foods, providing they are not contrary to medical instructions, will probably be the most popular. The child's illness needs to be considered when deciding what to give the child to eat; e.g. a child with a sore throat or tonsillitis will need foods which are soft and easy to swallow such as mashed potatoes, soup, jelly and ice cream.

Once the child is showing improvement, there is the opportunity to 'play out' the illness with the child through imaginative play and role play. The carer needs to be aware of this and be able to provide the props for this activity. When a nursery is experiencing a lot of children contracting the same illness, e.g. flu and chickenpox, there is a greater need for the illness to be talked about and provision made to enable the children to role play doctors, nurses, caring adults and others associated with the illness.

Scenario 6.1

The Bailgate Children's Centre has an outbreak of chickenpox. You are in charge of a room of 3-year-olds, half of whom have gone down with the illness.

How do you:

(a) Deal with Ranjit who appears to have a high temperature and is very tearful?
(b) Explain to the other children what is happening in the group?
(c) Provide activities which will help reassure the remaining children?

Hospitalization

To be admitted to hospital is a frightening experience for an adult so what must it be like for a child? The fear associated with the experience is the 'fear of the unknown'. We do not know about hospitals as they are not part of our everyday environment nor are they accessible to be explored in advance; the people inside hospitals often appear as white-coated strangers and uniforms are abundant. Hospitals are places where it is likely that you will experience physical hurt and pain, even though at the same time they may provide relief from pain. Many adults have a deep-rooted fear of hospitals that can often be traced back to a hospitalization experience during their childhood which may have involved themselves or a member of their family. This is not surprising and if you read Scenario 6.2 it will give you some idea of what admission to hospital used to be like for children.

In the 1960s the nursing staff were not deliberately unfeeling or unkind in their treatment of the children but were following the philosophy of the time which was based upon the physical aspects of the child's care and did not take into account the psychological aspects. Lack of understanding of child development or the importance of play and the attitude of the time which viewed children as 'mini-adults' led hospitals and nursing staff to take a clinical approach to children.

Hospitals are large institutions which expected those entering them to take on the role of the patient, a role which is beneath that of the medical and nursing staff. The medical knowledge of the staff who knew how to treat and cure disease engendered in them the power to decide what was best for the patient. Hospital wards were designed on 'Nightingale' lines, i.e. rows of beds, offering little privacy for the individual. In order to protect themselves from any emotional involvement with the

Scenario 6.2

In the 1960s, Monday morning on the paediatric ward was the day that children were admitted to have their tonsils removed. At a pre-arranged time approximately a dozen children aged between 3 and 10 years would arrive on the children's ward accompanied by their relatives. In an efficient and professional manner the nursing staff would send the relatives away (making sure they understood that there would be no visiting on operation day !!), strip the children of their day clothes, dress them in their nightwear and put them to bed. The children would be cared for by many nurses all involved in different activities and none of these people would have time to spend with individual children and were not encouraged to do so by their managers. This was just the beginning of a 4-day stay which often got worse for the children as the days went on.

How do you think these children felt during their stay in hospital?

patients, the staff donned uniforms to set themselves apart and were actively discouraged from getting to know patients in anything other than a clinical way. Patients were identified by their illness or their bed number and not their name and it was never considered that psychological factors could be capable of interfering with the healing process.

During the 1970s and 1980s there were radical changes taking place in the attitudes towards patients, a move away from the clinical approach towards a patient-centred approach. Such changes have come about as a result of research findings relating to the sociological and psychological effects of hospitalization. In many hospitals, nurses now adopt a procedure called the 'nursing process' which ensures that on admission each patient is assigned a nurse who is the patient's key worker. This nurse not only elicits the medical history of the patient but also talks to them about their home circumstances and any fears they may be experiencing about their hospitalization or illness.

Attachment and loss reactions

Parallel to the developments in the nursing and medical field there were significant research findings relating to child development. In the 1950s the work of John Bowlby put forward major theories about the effects upon children relating to their attachment to and any subsequent loss of their carer. Bowlby developed the theory that it is necessary for children to 'bond' with an adult in order for the child to have psychological stability in its early years. Bowlby's bonding theory in conjunction with the work of James and Joyce Robertson who filmed children in brief separation situations, including *A Two Year Old Goes to Hospital* (Robertson and Robertson, 1952), led to the major present-day theories regarding the attachment and loss reactions of healthy children. Bowlby's work on attachment and loss describes the three stages – protest, despair and detachment – which children go through when separated from the person with whom they are bonded. (Although more recent research has challenged the notion of 'one' carer, usually the mother, being responsible for the child's psychological health through bonding, it is true to say that there is a general consensus amongst child psychologists that multiple changing carers are detrimental to a child's stable development.)

The Robertsons' films of children being admitted to residential care and hospital reinforced Bowlby's theories and produced visual evidence of the three stages he put forward. During the first stage of separation the child will cry, become angry and demand the return of the mother or carer. This is the stage of protest and may last for several days; if a parent or carer returns during this period, it is unlikely to have done the child lasting damage. If the adult does not return then the child will enter the stage of despair whereby the child becomes quiet but is still preoccupied with the absent person and hoping for the adult's return. If the adult does return during this stage, it is likely to take the child some time before the relationship is rebuilt and the adult is trusted again. If the adult still does not return, then the child enters the final stage of detachment where all hope is given up and the child appears to have forgotten the adult. If the adult returns after this stage, the child may not recognize the adult and will not greet the adult as somebody to whom the child is related.

When children are hospitalized they will pass through the three stages of protest, despair and detachment if steps are not taken to avoid the separation of children from their carer or by the provision of a satisfactory substitute. The length of time of the separation will determine the number of stages the child may pass through and the amount of subsequent psychological damage that is done to the child.

The work of Bowlby and the Robertsons has done a lot to change the attitudes of the adults who deal with children in separation situations. Thanks to the work of Dr Hugh Jolly and organizations such as Action For Sick Children (prior to October 1991 they were known as the National Association for the Welfare of Children in Hospital – NAWCH) hospitals have totally changed their attitudes towards children who become patients. Parents and relatives are now allowed to stay with children when they are admitted to hospital, children are allowed to bring their favourite toys, wear their own clothes, are not confined to bed unless it is a necessary part of their treatment and have hospital play specialists working with them to encourage and develop play activities. The Department of Health Report 1991 'Welfare of Children and Young People in Hospital' recognized the value of play in the health care setting as part of the healing process. The Report states:

> Play is Essential to the intellectual, social and emotional development of children. It can also help them resolve stressful situations like admission to hospital where they may have to undergo painful procedures and suffer separation from family and friends.
>
> *Department of Health 1991*

During recent years, as a result of modern medical techniques and the availability of new drugs, the length of time that a child spends in hospital has lessened; e.g. the average length of stay for a child in Great Ormond Street Hospital is 2 weeks. Therefore even seriously ill or chronically sick children will have shorter hospital stays which may occur at frequent intervals over a long period of time. The average length of stay on a paediatric ward is now 2.5 days.

Prepared hospital admission

The majority of children going into hospital are admitted from the waiting list and therefore have the benefit of prior notice of the event. Before the admission they would have attended the outpatient department and would be familiar with the building and the doctor who will be treating them. Outpatient departments are likely to have children's waiting areas with toys and play equipment (there are specifically trained casualty and outpatient hospital play specialists), although this may depend upon the resources of the health authority. In some areas the Pre-School Learning

Alliance (PLA) run playgroups and playschemes inside hospitals. Ideally, the doctors, nurses and paramedical staff will have been trained about the best ways to handle children which will cause them the least amount of stress.

A child who is going to be admitted to hospital can be prepared for the event by parents, relatives, playgroup leaders, teachers, childminder or other carers. The first stage of preparation is to explain to children in the simplest way what is wrong with them and what the hospital treatment is likely to be; e.g. if a child is to have the tonsils removed it needs to be explained that it is the tonsils which have been the cause of previous sore throats and pain. Using a mirror and a tongue depressor, the child can be shown the tonsils. The child should be told that the tonsils will be removed whilst the child is having a special sleep and so will not feel anything happening. After breathing a special gas the child will have a very deep sleep and wake up when everything is over. When the child wakes up, the throat will be very sore. It is important that the explanations given are appropriate to the child's age and development. It is also important to be honest with children about the medical procedures and about pain, so that the child will know what to expect.

Dishonesty in these matters will lead to the child mistrusting the adult and this can permeate all future relationships with the child. A lot of treatments and operations will hurt the child and this needs to be explained in advance. In many cases, the short-term hurt will progress to long-term good health; however, in cases of children who are chronically sick, the pain will not be short-term and may not give them future good health but may enable them to live longer.

There are many story books about children going into hospital and these can be read to the child. A doctor's or nurse's outfit can enable a child to play out fears of hospital and a home corner can easily be adapted to represent a hospital in order to encourage role play. Talking to the child about the event is very important and can be done by all those concerned with the care of the child. It is also important to listen to the child and give the child the opportunity to talk about feelings and concerns. Preparing a child for hospital should be carried out with the co-operation of all the people who care for the child in conjunction with the child's immediate family. It is important that adults do not convey their own fears to the child as this will distress and frighten the child. Barnes (1997) states that:

> Many sick children feel unsure, suffer regression, lose their independence and lack self-confidence. Play helps children to overcome these feelings and regain mastery of the situation.

There has been a great deal of 'opening up' of paediatric wards and it is now possible to arrange a pre-admission visit so that the child can meet the nursing and medical staff, the hospital play specialist and the other children. Such a visit does a lot to allay a child's fears as the hospital then becomes a more familiar place. From this visit the child will know where the toilets are, that the lady in the blue uniform is called Mary and the boy with his leg in plaster is called Sanjeev.

Figure 6.1
Children playing in
hospital corner.

Figure 6.1
Children playing in hospital corner.

Admission

The night before admission the child should help to pack a bag and put in favourite toys and books. On the day of admission the parents or carers should accompany the child and one adult should be prepared to stay with the child. Most hospitals have facilities to enable at least one person to stay overnight and they do not restrict visiting on paediatric wards. Ideally, a parent or relative should stay with the child throughout the hospitalization period and most families are able to organize this on a rota basis with grandma, granddad, aunty and uncle all taking a turn. This is not so easy if a child is being fostered or has no relatives who live nearby. These children will need more attention from the hospital play specialist and nursing staff, particularly the key worker nurse. The constant presence of a parent or relative means that a child does not go through the trauma of loss as described by Bowlby nor does the child have to overcome the problems of having multiple changing carers. The parents should inform the staff of the child's likes and dislikes, any special dietary requirements, special, 'pet' words for 'toilet' and the child's sleeping patterns.

Emergency hospital admission

When a child is suddenly taken ill or has an accident requiring emergency admission to hospital there is no time to prepare the child for future events. In some instances the child may be unconscious upon admission or arrive at the hospital unaccompanied by a parent or relative. The events leading up to the admission are likely to have been traumatic for the child, i.e. a sudden severe pain, a fall or a road accident. The child will be very frightened and desperately in need of the presence of parents or familiar carers. It is likely that the child would have been admitted via the accident and emergency department and the staff there would have made every effort to contact the child's relatives. The child will not be left alone but the person with the child may be a stranger and they will encounter numerous other strangers such as doctors, clerks, radiographers and porters. It is good practice to assign one nurse or a hospital play specialist to stay with the child until its parents arrive. If the parents are with the child, they may be upset and shocked – perhaps they had not previously realized the extent of the child's illness – or feel guilty because the accident had happened when they were not with the child. Emergency admission can be as traumatic for the relatives as it is for the child, possibly leaving the parents unable to cope with comforting their child and needing a great deal of reassurance themselves.

It is the period following the child's admission and when the child is out of immediate medical danger that the greatest help can be given to the child to overcome the trauma and fears of past events. Barnes (1997) points out that 'play can be used within the health care setting as a coping mechanism'. It is at this time that the role of the hospital play specialist becomes crucial in helping the child to relieve pent-up emotions via a selection of play activities. These activities are designed to allow the child to explore different situations and roles through dramatic play and release tension through activities such as clay, dough, hammer and peg toys. In the clinical atmosphere of the hospital, many play specialists believe that messy play has a great therapeutic value.

The child may be feeling guilty knowing that its condition has for some reason upset its parents or knowing that an injury was the result of the child disobeying its parents or carers. Children need to be given the opportunity to talk about these things or work through their feelings using play as a therapy. The nursing staff or hospital social worker will be available to comfort and reassure the parents. The child needs to be told about its operation or injury and the future treatment explained. The child can be introduced to the other children on the ward, especially if there is another child who has had a similar operation or treatment. Once the child has mobility it needs to be shown all the facilities that it might otherwise have discovered on a pre-admission visit. Children are often very flexible to new situations once their fears are allayed and may quickly come to terms with their new environment.

Outpatient clinics

Following a period of hospitalization the child may need to attend the outpatient clinic in order for ongoing treatment to be monitored. Many children who have chronic illness such as diabetes, scoliosis, spina bifida or other physical disabilities will be regular attenders at these clinics. The staff get to know the children and in turn the children come to understand the routines and what is expected of them. Hospital play specialists have a particular role in the outpatient department as they are able to organize drop-in play facilities and become familiar with the children and are able to help allay their fears.

Chronic or terminal illness

Children who are suffering from chronic or terminal illness will have to face regular treatment and periods of hospitalization, the seriousness and extent of these depending upon the diagnosis and available treatment. For these children and their relatives there is continuous stress and anxiety which can place a strain upon family relationships. If the child's condition is due to a genetic defect, parents may feel very guilty and this may interfere with their relationship with the child. Although the actual periods of hospitalization may be short (the average length of stay for a child in Great Ormond Street Hospital is 2 weeks), they may occur on a regular basis over a long period of time. During these periods in hospital a child may be subjected to numerous tests and treatments, some of which may be painful, and it is easy to envisage how a child may fear the prospect of hospital admission. Parents and staff can do a great deal to alleviate the child's fears by discussing treatment procedures and allowing the child time to come to terms with its situation using play as a therapy. Although chronic or terminal illness may interfere with children's physical development, their psychological, emotional and social development may not be impaired and it is important that they are given appropriate activities to enable them to develop normally.

Long-term illness may mean that children are not able to be in control of their physical body so it is important to give them activities which allow them to make decisions and experience being in control of other situations. One way of doing this is to allow them to choose their food, clothes and toys and giving them games that encourage decision-making skills. Offering games and toys which are simple and meant for an age group younger than that of the child enables the child to accomplish these easily and feel a sense of empowerment and control.

Discipline can often pose problems for the parents and carers of these children as imposing rules upon children who may only have a short time to live or are undergoing painful treatments may appear cruel and unfeeling. Discipline and rules are often the very things that offer stability to a child when other things around the child are in a state of confusion. Provided that such discipline and rules are carried out with understanding and a certain amount of flexibility they are unlikely to be detrimental to the child's welfare.

It is important that these children have the love and support of their families and carers during their illness. Regular hospitalizations are disruptive to family life and may cause friction in relationships. The child's siblings may become jealous of the extra attention that the sick child is receiving. It is important that siblings are encouraged to be involved in the illness of their brother or sister and this can be done by explaining the illness and treatment, taking them on visits to the child in hospital and involving them in any special treats or trips that the sick child may have. It is significant that organizations such as 'Dreams Come True' or 'Make-A-Wish' which provide finance to enable chronic or terminally ill children to have holidays or once-in-a-lifetime trips, usually ensure that the money given allows at least one sibling or family member to accompany the sick child, and sometimes there is enough money granted to enable the whole family to go.

Scenario 6.3

Mandy is 5 years old and she knows that she is not well at the moment as she has 'bad' cells in her blood which are fighting the 'good' cells. The doctor has told her about the treatment she must have to get rid of the 'bad' cells and how this will make her hair fall out. Today she is feeling very tired and wants to be sick. When she woke up this morning lots of her hair had fallen out and was on the pillow. The nurses have given her a wig to wear. This was fun at first but it soon made her head hot and itchy so she took it off. Yesterday she had felt very cross and cut all the hair off her favourite doll and her mother had been angry with her about this and had shouted at her.

If you were Mandy's hospital play specialist, what activities would you devise for her that could help the way she is feeling?

Children who have contracted cancer will have particular problems associated with the treatment they will undergo. With the advent of chemotherapy and radiotherapy treatments, children with cancer now have a greater chance of a longer life and in some cases a complete cure. However, such treatments have side effects that are very distressing for the child such as loss of hair, nausea and vomiting. Some of the side effects will only last the duration of the treatment but it can take a considerable time for hair to grow back. It is important that children are told about the side effects of the treatment before it is started so that they know what to expect. Children are offered wigs to wear whilst their hair grows as this will be happening long after they have left hospital and when they have returned to playgroup, nursery or school. Some young children find wigs uncomfortable and refuse to wear them and they should not be forced to do so; a hat could be more useful. Children will need the support of their family and carers to help them overcome any worries that they may have about returning to the world outside the hospital and this is the time when there needs to be a good liaison system between the home, the school and the hospital.

Some children may have illnesses which require them to take steroids and the side effects of these drugs are likely to change the shape of the child's face into a 'moon shape' and their body may become fatter. Once again, it is important that the child knows why these changes are taking place and is told that the body will return to normal once the drug treatment stops. Any treatments which change the child's body shape can be frightening and a lot of preparation and follow-up support will help the child cope with the situation.

Coping with death

How do children cope with death? This may be their own forthcoming death owing to a terminal illness or the death of a close relative or significant person in their lives. Research shows that under the age of 5 years a child's reactions to the death of a loved one take on a similar pattern to those of the child who is separated from their parent or carer; they go through the stages of protest, despair and detachment. A young child's first encounter with death may be when a favourite pet dies; such experiences enable children to develop and rehearse emotional responses. How a parent or carer answers a child's questions about the death of a pet or death in general will be very important to the child's conceptual development. In a misguided desire to protect the child's feelings, parents may describe death as 'going to sleep' or 'going away'; such explanations will cause anxiety and confusion for the child, particularly when the child realizes that the person does not 'wake up' or 'come back'. It is important that the child is told that once animals or people are dead they will not return or participate in future activities. Explanations given to the child may also depend upon the cultural and religious beliefs of the family but there is a need to remember that explanations which refer to places in an afterlife can be equally confusing for small children. Television does not help children to develop a concept of the finality of death as characters in films and plays may die one day and then re-appear on the screen the next day. When children have talked about or encountered death it will often feature in their imaginative and fantasy play and this should not be discouraged.

A young child with a life-threatening illness may not be aware or may be unable to conceptualize what death will mean. In the USA there is a policy in many hospitals that children should be made aware of their illness, the treatment and if necessary be emotionally prepared for their own death. In the UK, the majority of doctors will make decisions with the parents regarding how much children should be told about their illness. For older children (8 years and upwards) there is a lot to be said for the idea that children should be made aware of their situation and thus enable them to prepare for their death. Adults have the opportunity to prepare for death by making wills and sealing relationships; in the same way children are likely to appreciate the opportunity to distribute their favourite toys and have last meetings with their friends.

There is little research on the reactions to death of children under 5 years, the extent to which a child is able to be prepared for death being dependent upon the child's ability to understand the concepts involved. Such understanding is probably linked with the Piagetian stages of cognitive development, children being more equipped to deal with these concepts when they are in the concrete operations stage which usually begins around the age of 6 years. Dr Cecily Saunders advocates that whatever the age of the dying child it is important that the child has a 'climate of security'. This may be difficult for parents and relatives to sustain at a time when they are feeling insecure, anxious and are probably least able to cope with the situation. The emotions of parents and relatives are quickly picked up by the child who may in turn become anxious and feel guilty that they are causing distress to their family. Children may become confused as they may not know what it is about them that is responsible for giving stress to their families.

Support for the child and family

There are many people and organizations that are available to offer support to the dying child and its relatives; however, it is not uncommon for adults to deny that the child is in a terminal condition. When this happens such denial may also lead to the rejection of offers of help and support. Within the hospital there may be social workers, bereavement counsellors or religious figures such as priests, vicars, rabbis and mullahs who are able to offer help. Parents and relatives need an opportunity to talk to someone, perhaps even another parent who has been through a similar experience. Staff in hospices (there are hospices for children) and the Macmillan nurses who undertake home-visiting are specifically trained in the best ways to offer support to the child and its family. Organizations such as the Society of Compassionate Friends are able to link relatives with somebody who has had a similar experience. If children are very young, they may miss out on getting support unless they are exhibiting behavioural problems and are referred to a psychologist. The hospital play specialist and nursing staff are the people most likely to be on hand in the hospital to support the child.

Parents and relatives may get comfort from being allowed to provide some of the care for the child and should be encouraged to help with feeding, washing, dressing and joining in with the child's play activities. Such involvement enables the adults to share the last moments of the child's life; these moments will become fond memories for the carers. By being involved in the care of the child the relatives will feel more adequate and will not be left with the feeling that there was nothing that they could do.

When the child has died it is important for the relatives to be allowed to see the body and go through the healing ritual of the funeral service. Following this there will be a period of grief and ways of expressing this will vary depending upon the cultural and religious beliefs of the family. Some cultures and religions have very specific mourning rituals which may involve certain periods of time, i.e. the Jews will sit 'shiva' for a week following a death and the full mourning period lasts for 1 year. Such ritualized expressions of grief may be a more healthy way of expressing feelings than the quiet, introverted process which may be encountered in the British culture. However, the public reaction to the death of the Princess of Wales may denote that the 'stiff upper lip' is no longer the British cultural norm. Colin Murray Parkes has studied and written about the grief reactions of white British adults and suggests the stages of grief are numbness, pining and depression. When a child has died suddenly the initial reactions of the relatives and carers are likely to be anger, aggression and guilt. Each stage of grieving has its own characteristics and differs from person to person, thus comfort for bereaved people comes via individualized and personalized counselling. For many people talking about the dead child will be a comfort and a major skill of bereavement counsellors is to be a good listener. It must be remembered that nothing can replace a dead child and the grief processes will be the same whether there are other children in the family or a new baby is born at a later date. Research carried out in this area with families who have lost a child through a cot death (sudden infant death syndrome) has found that even though the families have gone on to have another child, the memory of the dead child remains with them.

Role of the hospital play specialist

The majority of paediatric wards will have a hospital play specialist whose role is to work with the children in order to alleviate trauma and anxiety through the medium of play. Hospital play specialists may be qualified nursery nurses (NNEB) or hold other child care qualifications and they may also have the Certificate in Hospital Play Specialism. Their role is to design activities which will enable children to bring out any fears or misunderstandings that children may have about their admission to hospital and their treatment; e.g. one child when asked why he was in hospital replied, 'Because I stole sweets from my friend'. In this case the child was viewing his admission to hospital as a punishment. Another child when told that she was to have her blood taken was very frightened because she thought this meant all the blood

Figure 6.2
Hospital play in
action.

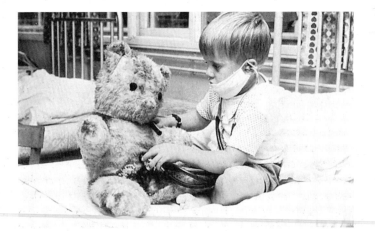

would be taken from her body. By establishing a good relationship and dialogue with the children in their care the hospital play specialist is able to ascertain and deal with such fears and misunderstandings through appropriately designed play activities and programmes.

Hospital play specialists work with individual children and groups of children and will choose toys and activities which satisfy the needs of all these children. Toys often fall into two categories: diversional toys and therapeutic toys. Diversional toys take the child's thoughts away from the illness and enable the child to develop new skills, be creative and gain enjoyment and satisfaction from the activity. Diversional toys are items such as paint, puppets, rattles, mobiles, board games, audio and video cassettes and video games. Therapeutic toys allow children to 'play out' their treatment and include medical kits, medical puppets, anatomically correct dolls, mirrors, tape recorders, clay, sand and hammer toys but can also include messy play.

As previously mentioned, children who are hospitalized are no longer in control of their bodies or their environment and a major role of the hospital play specialist is to provide activities that will give children opportunities to make decisions so enabling them to gain some self-esteem, control and the ability to engage in the healthy activities of fantasy and role play. For the very young child, the hospital play specialist needs to provide activities that will encourage normal development; e.g. an 18-month-old child will need activities to stimulate language development, motor co-ordination, fine manipulative movements, etc. Children in hospital are likely to regress in their development and will need a great deal of stimulation and encouragement in order for them to catch up with their peer group. Older children who regress may need to be given activities that are designed for a younger child so that they can complete these and thus have a sense of achievement and control.

For the child over 5 years of age, the long-stay, paediatric wards will have a teacher on hand and may even have a classroom. These teachers are provided by the local education authority and work closely with the hospital play specialists in designing a package of education and play for each individual child. Many hospital play specialists undertake an advisory and counselling role with parents and relatives, helping them to cope with the child's illness and suggesting appropriate toys and activities that they can share with the child.

There are no age limits to the children that the hospital play specialist may be working with and older children may welcome the opportunity to regress without losing self-esteem by joining in the activities provided. For children who are in hospital over a long period of time or are admitted at frequent intervals, there is a danger that they will become institutionalized. When this happens the hospital becomes their main environment and they lose touch with the outside world. There has been a great deal of research on institutionalization undertaken with children in residential care. Children who have become institutionalized have problems in coping with the environment outside the institution and are often deficient in their decision-making skills. Many hospitals have gone a long way to prevent this happening by allowing children to make decisions about food, clothing, allowing them to leave the ward on outings

Figure 6.3
Pastry making.

or weekends home, letting them visit the hospital shop and allowing unlimited visiting by friends and relatives. Hospital play specialists also help by enabling children to take the decision-making role in their play.

The role of the hospital play specialist is crucial and it requires very special skills as it involves the care of children who will make good recoveries and those who may die. A hospital play specialist may find themselves in a discussion with a child concerning to whom they wish to leave their treasured possessions when they die. Children may ask the hospital play specialist how best to deal with their parents or relatives who may be having more difficulty than the child in coping with the diagnosis. In a lighter vein, a hospital play specialist may have to organize a ward birthday party, to cope with the whole of Form 5A visiting Mary and to go shopping for presents on behalf of the child.

As children now spend less and less time in hospital there are now more hospital play specialists working in the community as members of the community paediatric team. Hospital play specialists have become valued members of the paediatric team both in the hospital and in the community, liaising with all the professionals within the team and acting as advocates for the children in their care.

Scenario 6.4

The hospital play specialist arrives on the ward with a box full of stuffed cloth dolls which have no features, clothes or hair. The children are invited to choose a 'patient' and to decide who it is, colour it with crayons and practise carrying out a 'treatment' on their patient. The children are allowed to be doctors, nurses, physiotherapists or whatever role they like.

What do you think is the value of this activity for the children?

Assignments

Assignment 1

Find out what facilities are available for children in the outpatient department of your local, district, general hospital. Do you think the facilities are adequate?

Assignment 2

Devise a programme of activities to occupy a 5-year-old with chickenpox in the home situation during the daytime hours. Give reasons for your choice of activities.

Assignment 3

The goldfish in your nursery has just died. Write an essay on the explanation of death that you will give to the children and a list of associated activities that you could carry out with them.

Assignment 4

Critically review one of the available children's books which tells the story of a child going to hospital.

Assignment 5

Write a leaflet for parents telling them about the nursery's policy on dealing with sick children and the administration of medicines.

References and further reading

Audit Commission Review. (1993) *Children First: a study of hospital services*. London: HMSO.

Barnes, P. (1997) Hospital play: the current position. *In Current Research in Early Childhood Update*, No. 89. UK: Organisation Mondiale Pour L'Education Préscolaire.

Bowlby, J. (1969) *Attachment and Loss, Vol. 1 Attachment*. Harmondsworth: Penguin.

Bowlby, J. (1969) *Attachment and Loss, Vol. 2 Separation, Anxiety and Anger*. Harmondsworth: Penguin.

Bowlby, J. (1979) *The Making and Breaking of Affectional Bonds*. London: Tavistock.

Davie, R., Butler, N.R. and Goldstein, H. (1972) *From Birth to Seven*. Harlow: Longman.

Hughes, J. (1981) *Questions Children Ask*. Tring: Lion.

Lansdown, R. (1980) *More Than Sympathy*. London: Tavistock.

Lansdown, R. (1996) *Children in Hospital: a guide for family and carers*. Oxford: Oxford University Press.

Lindley, K. (1984) *Helping Children Cope with the Loss of a Fellow Pupil*. Clwyd: School Psychological Service.

O'Hagan, M. (1997) *Geraghty's Caring For Children*, 3rd edn. London: Baillière Tindall.

Robertson, J. (1970) *Young Children in Hospital*. London: Tavistock.

Robertson, J. and Robertson, J. (1952) *A Two Year Old Goes to Hospital*. London: Tavistock.

Rodin, J. (1983) *Will This Hurt?* London: Royal College of Nursing.

Rutter, M. (1972) *Maternal Deprivation Reassessed*. Harmondsworth: Penguin.

Saunders, C. (1969) *The management of fatal illness in childhood*. Proceedings of the Royal Society of Medicine **62**: 550.

Ward, B. and Houghton, J. (1987) *Good Grief: Talking and Learning about Loss and Death*. London: Good Grief Associates.

Wells, R. (1988) *Helping Children Cope with Grief: Facing a Death in the Family*. Sheldon Press.

7: CHILD PROTECTION

Links

This chapter has links with:
- NVQ (EYCE) Units: C15; E2; M6, M20.

Introduction

Child protection is a basic right of all children. Article 19 of the United Nations Convention on the Rights of the Child states that the signatories of the present convention:

> ... shall take all appropriate legislative, administrative, social and educational measures to protect the child from all forms of physical or mental violence, injury or abuse, neglect or negligent treatment or exploitation including sex abuse while in the care of the parent(s), legal guardian(s) or any other person who has care of the child.

Child protection is an important role for child care workers, particularly as they may be the first person to notice that a child is showing signs of abuse or neglect or changes in the child's behaviour. All early years establishments are required to have a policy on child protection and with this should go a set of procedures clearly stating what workers should do if they suspect that a child is being abused.

Working in settings where some children may be on the 'at risk' register will require working with other professionals as a multi-agency team. This will require special training and skills on the part of the worker and an ability to adapt to different methods of working.

In these days of globalization, different forms of child abuse have been identified such as child pornography, sex tourism, child labour, street children and the abducting of children between one or more countries. More recently, in the UK, there have been cases where children in residential care have been abused. Although residential care in an institution is unlikely to be an option for children under 8 years of age as they are usually placed with foster families, residential care homes do exist for older children when foster care is no longer a viable alternative. As MacLeod 1997 points out, 'if the child protection scandals of the past 20 years have taught us anything it is that children cannot be protected by professional systems alone, essential as they are.'

A recent Department of Health Consultation Document (1998) on Working Together to Safeguard Children cites four situations which may lead to stress for a child and its family and thus make the child vulnerable to abuse:

1. *Social exclusion*
    Over half of the families caught in the child protection process lacked a wage earner or were dependent on income support. Poverty leads to poor diet, poor housing and poor health. Racial harassment can also be a source of stress.
2. *Domestic violence*
    Long-term exposure to domestic violence can have a serious impact on the development and well-being of the child. Where there is domestic violence, there is also likely to be child abuse.
3. *Mental illness of parent or carer*
    Parental depression and/or mental illness can lead to child abuse or have a damaging effect upon the health and development of the child.
4. *Misuse of drugs or alcohol*
    Substance-abusing parents find it difficult to give priority to the needs of their child. Substance misuse can result in chaotic lifestyles with children not getting the care and stability they need.

This chapter will look at the possible reasons for abuse, signs and symptoms of abuse and good practice in dealing with abuse.

Historical perspectives

Sociologists argue that the neglect and abuse of children are a social construct (how society assigns meanings and significance to individuals, groups and institutions over time). To understand this terminology we need to look at the way society has viewed and does view childhood. Historically, the period of life that we refer to as childhood has been defined in many different ways. Aries (1973) gives a very full account of the way European society has, over time, viewed the state of childhood; e.g. children have been treated as 'mini-adults', the property of their parents or other adults and have been handled accordingly. Most people are familiar with the Victorian adage that 'children should be seen but not heard', which is in total contrast to present-day attitudes that encourage adults not only to hear children but to listen to them. At the present time there is a movement towards the view that children should be treated as individuals with their own rights within society.

The way that society perceives children has a great bearing on the way that society will treat children and this is what sociologists mean by a 'social construct'.

Many classic novels, e.g. those by Dickens or Kingsley, offer descriptive examples of situations which today we would classify as child neglect and abuse. They are set in the era when children were viewed and treated as property. It is a reflection of those times that in 1875 the first case of child physical abuse was brought before a court in the USA under the laws relating to cruelty of animals. Even today, many child care campaigners feel that it is a reflection of present-day attitudes that the society for protecting animals has royal patronage (Royal Society for the Prevention of Cruelty to Animals – RSPCA) whereas the society for protecting children does not (National Society for the Prevention of Cruelty to Children – NSPCC).

An extract from a document produced by the Children's Legal Centre (1988) states:

> In our view the major cause of all kinds of abuse of children in our society … arises from the deeply rooted and negative attitudes to children.

In England the first laws to protect children from physical abuse were passed in 1889, but it took until the 1960s for child abuse to be taken as a serious subject and for researchers to start looking for causes. Part of the reason for this was that adults did not think that events in childhood had a lasting impression or affected the way that a person behaved as an adult. It was Sigmund Freud (1856–1939), the Austrian psychiatrist, who first argued that events in childhood could lead to mental disturbances, fears and phobias which, in time, resurfaced in the quality of relationships in adulthood.

In the 1960s, a number of researchers put forward important theories which argued that children had feelings and were affected by events such as the loss of, or abandonment by, their parents or carers. The work of John Bowlby on attachment and loss reactions in children was backed by the visual evidence of films made by James and Joyce Robertson which showed children's reactions to brief separations from their parents when they were taken into hospital or residential care (see Ch. 6).

At around the same time in America, Harlow undertook experiments with monkeys which clearly showed that the removal of the mother had severe effects upon their emotional development. The results of these pieces of research were to have a significant effect upon the way society viewed children.

In 1968, Kempe, an American pediatrician, put forward the idea of the 'battered child syndrome' and thus brought child abuse to the front of the research arena. Kempe also looked at abusing parents and put forward the idea of the 'cycle of abuse', whereby parents who had been battered in their childhood in turn battered their own children. In 1978, Kempe stated:

> Child abuse occurs in the presence of four factors…
> (1) the parents must have a background of emotional or physical deprivation and perhaps abuse as well;
> (2) a child must be seen as unlovable or disappointing;
> (3) there must be crisis;
> (4) there are no effective sources of aid at the moment of crisis.

For many years the pattern for intervention strategies in child abuse relied heavily on the work of Kempe, thus we saw programmes to break the cycle of abuse, therapy for abused children, crisis counselling and helplines for parents.

Present situation

It is often asked whether child abuse is more prevalent in the 1990s than it has been in the past; this is a difficult question to answer. In the past there were poor definitions of abuse; accurate records of incidents were not kept so there are no statistics to compare; children were often not believed if they made disclosures of abuse and may even have been blamed and punished for the incidents; society in general did not welcome the subject of abuse being raised privately or publicly. More recently, many of the above positions have been reversed; statistics are now kept; children are listened to and are most likely to be believed; professionals are trained to take a pro-active role in dealing with cases of abuse.

In the DoH Guide, *Working Together* (1991), it states:

> A child's statement about an allegation of abuse, whether in confirmation or denial, should always be taken seriously. A child's testimony should not be regarded as inherently less reliable than that of an adult. However, professionals

need to be aware that a false allegation may be a sign of a disturbed family environment and an indication that the child may need help.

Organizations such as ChildLine have been specifically set up to listen to children who may wish to disclose incidents of abuse. Professionals working with children and their families are now very aware of child abuse in all its forms and are able to keep a protective eye on the children in their care. Because of changes in society and in the facilities for reporting abuse, cases are more likely to become statistics, thus showing what may appear to be a sharp increase in incidence. Local authority social services departments keep 'child protection' registers where the names are entered of children/ families that are considered by the professionals to be at risk of abuse and therefore in need of protection. Such records are also likely to become part of the national statistics even though abuse may not have taken place.

Lastly, it is necessary to look at the role of the media in publicizing the more extreme cases of abuse. The production of television documentaries and the publication of sensational articles in magazines and the tabloid press have led to child abuse having a high profile in society. In turn, this may lead people to believe that there is a much higher incidence of abuse within the society than there actually is.

Always look carefully at any statistics before drawing conclusions, particularly the definitions of abuse that the researchers are using. It is important that workers with young children and their families are not influenced by sensationalism in media reports. Incidence rates and statistics should never be put before believing a child. Later, this chapter will examine the concept of family dysfunctioning which is a contributory factor in child abuse; such dysfunctioning can occur in *any* family.

Definitions of child abuse

There are many definitions of child abuse and it would not be useful or possible to reproduce them all in this chapter. The government department that deals with matters relating to child abuse is the Department of Health. Using the Guidelines laid down by the Department of Health, each local authority draws up its own policy on child protection. The Department of Health makes it clear that its definitions are just one of many and it does not necessarily mean that other definitions are wrong.

The Open University uses the NSPCC definitions with some enhancements to include examples which enable people to understand them more easily; these are as follows:

> **Neglect:** where parents (or whoever else is caring for the child) fail to meet the basic essential needs of children, like adequate food, clothes, warmth and medical care. Leaving young children alone and unsupervised is another example of

neglect. Refusing or failing to give adequate love and affection is a case of emotional neglect.

Physical Abuse: where a parent (or somebody else caring for the child) physically hurts, injures or kills a child. This can involve hitting, shaking, squeezing, burning and biting. It also involves giving a child poisonous substances, inappropriate drugs and alcohol, and attempted suffocation or drowning. It includes the excessive use of force when carrying out tasks like feeding or nappy changing.

Sexual Abuse: when adults seek sexual gratification by using children (boys or girls). This may be by having sexual intercourse or anal intercourse (buggery), engaging with the child in fondling, masturbation or oral sex; and includes encouraging children to watch sexually explicit behaviour or pornographic material, including videos.

Emotional Abuse: where children are harmed by constant lack of love and affection, or threats, verbal attacks, taunting or shouting.

Open University (1989)

In addition to the above, the Department of Health defines one more category:

Grave Concern: This category should not be used lightly and should be needed only in exceptional circumstances for children whose situations do not currently fit the above categories. This may be where there is an explicit and serious concern that the child is not developing as would be expected (and all medical causes have been eliminated) or there is a sudden, unexplained change in that child's normal behaviour pattern. If the cause of the child's condition is later established as fitting one of the above categories, a case conference should amend the cause of registration.

Working Together (1991)

It is sometimes difficult to distinguish between neglect and abuse and those working in the field of child protection are trained to be able to make such fine-line distinctions. For the majority of child care and education workers it is sufficient for them to be able to recognize that something is happening to a child and to know to whom to pass that information in order to ensure that the child is protected. All local authorities have policies and procedures for dealing with child protection and you should make sure that you are familiar with your local policy.

Difficulties in defining abuse

Whilst the above definitions are those used in common practice, there still remain difficulties in defining abuse. MacLeod (1997) explores this area and asks the following questions, 'At what point does reasonable chastisement become physical abuse? When does exposure to pornography, peeping or looking or flashing become sex abuse?' Whipple and Richey (1997) reported on an American study which suggested, on the basis of fieldwork, that parents who spank their children 0–5.73 times in a 24-hour period could be classified as falling within the normal range, whereas those who spank 6 or more times in a 24-hour period may be more at risk of crossing the line into physical abuse.

This shows just how difficult it is to quantify definitions in a legalistic way which takes no account of the child's behaviour, parental interpretation of that behaviour and the environmental circumstances. If a parent or carer does not normally smack a child and then one day does smack them, the child receiving the smack may well feel that it has been abused.

It is necessary to have legal definitions so that abusers can be prosecuted and child protection workers have a yardstick to work with. However, the difficulties surrounding the area of definition should not be forgotten.

Theories on the causes of child abuse

There are numerous theories offering explanations as to why adults abuse children, but only a few will be mentioned in this chapter.

The medical model

Early researchers such as Kempe and Kempe (1978) coined the phrase, the 'battered child syndrome', which led to the causes of child abuse being viewed as a disease with specific signs and symptoms (see Kempe's four factor's for child abuse on p. 218). The medical model was heavily criticized and in 1976 Kempe and Kempe changed their terminology to 'child abuse and neglect'. By presenting child abuse as if it were a disease, it led people to believe that it was predictable, preventable and curable just as any other disease, but as we know it is not.

The sociological model

Sociological research has concentrated on the changing patterns of society and how these have affected the functioning of the family. Unemployment, poverty, poor housing, poor health care and social exclusion are given as reasons for people abusing their children (Parton, 1985). If this were true, then one would expect all child abuse to occur in families who were Social Class 5 on the Registrar General's social scale (market research scale E); however, the statistics show that child abuse occurs in families from all social classes.

The psychological model

Psychologists have put forward theories which relate to the way a household functions as a family and refer to the breakdown of these relationships as 'family dysfunctioning'. This theory hinges upon the idea that family therapy can repair poor relationships and thus prevent child abuse. Alongside this theory goes the idea of 'scapegoating' whereby all the aggression and frustration of poor family relationships is directed towards one member of the family (often the weakest) and that is the person who will be abused. Whilst there is no doubt that in some abusing families one particular child may be the recipient of the abuse, there are cases where all the children in a family have been abused.

The feminist model

With the advent of sex abuse being openly discussed, a number of theories relating to this have been put forward by the feminists. These theories are mainly based upon sexual politics and examine power relationships between men and women. The fact that it is the men who are the main perpetrators and men who are the judges of these perpetrators enables the feminists to put forward very convincing theories. In her account of the Cleveland case Campbell (1988) wrote:

> ... the gender factor was salient to Cleveland.

She then proceeded to illustrate how the whole affair challenged society's stereotypes of doctors, abusers and victims. Whilst offering powerful arguments in relation to the causes of sex abuse, the feminists ignore the fact that some 10% of sexual abusers are women, and that victims can be both male and female. Although the feminists' arguments concerning power relationships are extremely valid, they do not appear to have really tackled the questions raised about physical and emotional abuse, although Miller (1983) does make an attempt to do so by examining how punishment and sanctions against children are inculcated in our child-rearing practices and legitimized as being 'for the good' of the child.

In spite of the large number of theories that are put forward, there is no one theory which is able to be applied to all cases of child abuse. Each situation is different and occurs for different reasons and therefore needs to be viewed individually. The use of theories, however, may aid interventionists to draw up risk assessment lists. By weighing one risk against another, interventionists are able to draw up a risk analysis list which will show the best and worst scenarios and enable them to judge the risk attached to each of these developing and to calculate how specific types of intervention could lessen the risk. The theories that appear to be the most popular with child protection workers are those relating to family dysfunctioning. This may be because they enable child protection workers to offer intervention in the form of family therapy whereas many of the other theories would require major changes in society's attitudes or government intervention to improve the structure of society.

Variations in family functioning

In present-day society it is very difficult to define the term 'family' as it is likely to mean different things to different people. Sociologists have defined three types of family that they maintain represent the normal household unit in the UK:

- *The extended family:* parents, children, grandparents, aunts, uncles and cousins all living in close proximity.
- *The nuclear family:* parents and children living together.
- *The one-parent family:* a mother or father living alone with their children.

There are many other combinations of relationships that may go to form a household and describe themselves as a family unit but which do not fit the above descriptions. The high divorce rate in the UK means that many children may live in a family where one of the parents is not their natural parent; step-parenting is a common situation. (It is probably significant that the Children Act 1989 enables step-parents to apply for parental responsibility. See Ch. 8.) The people that make up a family unit and the roles that they undertake within it are not important provided that the family is able to operate as a cohesive group and is able to meet the needs of all its members, particularly the needs of the children. It is when needs within the family are not met or when adult needs are met at the expense of the needs of the children that problems will arise.

Scenarios 7.1–7.3 illustrate the situations that may place stress upon a family unit.

In other situations, such as an extended family, where the senior male may take on the role of decision-maker for all the family but does not take into account the

Scenario 7.1

Mr Brown is unemployed and Mrs Brown has a full-time job as a cashier at the local supermarket. Although Mr Brown is at home all day, it is Mrs Brown's responsibility to organize all the childcare for their two children and run the household. Mr Brown is not the sort of man who participates in these activities; in fact he feels that to be seen hoovering or looking after the children would make people think he was not a 'real man'. The Browns do not have any family or relatives living nearby who could help out with the children. There are frequent quarrels between the parents and Mrs Brown is often depressed because she is unable to meet the demands placed upon her. Often the children are blamed for being so demanding and Mr Brown has little patience with them. This is a potentially explosive situation.

Using a risk analysis list, write a sequel to this scenario that either offers the Browns help with their predicament or leads to a crisis.

Scenario 7.2

Mr Bolton has a poorly paid job and Mrs Bolton tries to subsidize the family income by doing early morning office cleaning. They have three children, aged between 8 years and 3 years; the eldest two attend the local primary school and the youngest has a part-time place at the local nursery school. The family receives income support and it is a daily nightmare for the parents trying to manage their financial affairs. Recently, the eldest child demanded his parents buy him a computer so that he could play games like his friends. The parents agreed to his demands and are paying for it under a hire purchase scheme. Yesterday, the middle child, aged 6 years, demanded a pair of designer label training shoes which cost £70, refusing to go to school until he got them. Mrs Bolton bought these using an in-store charge card. The family are seriously in debt and each day seems to bring more financial problems. Mr Bolton, jealous of the fact that a lot of his hard-earned money is being spent on the children, has taken to nightly visits to the pub. Mrs Bolton, tired from her daily work, rents videos to watch while her husband is out. There have been numerous quarrels about money and Mrs Bolton feels that Mr Bolton is taking it out on the children, particularly the youngest child.

Make a list of the risks you think are involved for the children and the family. Using this risk analysis list, write a continuation of this scenario which either helps the Boltons to solve their problems or leads to a situation which requires intervention by the social services department.

feelings and opinions of individual members, there can be a considerable amount of family conflict. In a one-parent family where the parent has no help from relatives or friends, the single parent may find it difficult to cope with all the responsibilities.

Our present society exerts a great deal of pressure upon the family unit and it is easy to 'scapegoat' the stress onto one particular family member.

Housing is a problem in some areas, and families with children may find themselves in unsuitable high rise blocks, temporary short-life accommodation or living in bed and breakfast situations in hotels or hostels. None of these is conducive to bringing up children and places considerable strain upon family relationships. These situations do not make it easy for parents to answer the needs of their children.

In addition to the social problems that people might face there are some families who have inadequate or undeveloped parenting skills (it was Winnicott (1964) who first coined the term 'Good enough parenting'). Parenting skills are not a subject that is on the secondary school curriculum although some schools do have child development as a curriculum subject. In the past, if people found that they were unable to cope as parents, they could hire a nanny or rely on members of the extended family to show them how things are done and offer care and support during times of stress. Today many families have nobody to ask for advice if their child gets 3-month colic

Scenario 7.3	

Gillian and her two children, aged 3 years and 7 years, are living in bed and breakfast accommodation in a shoddy hotel in a poor district of the city centre. Her husband Bill is not allowed to stay there and is sleeping on the floor at a friend's house. They had been living in a nice, three-bedroom flat which they were buying from the local council. When Bill was made redundant from his job, they were unable to meet the mortgage repayments and the building society repossessed the flat. Since that time Gillian and the children have been living in bed and breakfast accommodation. Gillian is suffering from depression and spends most of her days in the small hotel room with the children. The only cooking facilities are a small gas ring in the room where she can boil water or soup. The eldest child has not attended school since they moved into the hotel as they now live too far away from the school and Gillian has not got the money for bus fares. There have been complaints from the hotel management about the noise the children make running up and down the corridors. Recently Gillian has lost her patience with the children and frequently hits them and shouts at them in order to get them to be quiet. Gillian is also worried about Bill as he is visiting less and less frequently and she is afraid that he may have found another woman.

Write a sequel to this scenario which either shows how Gillian can be helped or depicts what the next steps may be in the way Gillian handles the children.

or how to deal with temper tantrums, so parenting can become a 'hit and miss' affair. In many cases parents may rely on treating their child as they themselves were treated by their own parents. This is all right unless their parents were abusers, in which case you then have the possibility of Kempe's 'cycle of abuse' taking effect.

The concept of 'good enough parenting'

Pugh and De'Ath (1984) maintain that parents need certain skills and abilities if they are going to adequately care for their children; these fall into the following categories:

the ability to love and undertake relationships, to care, to support and nurture other people, to be sensitive to their needs;

flexibility of mind and thinking, the ability to respond and to adapt to changing needs and demands;

consistency of attitudes and behaviour, a reliable and dependable behaviour that provides a stable and secure environment where responses can be anticipated and rules are clear;

the ability to communicate, through active listening, giving appropriate non-verbal and verbal messages, reflecting on feelings, and negotiating;

the ability to make decisions and to accept responsibility for them;

the ability to cope with stress and deal with conflict;

the ability to apply knowledge and information, for a theory on how to cope with temper tantrums is no use unless it can be put into action.

It is unlikely that the average family would have acquired all of these skills and abilities by the time that their first child arrives; however, it is possible for parents to increase their knowledge by talking to relatives, friends, professionals or reading books and magazines on child rearing. Research has shown that there are a number of features which have been associated with adults who are likely to be poor parents and/or neglect and abuse their children:

Parents who themselves have been abused as children

These are the people who Kempe (1978) referred to as being caught in a cycle of abuse. As children, there was probably in their lives a close association between love and violence, e.g. a parent hits a child too hard and is immediately sorry, so hugs and cuddles the child and tells them that they love them. This establishes an association between the two emotions, the receiving of violence going hand in hand with the receiving of love. These people need a lot of help in order to disassociate the love and violence factors in their lives.

Another aspect of this is those parents who as children were severely chastised/abused and who take the attitude, 'It didn't hurt me so it won't hurt them.' This is more difficult to deal with as the severe chastisement as a child had harmed them but they are unable to recognize the damage that it had done to them.

Parents who have had poor parenting

For these people their mother or father may have been a cold, unemotional person, unable to show love to their child, inconsistent in their dealings with the child, making demands upon the child, seeking attention for themselves and denying the child's needs. All of these things would have affected the child and are likely to be reflected in the way as adults they treat their own children. For many people the only example they have of the role of a parent is the way that their parents behaved towards them. As their own parents have been lacking, so this is perpetuated by them becoming poor parents.

Very young parents or a child being born to young parents during the first year of marriage

Some teenagers who become parents have great difficulty in coping as they themselves are still growing up. Often they find themselves in a conflict situation, wanting the freedom of the teenage years but having the responsibility for a small child. They are unable to meet the needs of their children because they are unaware of what those needs are. When people marry or live together at a young age and a child is born very early in the relationship it can create problems. In this situation the two young people have probably not really come to terms with their relationship with each other when suddenly they find that they are thrown into the responsibility of having a child to rear. These situations are likely to cause fewer problems if the couple are part of an extended family which is able to offer them advice and support.

Parents who have unrealistic views of their child's behaviour

A number of people have the idea that children should behave impeccably as long as they are well fed and kept clean. These people have no idea about stages of child development and they are likely to place unrealistic demands upon their children. When the children are unable to come up to these expectations they are punished and in some cases this punishment may be severe. In these situations love may be conditional depending upon the behaviour of the child.

Parents who are on a low income

For people who are caught in the poverty trap it can be a daily nightmare trying to manage a family budget. Making decisions about paying rent, buying the right sort of food or spending money on videos, cigarettes and alcohol do not come easily to some people. Being unable to make reasoned decisions which may mean going without certain items can lead to the family amassing large debts with no hope of ever paying them off. Whilst this process is going on, food may not be bought, clothes may not be bought, heating and lighting bills may not be paid and the child may suffer. One member of the family may be selfish and object to going without and this can lead to added stress for the rest of the family. Sometimes this situation can lead to a child being 'scapegoated' and neglected or abused by the parents who may feel that it is the extra expense of the child that is responsible for their poor financial state.

Parents who demand affection from their children but who are unable to return this by showing affection to the child

Some people are very demanding of affection from all the people around them but they themselves are unable to give affection to others. This may lead to them using emotional blackmail with their children in order to get their own needs answered. They are likely to tell their children that if they behave in a certain way it must mean that they do not love their mother/father. This type of behaviour by adults totally confuses children emotionally.

Parents who have low self-esteem

Many things in life can lead to a person having low self-esteem. It may come about as the result of events that happened in their childhood, e.g. not being able to live up to parental expectations, or it may be due to events that have happened in adult life, e.g. the desertion of a husband/wife to live with someone else. In some families it can be associated with gender, e.g. the males behaving in a superior fashion and perpetually 'putting down' the female family members. Redundancy from a job can lead to a loss of self-esteem. When low self-esteem leads to the adults blaming the children for their situation or adults trying to raise their self-esteem by insisting on unrealistic behaviour from their children, it can lead to the child being neglected or abused. Adults who sexually abuse children often have low self-esteem and are probably unable to make adult sexual relationships.

Parents who are addicted to alcohol or drugs

The behaviour of people who have a problem with alcohol and drug abuse will affect the whole family. Many cases of family violence are associated with alcohol abuse, one member of the family getting so drunk that they are unable to control their reactions to normal family situations. Drug abuse can also lead to violence but in many instances it is more commonly associated with neglect. Children are often neglected because the parent is spending all their income on drugs or alcohol rather than buying food and clothes. The effects of drugs often lead to addicts spending most of their time in a state of inertia and neglecting the basic needs of themselves and their children.

Parents with mental illness

If a family member has a mental illness this will place stress upon the whole family. Adults exhibiting bizarre behaviour patterns and severe mood swings can be very distressing for children. In some cases the moods may be violent and this may lead to the child being abused. If there is a history or diagnosis of depression, the parent may be totally unable to cope with the responsibilities of child rearing and may neglect the child. Following the birth of a child, a woman may suffer from postnatal depression and this can lead to her being disinterested in the baby.

None of these categories is clear cut nor able to be applied to every adult that neglects or abuses their children, but they are worth considering when explanations are being sought.

Features of child neglect and abuse

Statistics show that the highest incidence of child abuse (other than sex abuse) occurs in children in the age range 1 to 4 years. It occurs in all social classes and the people most likely to be perpetrators are parents, co-habitees who are not the child's natural parent, siblings and strangers. Research has identified features which may be associated with children who are likely to be at risk of neglect and abuse:

- *children born prematurely*
- *children separated from their mother for some period following their birth*
- *children with disabilities*
- *children who cry a lot*
- *children who are difficult to feed*
- *step-children*
- *children who are not the sex wished for by the parents.*

General indicators of child neglect and abuse

There are a number of indicators that have been put forward by professionals in the field of child protection in order to raise awareness in those who are working on a daily basis with children and their families. The following lists have indicators which apply to children and their parents. It is most likely that your local authority policy and practice documents clearly state the local guidelines; the following are generalized indicators.

Parents who may neglect or abuse their children may exhibit the following:

- *rejection of the child*
- *rough handling of the child*
- *failure to keep appointments with child care staff*
- *frequent visits to the medical services with trivial complaints about the child or themselves.*

Children who may be suffering from neglect or abuse may exhibit the following:

- *unexplained failure to thrive*
- *injuries that are inconsistent with the accident as described by the parents*
- *frequent bruising, cuts or burns to the body*
- *frozen awareness, when children carefully watch adults' expressions and movements*
- *reluctance to be alone with their parent/s*
- *sudden unexplained changes in their reactions towards their carers.*

Not all children who have been neglected or abused will show all of these indicators and one indicator alone may not denote that a child is being neglected or abused. A number of children may exhibit 'failure to thrive' and doctors may not be able to find any reasonable explanation for this but this does not necessarily indicate that these children have been victims of abuse. A child with a combination of indicators who has a parent who is also exhibiting one or more of the adult indicators could lead a carer to suspect that the case was indeed one of abuse or neglect.

In the area of child sexual abuse there are a different set of indicators, most of which are related to the behaviour of the child:

- *sudden changes in personality such as wanting constant attention and reassurance*
- *lack of trust of a familiar adult*
- *aggressive or compliant behaviour*
- *withdrawal, listlessness, sadness*
- *regression in toilet training*
- *sleep disturbances and nightmares*
- *fear of being alone*
- *showing affection in a sexual way inappropriate to their age*
- *exhibiting sexual promiscuousness in their imaginative play*
- *frequent urinary tract infections and other ailments related to the genital area*
- *eating problems, loss of appetite, problems swallowing, excessive eating.*

Specific indicators of various forms of child neglect and abuse

Neglect

Physical indicators
- *Poor hygiene*
- *Inadequately clothed, dirty, torn or inappropriate clothing*
- *Untreated medical problems*
- *Poor nourishment/failure to thrive*
- *Emaciation.*

Behavioural indicators
- *Tired or listless*
- *Low self-esteem*
- *Always hungry*
- *States that there is no-one at home to look after them or indicates that they spend a lot of time at home alone.*

Physical abuse

Physical indicators
- *Unexplained bruising in places where an injury cannot easily be sustained or explained*
- *Facial bruising*
- *Hand or finger marks or pressure bruising*
- *Bite marks*
- *Burns (particularly cigarette burns), scalds*
- *Unexplained fractures*
- *Lacerations or abrasions.*

Behavioural indicators
- *Shying away from physical contact*
- *Withdrawn or aggressive behaviour*
- *Sudden changes in behaviour, i.e. from extrovert to introvert.*

Sexual abuse

Physical indicators
- *Bruises or scratches inconsistent with accidental injury*
- *Difficulty in walking or sitting*
- *Pain or itching in the genital area*

- *Torn, stained or bloody underclothes*
- *Bedwetting, sleep disturbances*
- *Loss of appetite.*

Figure 7.1
Signs of physical abuse:
(a) facial squeezing; (b) diffuse facial bruising; (c) pinch marks; (d) grip marks; (e) body bruising; (f) identifiable lesions; (g) bite marks; (h) burns or scalds; (i) cigarette burns.

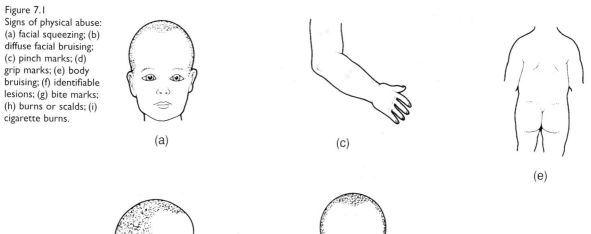

(a)

(c)

(e)

(b)

(d)

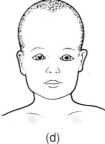

(f)

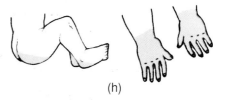

(h)

(g)

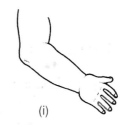

(i)

Behavioural indicators
- *Hints of sexual activity through words, play, drawings*
- *Sexually precocious, uses seductive behaviour towards adults*
- *Uses sexually explicit language*
- *Excessive pre-occupation with sexual matters*
- *Informed knowledge of adult sexual behaviour*
- *Poor self-esteem*
- *Withdrawn or isolated from other children.*

Emotional abuse

Behavioural indicators
- *Attention-seeking*
- *Withdrawn*
- *Tells lies*
- *Inability to have fun*
- *Low self-esteem*
- *Tantrums past the age when they are part of normal development*
- *Speech disorders, e.g. stammering*
- *Inability to play*
- *Indiscriminately affectionate.*

Other forms of child abuse

There are other forms of child abuse which are not mentioned above but which are worth noting. Some of these are mentioned earlier in this chapter, e.g. child pornography, child abduction, sex tourism, child labour and street children. There has been a lot of media attention given to what has been termed ritual abuse, a situation whereby children are abused during pseudo-religious ceremonies. Extensive research into ritual abuse was undertaken by Jean La Fontaine, but her report notes that in no case that she investigated could a link be found between the abuse and rites or ceremonies. There is also the problem of children who abuse other children physically, sexually, by bullying or by racial harassment. This is a very complex area as the abuser may be both victim and perpetrator. Bullying is now being taken very seriously in society, and schools and other institutions have anti-bullying policies and implementation programmes. Racism is also being tackled in schools and institutions in addition to the requirements of the Race Relations Acts and the Children Act. However, it is very difficult to change attitudes when the child's home may be a climate of bullying or the area where they live may be overtly racist.

Good practice for dealing with child neglect and abuse

What to do if you are caring for a child who exhibits indicators of neglect or abuse

1. Be sure of your facts. One way of ensuring that you know exactly what indicators the child is showing is to undertake systematic observation of the child's behaviour over the period of a day for a number of days.
2. Report your suspicions to a senior member of staff who will know the local authority's procedures for child protection.
3. Continue to observe the child and build up a picture of the indicators in preparation for writing a report.
4. Make a special point of trying to involve the child in play activities, particularly those that will enable the child to let out aggression or those that will help to raise the child's self-esteem.

The situation of what to do may be more complicated if you are working alone in a family or may be a childminder. A childminder is able to make contact with the family's health visitor or social worker in order to seek advice whereas a nanny does not have this facility. In either case you should keep records of what you have seen, when you have seen it and observations of the child's behaviour. You should then discuss these things with the parent/s, as another member of the family or family friend could be responsible for the abuse. If, after a period of time, you are still unhappy and suspect that the abuse is continuing, then this may necessitate talking with the health visitor or social services. It is important if you work alone to keep very detailed records of what you have observed, the action that you have taken, the parents' response to that action and any further action that you may take.

What to do if a child tells you that they have been abused

In some textbooks this is referred to as 'disclosure'; however, the Cleveland Report (1987) made the point about 'the undesirability of calling them 'disclosure' interviews, which precluded the notion that sexual abuse might not have occurred.' In other words, the actual word 'disclosure' assumes the child has something to disclose. This has led to the word 'disclosure' being phased out of the child protection terminology.

1. Reassure the child, telling them that you are glad they have spoken to you.
2. Tell the child that you believe them and that you will do your best to protect them.

3.   Let the child know that it is the adult who is to blame not the child.
4.   Be ready to listen to what the child has to say but do not ask the child questions.
5.   Report the matter to a senior member of staff so that the local authority's policy on child protection can be put into practice.

The case conference

When there is reason or suspicion to think that a child has been neglected or abused and the matter has been reported to the relevant senior staff member, it is likely that a case conference will be called.

The Department of Health document *Working Together* (1991) defines a case conference as:

> a forum for the exchange of information between professionals involved with the child and family ... that allows for ... multi-disciplinary discussions of allegations or suspicions of abuse; the outcome of investigations, assessment for planning; an action plan for protecting the child and helping the family and reviews of the plan.

The people invited to attend a case conference are those people who are 'key workers' with the child and family, e.g. health visitor, social worker, head teacher, teacher, nursery nurse, nursery officer, playgroup leader, general practitioner and paediatrician. Sometimes case conferences will involve the police, particularly if they have had past dealings with the family. Case conferences focus upon the child whose interests and safety are paramount to all other considerations. The proceedings at case conferences come under strict rules of confidentiality. Parents/carers of the child are informed about the case conference in advance and their views sought on the issues to be raised. Whether they are invited to attend the case conference or not is a decision made by the case conference chairperson and this decision will be based upon what is in the best interests of the child. The outcome of the case conference will be an action plan for dealing with the situation, which may range from placing the child's name on the Child Protection Register to seeking court protection for the child. The parents/carers must be informed of the outcome of the case conference.

At the case conference each person will be given the opportunity to report on the particular area they are dealing with; there is then likely to be a full discussion about the best way to proceed to ensure that the child receives maximum protection. The action plan is then drawn up. As a child carer you may be asked to attend case conferences relating to children in your care. It is important to take with you any observations or notes that you may have made on the child's behaviour or meetings with the child's parents. The members of the case conference will want valid evidence relating to the child or the child's family and it is on this that they will base their action plan. Case conferences are formal proceedings but are often run on informal lines in order to gain the maximum information about the child without making the participants feel intimidated.

Area child protection committees

Area Child Protection Committees (ACPCs) are not statutory bodies but have been set up as a result of the guidelines in Part Two of the document *Working Together* (1991). Their aim is to form a close working relationship between all the agencies who share a common aim of protecting children at risk. They offer a joint forum for social services departments, the police service, health, education, voluntary organizations and other interested parties. They are a valuable catalyst for developing shared child protection policies. The ACPCs produce an annual report which should form part of the Children's Services Plan of the local authority. (Children's Services Plans 1996 come under Part III of the Children Act 1989 and they need to include the Child Protection Services.) Annual reports are also submitted to the Department of Health and the Welsh Office.

The law relating to child protection

The Children Act 1989 not only brought together a number of previous Acts but also re-wrote the laws relating to child protection to ensure that there are proper safeguards for children and reasonable opportunities for the parents/carers of the child to challenge any action that the courts may take. The term 'significant harm' is used in the Act and this is defined as:

> Harm is defined as 'ill treatment or the impairment of health or development.
> Development as meaning physical, intellectual, emotional, social or behavioural development.
> Health as meaning physical or mental health.
> Ill treatment as including sexual abuse and forms of ill treatment which are not physical.'
>
> *Department of Health (1991)*

Child assessment order

This may be applied for by the local authority or the NSPCC and enables the applicant to assess the state of the child's health or development. To obtain an Assessment Order the applicant must satisfy the court that there is reason to suspect that a child is suffering or is likely to suffer significant harm and that an assessment needs to be carried out in order to determine such harm. Once the Order has been granted, the applicant has up to 7 days to carry out the assessment. A Child Assessment Order is likely to be used when a child's parents or carers are unco-operative and there is reason to believe that a child's needs are not being met but that the situation is not serious enough to require an Emergency Protection Order (EPO).

Emergency protection order

This has replaced the 'Place of Safety Order'. It is applied for and issued by a court or an individual magistrate in cases where there is reasonable cause to believe that a child will suffer significant harm if not removed from the place of residence. Anyone can apply for an EPO and although most applications are likely to come from social services departments, it is possible for a concerned relative, a teacher or a neighbour to make an application.

The person applying for the EPO will need to satisfy the court or issuing magistrate that there is evidence to necessitate such a drastic step. Once an EPO has been granted, the person applying for the order is given rights of parental responsibility and is able to move the child to a safe environment. The EPO has effect for a period of 8 days and a court may extend this by a further period of 7 days. An application may be made to the court for a discharge of the EPO but this can only be done after 72 hours have elapsed from the beginning of the order.

Police powers of protection

Under Part V of the Children Act, police have been given special powers for dealing with child protection cases. These allow the police to remove a child whom they consider is in a position of significant harm or to ensure that a child stays in a place where it is safe. Such orders last for a period of 72 hours and the police must inform the parents/carers and the local authority of the steps they have taken.

Once a child is the subject of an EPO or under police protection, it is the duty of the local authority (this includes social services, education, health or the NSPCC) to investigate the situation of the child to determine what, if any, future action should be taken. One such action that may be taken is for the local authority to apply for a care or supervision order.

Care order

This order places the child in the care of the local authority or the NSPCC and only these bodies can apply for such an order. A Care Order gives the applicant rights of parental responsibility for the child and can last until the child is 18 years of age. Care Orders are granted when it has been proven to the court that the child is likely to suffer significant harm or that there is a likelihood of the child suffering significant harm if the child is left in its present environment.

Supervision Order

This puts the child under the supervision of the local authority or a probation officer. The person undertaking the supervision on behalf of the local authority or probation service is charged with specific duties, the main one being to assist and befriend the child. The person who has parental responsibility for the child must take reasonable steps to ensure that the child complies with the Supervision Order. A Supervision Order is given for a period of 12 months but it can be extended up to a maximum period of 3 years and it can be converted to a Care Order.

Reforms to the law about child evidence

The Criminal Justice Act 1991 made changes to the law about child evidence and procedure. In 1992 the Home Office and Department of Health issued a joint document called *The Memorandum of Good Practice on Video Recorded Interviews with Child Witnesses in Criminal Proceedings*. This document recommended that police and social workers should conduct joint interviews with children and they should have joint training for interviewing and carry out joint investigations.

Family Law Act 1996

This Act amends the Children Act 1989 to enable the courts, on the application of the local authority and others in certain proceedings, to order the removal of the violent person from a household as an alternative to removing the child.

Sex Offenders Act 1997

This Act was brought about by the growing concern of the dangers posed to children by sex offenders. The Act requires anyone convicted or cautioned for specified sex offences to notify the police of their names and addresses and any subsequent changes to these. Offenders who do not register within 14 days of the conviction or caution will be committing a criminal offence and will face penalties of up to 6 months in prison or a £5000 fine. The registration is applicable throughout the UK, not subject to appeal or review unless a conviction is quashed on appeal and subject to a minimum period of 5 years for non-prison sentences and life for those given prison sentences of 30 months or more. The Act also empowers the UK courts to prosecute people who commit sex offences against children abroad.

Voluntary organizations involved in child protection

There are many voluntary organizations that carry out work on child protection in addition to their main areas of responsibility but there is not space to mention them all. It is a good idea to become familiar with the organizations which operate in your particular area. The following section is about three national organizations that specifically deal with child protection and that have this as their sole aim.

National Society for the Prevention of Cruelty to Children

The NSPCC is probably the best known and the oldest voluntary organization that is involved in child protection in England, Wales and N. Ireland (Scotland has its own organization, the Royal Scottish Society for the Prevention of Cruelty to Children – RSSPCC). The Society was founded in 1884 by Revd Benjamin Waugh and had Lord Shaftesbury as its President. By 1889 there were 31 branch offices and in 1895 the Society was granted a Royal Charter. The Royal Charter placed upon the organization, '… a duty to ensure an appropriate and speedy response in all cases where children are alleged to be at risk of abuse or neglect in any form.' As a consequence of this, the NSPCC (along with local authorities) has for many years had statutory powers which enable the organization to apply to the court for relevant protection orders for children. Under the Children Act 1989 the NSPCC is allowed to apply for Child Assessment Orders, Emergency Protection Orders, Care Orders and Supervision Orders.

The NSPCC operates on a regional basis with a Regional Social Work Manager as the leading professional officer. Social workers operate in teams and undertake therapeutic work with children and their families as well as carrying out a preventative role. Local NSPCC social workers liaise closely with the local social services departments and other child protection agencies.

The NSPCC has a national research unit which holds comprehensive statistics and undertakes studies based on reported cases. The NSPCC has its own Child Protection Register from which it is able to transfer and interpret data in order to prepare national statistics.

The most recent innovation from the NSPCC is a free telephone help line which children who need protection or adults who need advice can contact.

ChildLine

This is a national charity started in 1986 by the television personality Esther Rantzen. It offers a free, 24-hours telephone advice service to children. It is staffed by trained volunteers and social workers who are able to counsel the caller. It is claimed that ChildLine has an average of more than 20000 calls per year but this number is said to increase to many more thousands if the number of attempted calls are added to the figure. In additon to calls from children, ChildLine also has a large number of adults contacting them. MacLeod (1997) reports that in 1996 ChildLine advised 6991 adults by telephone and 224 by letter. The majority of them were ringing to say they were worried about their child or a child known to them or about an adult who may be abusing.

There are two main factors that make telephone helplines attractive to callers: (1) the assurance of anonymity which removes the fear of the abuse getting worse because they have told somebody and (2) the assurance of confidentiality. Callers do not have to give their name, address, location where they are calling from or any other details which could identify them. The counsellors who answer the telephones do not pressurize the caller into revealing their identity unless it would appear that the person is in imminent danger. A major criticism of telephone helpline schemes has been the small number of cases which actually get followed up in comparison to the incredibly large numbers of phone calls received. The numbers of prosecutions resulting from information that originated from a telephone helpline call are very small. However, the main justification for this type of service is that it enables access to advice and counselling to a very large number of children. The children are offered advice on the best way to tackle the problem and this may empower the child to say 'No' to an abusing adult and seek help from sympathetic adults in the immediate locality.

Kidscape

This is an organization which originated in the USA and Canada and was brought to the UK by Michelle Elliott. It has now been established as a charity and works with schools and youth clubs offering children strategies for keeping themselves safe. The philosophy of the organization is that children should be given the tools to be able to keep themselves safe from danger and abuse. By using interactive teaching methods, children are encouraged to become more assertive and to not be frightened to say 'No' to adults and others who may be causing them distress. It also teaches children that they are allowed to do things that they normally would not be allowed to do in order to keep safe, e.g. kicking, biting, screaming, breaking windows. One area where Kidscape has had a great deal of success is teaching children how to protect themselves against bullying, a not uncommon form of child abuse inflicted upon children by other children.

Kidscape has produced a number of videos and books for children on how to stay safe and is able to send teams of teachers to schools and youth clubs to carry out its programmes with the children.

Help for children who have been neglected or abused

Wherever possible, children who have been the subject of neglect or abuse are kept within their families. The Cleveland Report (1987) made reference to children being doubly punished, once by being the subject of abuse and then by being taken away from their families and placed in the care of the local authority. Hence the Family Law Act 1996 which now allows the abuser to be removed. Support is given to the family by involving a number of agencies such as health visitors, social workers, educational welfare officers and psychologists. The child is likely to be given an immediate place in a day nursery, family centre or one of the specialist therapeutic nurseries run by the health service which are available in some parts of the country. Within these establishments the staff will work with the child and in some cases the whole family to help them work through their relationships and problems.

The key worker

Family centres and day nurseries will often operate a system whereby a member of staff is assigned to work with specific children and their families. This has the advantage of the key worker becoming a familiar figure to the child, somebody they can trust and relate to. The key worker is able to build up a meaningful relationship with the child and offer the child the type of play experiences which will help the child to come to terms with past experiences. The key worker is also able to build relationships with the parents and advise them on the best ways to deal with their child. A key worker will monitor the children they are assigned to and will be able to spot changes in a child's behaviour which may indicate that there is a deterioration in the home situation.

Play therapists

Some local authorities employ play therapists who visit the nursery or family centre to undertake one-to-one work with children who have been neglected or abused. Unfortunately there are very few play therapists and the children referred to them are often those who exhibit the most disturbed behaviour. The therapist's role is to encourage children to play and through their play to express their feelings.

Therapeutic nurseries

In some authorities there are specialist therapeutic nurseries designed specifically to deal with children and families where neglect or abuse has taken place. They are often joint ventures between the local social services and the health authority. Children are referred to them by social workers or through the local hospital or GP service. Staff in these nurseries comprise an inter-disciplinary team of people such as child care workers, psychologists, play therapists and social workers.

In general, children who have been the victims of neglect and abuse are likely to be very mistrustful of adults. Staff who care for them need to spend a lot of time rebuilding the bonds between adult and child. This is best done by ensuring that the child has to deal with as few adults as possible. The child will need to be encouraged to play and mix with other children and this is likely to take time. Children who exhibit very disturbed behaviour patterns will need a great deal of help to channel their aggression into play activities. Children will need a lot of praise and affection and this will need to be reinforced regularly in order to help them build up their self-esteem. The child care worker will also need to be alert to any changes in the child's behaviour or physical condition which may indicate that the neglect or abuse has restarted. It is important to talk to children about normal everyday things and listen carefully to what they have to tell you.

Assignments

Assignment 1

Miriam is aged 3 years and attends your playgroup five mornings a week. She is normally a quiet, timid child who has difficulty relating to other children. Recently she seems to have become more withdrawn and Pat, the playgroup leader, is concerned about her. She has talked to her mother who insists that nothing has changed at home. Whilst helping Miriam to undress for gymnastics, Pat notices finger-mark bruising on Miriam's buttocks. If you were Pat, what action would you take concerning these findings?

Assignment 2

Sharon is a precocious 4-year-old, outgoing, chatty and inclined to be bossy with the other children. She has a full-time place at your nursery because she is on the Child Protection Register. You are carrying out child observations for a college project and spend some time observing Sharon in the hospital corner. Sharon lies on the bed and begins to behave in a sexually promiscuous manner, inviting the boys to come and examine her. You complete your observations but are worried about Sharon's behaviour. Explain why the nursery workers might be concerned about Sharon's behaviour and describe what action they should take.

Assignment 3

You are a worker at the local 'One O'Clock' club situated in an inner city park. Recently Paula and her three children have been attending on a regular basis. You are rather concerned as two of Paula's children are over the age of 5 years and should be at school. Paula seems very depressed and you have been trying to establish a relationship with her but you have not mentioned your concern about the older children. Today, in conversation with Paula, you find out that she is living in bed and breakfast accommodation. Does this information help you to understand why Paula brings all her children to the club? Is there any advice that you can give Paula which may help her and her children?

Assignment 4

Mary is 23 years old; she has two children: Robin, aged 3 years, and Katy, aged 18 months. Mary's partner left her when she was pregnant with Katy. Mary very rarely goes out, but recently she has met up with some of her old school chums and they have invited her to go to a club with them. Mary cannot afford a babysitter and she knows that both children usually sleep through the night from 8 p.m. to 6 a.m. Mary decides to go out with her friends and leave the children on their own as she is sure that the children will be all right and sleep through. While she is out Katy wakes up and starts to scream; this wakes up Robin who also starts to cry and call for his mother. The next-door neighbours hear the children and knock on Mary's door. When they get no reply, they call the police. What can the police do? Is Mary's action considered as child abuse?

Assignment 5

You are a nursery nurse in an infant school, working with Year 2 children. Glen is a tall, well-built boy for his age with a loud voice and a rather 'pushy' manner. Recently you have noticed him hitting other children, shouting at them, taking their sweets and calling them names such as 'Paki', 'Four eyes' and 'Fatty'. Describe the school's anti-bullying policy and how you will implement this with Glen.

REFERENCES AND FURTHER READING

Allen, A. and Morton, A. (1961) *This is your Child: The Story of the National Society for Prevention of Cruelty to Children.* London: Routledge and Kegan Paul.

Aries, P. (1973) *Centuries of Childhood.* Harmondsworth: Penguin.

Bradshaw, J. (1990) *Child Poverty and Deprivation in the UK.* London: National Children's Bureau.

Butler-Sloss, E. (1987) *Report of the Inquiry into Child Abuse in Cleveland.* London: HMSO.

Campbell, B. (1988) *Unofficial Secrets: Child Sexual Abuse: The Cleveland Case.* London: Virago.

Children's Legal Centre. (1988) *Child Abuse Procedures: The Children's Viewpoint* London: Children's Legal Centre.

Department of Health. (1991) *Working Together: Under the Children Act 1989.* London: HMSO.

Department of Health. (1995) *Child Protection. Messages from Research.* London: HMSO.

Department of Health. (1998) *Working Together to Safeguard Children. New Government Proposals for Inter-agency Co-operation Consultation Paper.* London: Department of Health.

Hobart, C. and Frankel, J. (1998) *Good Practice in Child Protection.* Cheltenham: Stanley Thornes.

Hollows, A. and Armstrong, H. (Eds) (1991) *Children and Young People as Abusers.* London: National Children's Bureau.

Kempe, R. and Kempe, H. (1978) *Child Abuse.* London: Fontana.

La Fontaine, J. (1990) *Child Sexual Abuse.* Cambridge: Polity Press.

MacLeod, M. (1997) *Child Protection Everybody's Business.* Sutton: Sutton Community Care.

Miller, A. (1983) *For Your Own Good.* London: Virago.

Newell, P. (1991) *The UN Convention and Children's Rights in the UK.* London: National Children's Bureau.

Open University. (1989) Unit P554. *Child Abuse and Neglect.* Course material. Milton Keynes: Open University Press.

Parton, N. (1985) *The Politics of Child Abuse.* Basingstoke: Macmillan.

Pugh, G. and De' Ath, E. (1984) *The Needs of Parents.* London: National Children's Bureau.

Rogers, W.S., Hevey, D. and Ash, E. (1989) *Child Abuse and Neglect: Facing the*

Challenge. Milton Keynes: Open University Press.

Whipple, E. and Richey, C. (1997) Crossing the line from physical discipline to child abuse: how much is too much? *Child Abuse and Neglect* **21**(5): 1–444

Wilson, K. and James, A. (Eds) (1995) *The Child Protection Handbook.* London: Baillière Tindall.

Winnicott, D. (1964) *The Family, the Child and the Outside World.* Harmondsworth: Penguin.

8: CHILD CARE WORKERS AND THE LAW

Objectives

- Race Relations Act 1976
- Race Relations (Northern Ireland) Order 1997
- Children and racism
- Fair Employment (Northern Ireland) Act 1989
- Children Act 1989
- Parental responsibility
- Divorce and separation of parents
- Local authority responsibilities
- Day care – registration of services
- Foster care
- Children's services plans
- Education Reform Act 1988
- National Curriculum
- Local management of schools
- Education Act 1996 (incorporating Education Act 1993)
- Code of practice
- Early years development plans and partnerships (child care partnerships)
- Sex Discrimination Act 1975
- Gender issues in child care
- Sex Offenders Act 1997
- Disability Discrimination Act 1995

Links

This chapter has links with:
- Most NVQ (EYCE) Units and the underlying principles of the Early Years Care and Education National Standards.
- CACHE Diploma Module Q.

Anyone who is responsible for other people's children needs to be aware of the laws which may relate to the delivery of that care.[1] During the last 20 years there have been a number of such pieces of legislation, including what is probably the most important legislation enacted this century, the Children Act 1989.

---

[1] Chapters 5 and 7 also contain references to the law relating to child care workers.

The laws referred to in this chapter relate to the UK but it needs to be noted that there is other legislation that relates to children, namely, the European Social Charter, the European Convention on Human Rights and the United Nations Convention on the Rights of the Child, and specific references may be made to these. The laws which are looked at in depth are predominantly those for England as Scotland, Wales and N. Ireland often have their own laws or orders and amendments to existing English laws, particularly those relating to educational matters.

Whilst legislation can make people aware of situations and the legal requirements placed upon them, it is not able to change people's attitudes and this is most significant when dealing with the areas of sex discrimination and racial discrimination. When working with children and their families, it is important for the child carer to be committed to the concepts which underpin the legislation rather than acting in a certain way in order not to break the law. The laws discussed in this chapter require readers to think beyond 'the letter of the law' and to be aware of their own attitudes and values relating to the subject. Child care is a public service and it is the responsibility of all child care workers to offer a high quality of service to children and their parents. This will require them to incorporate the legislation and positive attitudes into their practice.

Race Relations Act 1976

Racial inequality is one of the areas that UK society has not successfully combated. Whilst we do have legislation that prevents people discriminating against others on the grounds of racial origin, we cannot have laws which prevent people from holding negative and discriminatory attitudes towards those from different racial and ethnic groups. We live in a pluralistic society and all children within that society should have the right to grow up holding good positive images of themselves.

Section 1(1) of the Race Relations Act defines discrimination as:

> (a) on racial grounds he treats that other [person] less favourably than he treats or would treat other persons ... [author's brackets]

The Act defines 'racial grounds' as colour, race, nationality, citizenship or ethnic or national origins (this includes groups with a long shared history and a cultural tradition of their own, e.g. Sikhs or Romany Gypsies). It does not include culture or religion; however, both of these are mentioned in the Children Act 1989.

The above definition refers to direct discrimination which is exactly what it implies: treating or telling people that they cannot do something or have something on the grounds that they are of another race, colour or nationality; e.g. a child care worker telling a child that the child cannot go on a nursery outing because the child is black or Irish would be direct discrimination. This example also applies conversely, e.g. if the worker said that the only children who could attend the outing were those who were black or Irish. In both of these examples the worker would be breaking the law.

Indirect discrimination is dealt with under Section 1(1)(b) of the Race Relations Act and occurs when rules or regulations are put into practice which are impossible for members of a particular group to conform to. The following example of this is one which was quoted by Sir Peter Newsom when he was the Chairman of the Commission for Racial Equality. A USA State Fire Brigade required all applicants to be 5′11″ to 6′ tall and this prevented people applying for jobs if they came from races which had small stature, e.g. Asians, Chinese, Filipinos. If a child care establishment imposes rules that mitigate against certain people in the community, then it would be breaking the law; e.g. if a nursery school had a rule that no hats were to be worn inside the building, then this would prevent Sikh, Rastafarian, Muslim and Jewish children gaining a place in that nursery as it would be impossible for them to conform to this rule. The rule would be unlawful under Section 28 of the Act which refers to discriminatory practices. Indirect discrimination is not always deliberate and may arise because people have not thought about the implications of the rules they are making; however, whether it is intended or not, it is still unlawful and ignorance is not an acceptable defence in law.

Section 1(2) of the Act states:

> segregating a person from other persons on racial grounds is treating him less favourably than they [others] are treated. [author's brackets]

This means that a child care worker who sat children at tables according to their colour or racial origin would be breaking the law by treating one group of children less favourably than another. Although most child care workers would not dream of doing this, it is not unknown for parents to request that their child should not be sat next to a black or Asian child. The parents, by making the request, would be in breach of Sections 30 and 31 of the Act which state that it is unlawful to instruct or pressurize a person to discriminate against others. The child care worker, by carrying out the request, would be in breach of Section 1(2) of the Act by segregating the children.

When advertising a pre-school facility, care must be taken to ensure that the wording of the advert is such that it does not discriminate against certain groups. Section 29 of the Act deals with this area and the word 'advertisement' is widely defined and covers the display of notices, signs and labels whether public or not. An example of this is given by Lane (1996):

> It would be unlawful to publish a list of child minders known to be prepared only to mind children from a particular racial group.

Child care workers, except foster parents who are not covered by the Race Relations Act, are under a legal obligation to provide the same goods, facilities or services to all members of society (Section 20 of the Act). This applies to all pre-school provision whether it is statutory, voluntary or private. However, it would be lawful for a parent to ask for a childminder with particular characteristics if the parent was able to show a special need. An example of this would be a foster parent or childminder who speaks the same language as the child and the child's family.

Other sections of the Act deal with employment, education and local authorities. The body responsible for implementing the Act is the Commission for Racial Equality (CRE) which has the power to investigate alleged discrimination.

The Act makes it clear when it is lawful to discriminate in order to redress the balance within a particular section of society. If an employer wishes to encourage black people to apply for specific posts, the employer is only able to do so legally if it can be shown that there is under-representation of people from particular ethnic backgrounds in the posts. Most employers do not use positive discrimination advertisements but show their intent to employ a black person by placing their advertisements in ethnic minority newspapers.

An employer requiring a worker who is fluent in a particular language may advertise for a person with that skill. This may encourage members of ethnic minorities to apply but it does not prevent a white person who is fluent in that language from applying.

Section 22(5)(c) of the Children Act 1989 states that local authorities have to give due consideration to the religious persuasion, racial origin and cultural and linguistic background of any child that comes into their care. This means that during discus-

Figure 8.1
Multi-cultural
child care.

Scenario 8.1

The Rainbow Nursery/Playgroup is in a multi-cultural, inner city area and the manager is very aware that they do not have any black members of staff. They now have a staff vacancy and the manager places the following advertisement in the local newspaper:

'Rainbow Nursery/Playgroup requires a black, Bengali-speaking worker for 36 hours per week. Please send C.V. to Mrs Trent, Manager,...'

Is this advertisement legal? If you think it is not legal, then say why not and which sections of the Race Relations Act you think it may be contravening. If you think that the manager could have approached this situation in a different way in order to encourage applications from members of ethnic minority groups suggest what could have been done.

sions on what might be the most suitable placement for a child they must take all the above factors into consideration. It is worth noting that this Act goes beyond the Race Relations Act as it refers to culture, linguistic background and religion. The Children Act also makes it clear that a person's registration to care for children can be cancelled if a care provider has not answered the needs of a child. In its definition of 'needs', the Act includes the categories mentioned above. This means that when registering people who are deemed under the Children Act to be 'fit' to care for children, local authorities will need to take into account those persons':

> knowledge of and attitude to multi-cultural issues and people of different racial origins.
>
> *Guidance and Regulations to the Children Act*, Volume 2 (1991)

Race Relations (Northern Ireland) Order 1997

This Order now makes it illegal to discriminate against anyone on the grounds of race in Northern Ireland. This legislation covers all ethnic and racial groups, from people of Chinese, Asian and African origin to members of the Irish travelling community. The law does not cover religious groups other than Sikhs and Jews who are recognized as racial groups. With the introduction of the Order came the setting-up in Belfast of the Commission for Racial Equality for Northern Ireland.

Children and racism

Underpinning the Race Relations Act and the above sections of the Children Act is the knowledge that racism has detrimental effects upon children and their families. Milner (1983) points out that from the age of 2 years children begin to notice the differences in skin colour and as they get older begin to internalize the differences in treatment that they may receive because of their skin colour. Children are not racist by nature but many children are open to learning racism from adults and other children. Children may ask questions about skin colour arising from their natural curiosity, and they should be given honest answers to these questions. Unfortunately, parents can transfer their own feelings and attitudes about colour and race to their children and sometimes children will repeat these in the school or nursery. It is important for the self-esteem of the black children in the establishment that racist or cruel remarks made by children should not be ignored but dealt with by the staff in a sensitive manner. To ignore such remarks is to condone those remarks and this would be unacceptable child care practice.

Stereotyping is another dangerous practice and should not be indulged in by child care workers. Stereotyping is done by ascribing certain characteristics to certain races and then treating people accordingly; e.g. there was a myth that Afro-Caribbean children were exceptionally good at sports and this resulted in large numbers of children being encouraged into sporting activities at school and not being directed towards the academic subjects. Research does not show that black people are any better than white people at sports, music or other areas that they have been stereotyped to fit into. In the past young black children were categorized as being hyperactive and difficult to control and as Coard (1971) reported this resulted in many of them being labelled as educationally sub-normal (ESN). Fortunately, we are now very aware of the effects upon children of stereotyping and labelling and conscious efforts are made by most child care workers to ensure that black children are able to develop positive self-images.

The damage that can be done to children by racism and discrimination is clearly recognized in the United Nations Convention on the Rights of the Child which was adopted by the General Assembly in November 1989; in Article 2 it states:

> the Principle that all rights apply to all children without exception, and the State's obligation to protect children from any form of discrimination. The State must not violate any right and must take positive action to promote them all.

Scenario 8.2

Michael, aged 3 years, is playing in the home corner with Ranjit, aged 4 years. Michael puts a plate in front of Ranjit and says, 'There you are, one smelly curry for your dinner.' Ranjit looks upset and walks out of the home corner and tells you that Michael does not like him because he is smelly and eats curry.

(a) How do you deal with this situation?
(b) What changes could you suggest to the nursery manager that might prevent this situation arising in the future?

Fair Employment (Northern Ireland) Act 1989

The position of Northern Ireland in relation to Acts of Parliament is often different from the position of the rest of the UK. Not all Acts apply to Northern Ireland and there are Acts which apply only to Northern Ireland. Discrimination (predominantly in the area of employment) against some sections of the population in Northern Ireland who belong to particular religious groups has a long history and the Fair Employment Act 1989 was brought in to eradicate such discrimination. The Act requires all employers with more than 25 employees (from 1992 this included all private sector employers with more than 10 employees) to be registered and to submit monitoring returns which show the religious composition of their workforce. If the monitoring shows that Catholics are under-represented in a particular workforce, then mandatory affirmative action must be taken in order to redress the balance.

Whilst the Act only covers employment and therefore does not specifically relate to children, the quality of life for some children and their families would be considerably enhanced if it was easier for their parents to find employment.

It is also applicable for child care workers who may be seeking employment or who may become employees in Northern Ireland. In the 1989 Annual Report of the Commission for Racial Equality, the Chairman, Michael Day, praised the Act and stated:

> We have watched with much interest, and not a little envy, the introduction of fair employment legislation in Northern Ireland. We believe that the kinds of obligations placed upon employers to avoid discrimination on the ground of religion should be matched here by equivalent provisions on race...

Children Act 1989

When the Lord Chancellor introduced the Act when it was at the Parliamentary Bill stage, he described it as being 'the most comprehensive and far-reaching reform of child law which has come before parliament in living memory.' The Act not only brought together existing legislation but it also took into account the major reforms that were needed in the areas of child protection and family breakdown. For the first time, the Act placed duties upon social services and education departments to provide for children in need. It should be noted that the Children Act 1989 only applies to England and Wales; the Children (Scotland) Act got royal assent in 1995 and N. Ireland is covered by the Children (Northern Ireland) Order 1995. Whenever this section refers to 'the Act' it means the Children Act 1989 (England and Wales).

The Act is complex and covers all areas of child care so it is imperative that child care staff become familiar with those parts of the Act which directly relate to their establishment and their work. In order to help people through the maze of the Act, the Department of Health has produced *Guidance and Regulations* in a number of separate volumes each covering a different area, e.g. Family Support and Day Care; Children with Disabilities; Family Placements. It is recommended that child care and education workers consult the *Guidance and Regulations* volume which deals with their area of work.

When the Children Act was written the following principles were seen as predominant:

1. *The child's welfare is paramount and as a priority this must be promoted and safeguarded.*
2. *There is a duty upon local authorities to ensure that services are provided for children 'in need'.*
3. *There must be avoidance of delay in court resolutions and in the provision of services.*
4. *Those providing services must work in partnership with children, parents, those with parental responsibility or other people who have a relevant relationship with the child/children.*
5. *Those providing services must take into account the religious, racial, cultural and linguistic needs of the child/children.*

The Act introduces new terminology which encompasses the new concepts of the Act. The following are definitions of some of the most important terminology (those which specifically relate to child protection can be found in Ch. 7).

- *Children in need.* These are children who need services to secure a reasonable standard of health and development and include children with disabilities.
- *Health and development.* Health means physical or mental health and development means physical, intellectual, emotional, social or behavioural development.
- *Parental responsibility.* This refers to all the rights, duties, powers, responsibilities and authority which by law a parent of a child has in relation to the child.
- *Guardian ad litem.* This is a person appointed by the court to represent a child in certain court proceedings. The guardian *ad litem* has access to all local authority records concerning the child and may be asked to advise the court in order to ensure that decisions made are in the child's best interests.
- *Family proceedings courts.* These are the new magistrates' courts which have been set up to hear proceedings under the Children Act. The magistrates who sit in these courts are chosen for their expertise in children and family affairs and will have undergone a special training course on the Children Act.

Parental responsibility

A person who has parental responsibility is empowered to take most of the decisions in the child's life. Parental responsibility cannot be taken away and remains until the child is 18 years of age. The person with parental responsibility may not necessarily be the child's parent or relative as a court may give parental responsibility rights to a person unrelated to the child, e.g. a step-parent.

The mother of a child automatically has parental responsibility and the father would also have this if he were married to the mother. A father who is not married to the mother of his child can obtain parental responsibility for the child by taking out a formal agreement with the mother or by applying to the court. However, the present government is looking at ways to change the law so that unmarried fathers are given certain rights in relation to their child/children.

Other people may get parental responsibility by making an application to the court or by the court appointing them or by the enactment of a court order. A parent may legally appoint someone to undertake parental responsibility of their child; this is often written into wills. In the Act, a person who has been given parental responsibility in a will can only exercise this when the child has no other living person who has parental responsibility. Another way of gaining parental responsibility is when a court makes a residence order in favour of a person who is not the parent or guardian of the child. A person who has a residence order in their favour may also gain parental responsibility.

The family of a child is considered under the Act to be any person with parental responsibility and anyone with whom the child has been living.

The Act enables people such as grandparents, uncles, aunts or other relatives with whom the child may have been living to apply for parental responsibility whereas prior to the Act these people would have had to apply to become foster parents in order to take on this role.

Divorce and separation of parents

When a family splits up there are a number of orders that the court can make in respect of the child; these replace the former custody and access orders. The child is considered by the court as a child of the family and all decisions are made with this in mind.

- A Residence Order is made to settle the question of whom the child shall live with.
- A Contact Order is made requiring the person who is caring for the child to allow the child to stay with or visit or have contact with the person named in the contact order.

- A Prohibited Steps Order is taken out by a parent who wishes to deny the child contact with the person who has a contact order.
- A Specific Issue Order can be taken out to resolve a particular issue when those with parental responsibility are unable to agree on, e.g., the child's education or medical treatment. In these cases the court would resolve the issue and give directions to those with parental responsibility to carry out the order.
- Finance Orders make provision for maintenance agreements. One of the major changes that the finance order brings about is that maintenance orders may be in respect of married and unmarried parents and against people who are not the mother or father of the child. In the case of the latter, the court will take into consideration whether the person assumed any responsibility for the child and the extent and length of time of that responsibility, e.g. step-parents who had been living with and supporting a step-child for 5 or 6 years may find themselves being expected to contribute to the continued maintenance of the child.

Residence and contact orders can cover a wide range of people such as step-parents, a person the child has lived with for at least 3 years or any person who has a genuine concern about the child's welfare, which can include foster parents. The court is empowered to grant these orders if it is in the best interests of the child to do so. Children themselves may apply for a residence or contact order providing they have sufficient understanding to make the application.

Scenario 8.3

Gary, aged 5 years, and Sharon, aged 3 years, spend a great deal of time living with their grandparents, Mr and Mrs Brown. They are the children of the Browns' daughter, Tracey, who works on a cruise liner as a waitress and so is often away for long spells of time. Tracey is divorced from the children's father, Bill. Recently, Bill has read about parental rights under the Children Act and has arrived at the Browns' house demanding to see his children. The children do not like their father very much; in fact they hardly know him as until recently he rarely visited them, and they were very young when their parents split up. The Browns have become increasingly worried about Bill's behaviour and are frightened that he will try to take the children away.

What would you advise the Browns to do and which sections of the Children Act could they use to help the children?

Local authority responsibilities

The services that the local authority must provide for children and their families are clearly stated in Part 3 of the Children Act 1989. Such services must be targeted towards children in need and their families.

Local authorities have a duty to identify the children in need in their areas and they must publish information about the services they provide. They must keep a register of children with disabilities within their area and services for the disabled must be integrated with those provided for other children in need. Local authorities must also take steps to prevent children in their area suffering neglect or ill-treatment.

There are a number of orders in the Act which put children under the care of the local authority.

- *Supervision Orders*. These require the child to be supervised by somebody appointed by the local authority. The role of the supervisor is to befriend, to advise and to assist the child and to have reasonable contact with the child. The supervision order places obligations upon those who have parental responsibility to ensure that the child conforms with the order. The supervisor can give directions for the child to submit to medical or psychiatric examination or treatment. The reports on such examination or treatment are given to the supervisor. Supervision orders are most likely to be used for older children, but they can be used for younger children, particularly in cases of child protection (see Ch. 7).
- *Education Supervision Orders*. These are similar to the above orders but relate to ensuring that the child attends educational provision. This type of supervision order is most likely to be used for children who persistently truant from school and whose parents take no preventative action. Supervision orders last for 1 year but can be extended for up to 3 years; they can also be changed into a care order.
- *Care Orders*. This places the child in the care of the local authority and can last until the child is 18 years of age. (For further details on care and supervision orders see Ch. 7.)

Day care

Under the Children Act the local authority has a duty to provide day care for children in need and those children who have disabilities. Day care consists of the provision of family centres or other day care services and supervised activities for children out of school hours. In the document *Guidance and Regulations* Volume 2 (DoH, 1991) there are clear guidelines on the standards of services for the under-8s and educational provision for under-5s. The minimum standards for each type of establishment are clearly stated and include staff qualifications, staff/child ratios, standard of the premises and the services that each establishment should provide. Some local authorities have chosen not to run their own day care facilities but instead have taken out Service Provider Contracts with voluntary or private establishments in order to buy in places for children in need.

Registration of day care services and childminding

Local authorities are responsible for the registration and inspection of day care and childminding facilities in the public, voluntary and private sectors. Anyone who looks after children under the age of 8 years on domestic premises for reward or non-domestic premises for 2 hours or more must be registered with the local authority. Those who are exempt from registration are relatives looking after the child, people who have parental responsibility for the child, foster parents, a person employed by the parent to look after the child in the child's home (nanny) and a person employed by two sets of parents to look after the children from both families in one of the homes (shared nanny).

One of the conditions attached to registration is that the person applying to be registered must satisfy the local authority that they are fit to be in the company of children under 8 years of age. In deciding that somebody is a 'fit person' the local authority are advised to take the following into account:

- Previous experience of looking after or working with young children or people with disabilities.
- Qualification and/or training in a relevant field such as child care, early years education, health visiting, nursing or other caring activity.
- Ability to provide warm and consistent care.
- Knowledge of and attitude to multi-cultural issues and people of different racial origins.
- Physical health.
- Mental stability, integrity and flexibility.
- Known involvement in criminal cases involving abuse to children.

Guidance and Regulations, Volume 2 (DoH, 1991)

With persons living or working on the premises the points are:

- Previous records.
- Known involvement in criminal cases involving abuse to children.

Local authorities are also required to inspect the premises where the child care will take place, including mobile facilities such as playbuses. Registration must be reviewed annually with inspections taking place prior to re-registration. The local authority also has a right of entry in order to carry out an inspection at times other than the annual review. Childminders and other day care establishments will be registered to take a certain number of children and there is a duty on the registered person to inform the local authority of any changes in staffing or numbers of children being cared for. A local authority may impose mandatory or discretionary requirements on a person or establishment as part of the registration procedure.

Registration can be refused or removed but the reasons for the decision must be clear and supported by evidence that would stand up in court. The local authority must give 14 days' notice of the refusal to register or the cancellation of registration. There is a right of appeal and this can be made to a court or to the local authority.

Once registration has been agreed, the person concerned is issued with a certificate of registration and the person's details are entered into the local authority register which must be available to the general public.

Scenario 8.4

Mrs Green is a childminder and has applied to the local authority for registration under the Children Act. Her 25-year-old son, Matthew, lives with her and helps her with the children. When Mrs Green received the forms to fill in for registration there was a question about declaring any criminal record of anyone resident on the premises. When Matthew was 19 years of age he was found guilty on a charge of possession of dangerous drugs and served a short prison sentence. Mrs Green is in a dilemma as she is basically an honest woman but is worried that if she mentions Matthew's previous conviction, she will not get her registration. She seeks the help of her health visitor.

What advice do you think the health visitor will give her and is it likely that Matthew's previous offence will prevent Mrs Green from being registered?

Foster care

When a Care Order is made on a child, it is the duty of the local authority to provide accommodation for that child. One option is to place the child with local-authority-approved foster parents. Foster parenting is a skilled task and to this end local authorities provide what is termed as a fostering service which includes recruitment, preparation, training and support for foster parents. Local authorities must also set up procedures for assessing and approving foster parents. Only when a foster parent has gained approval and entered into a foster placement agreement with the local authority will children be placed with them. When placing children with foster parents, it is expected that factors such as race, culture, religion and linguistic background will be taken into consideration when choosing the foster family. The number of children being fostered is usually limited to three but may be more if the children are all from the same family. The needs of the foster family's own children are taken into account when deciding upon the number and ages of the children who will be placed with the foster parents.

When children are taken into the care of the local authority, they must be allowed reasonable contact with their parents or other significant adults. Foster parents play a major role in promoting good relationships between children and their parents.

When considering the suitability of people for fostering, similar criteria to those relating to the 'fit person' are used. In addition, the following factors are also taken into consideration, marital status, religious persuasion and the degree of religious observance, racial origin and cultural and linguistic background, past and present employment, leisure activities and interests.

It is the duty of the local authority to regularly review the situation of all the children in its care and this includes children who are fostered. In cases where a child is not visited by their parents or where the relationship between the parents and child has broken down, the local authority may decide that it is in the child's best interests to appoint an independent visitor for the child. This person will befriend the child and visit the child on a regular basis and in some circumstances undertake an advocacy role on behalf of the child.

Children's services plans

In March 1996 the Secretary of State for Health made an order under section 17(4) of the Children Act 1989 which required all local authorities to draw up children's services plans. In order to do this the local authority had:

- to assess the need for provision in its area of services under Part 3 of the Children Act
- to consult with various bodies in planning how that need will be met
- to publish the resulting plans.

The aim of children's services plans is to deliver a better service to children. Social services departments were expected to take the lead within the local authority for drawing up the plans and should do this in conjunction with other key agencies in order to establish the most effective range of services. Children's services plans are not specific to the under-8s as they deal with all age groups of children covered by the Children Act 1989. Initially it was intended that children's services plans should focus on those children most at risk (children in need). As Sutton (1995) points out:

> At their most ambitious, children's services plans can become visions or mani-
> festos for the whole child population in a given area. At a more prosaic level they
> can be a statement of how the social services department intends to carry out its

statutory functions and how other agencies will assist in the exercise of its functions.

General points about the Children Act

As previously stated, the Children Act is a complex document that has brought together 20 or more pieces of previous legislation to form a cohesive statute. There has been some criticism of the Act in terms that it did not go far enough by laying down specific minimum standards for child care or state the minimum qualifications or training needed for those looking after children. The Act and the accompanying Guidelines have gone much further than any previous legislation in working towards a better standard of care for children. The underlying principles of the Act should also ensure that the welfare and interests of the child are put first and this should avoid the situation whereby children have become pawns in family disputes. All child care and education workers need to have a commitment to work as closely as possible to the Guidelines when implementing the Act as this will ensure that children will get the best out of the Act. It is inevitable that lawyers and others will find 'loopholes' in the Act which could be to the detriment of the child. At present, however, we still have little case law in this area to draw any conclusions.

Education Reform Act 1988

The Education Reform Act was responsible for significant changes throughout the education field: the National Curriculum, new responsibilities for school governors, new methods of financing schools, schools opting out of local authority control, the reorganization of the Inner London Education Authority (ILEA), to name but a few.

For children in the infant school age range, the most significant sections of the Act have been those relating to the National Curriculum and the local management of schools.

National Curriculum

Part 1 of the Education Reform Act deals with the school curriculum and the arrangements for assessment and examinations. The Act states:

> the curriculum should be balanced and broadly based and should:
> (a) promote the spiritual, moral, cultural, mental, and physical development of pupils at the school and of society; and

(b) prepare such pupils for the opportunities, responsibilities and experiences of adult life.

Education Reform Act 1988, Chapter 40, Section 1(2)

There are three core subjects: mathematics, English and science; and a number of foundation subjects: history, geography, technology, music, art and physical education. For older pupils, there is also the requirement of a foreign language. For each subject, there are attainment targets which represent the level of knowledge and understanding that a pupil should have at each key stage. There are arrangements for assessment for testing pupils in these subjects at the end of each key stage. There are four key stages:

Key stage 1 at the age of 7 years
Key stage 2 at the age of 11 years
Key stage 3 at the age of 14 years
Key stage 4 at the age of 16 years.

The ages relating to the key stages are those of the majority of pupils in a class. A child who is under or over the age of that stated for the key stage test would be tested with the majority of the pupils in the class if the child was in the minority age group of that class.

The Act established the National Curriculum Council (NCC) which was responsible for setting up working groups to determine the attainment targets and assessment tasks for each subject at each key stage. The NCC became the Schools Exams, Assessment and Curriculum Authority (SEAC), which then became the Schools Curriculum and Assessment Authority (SCAA). In October 1997, SCAA merged with the National Council for Vocational Qualifications (NCVQ) to form the Qualifications and Curriculum Authority (QCA). The National Curriculum was introduced on the basis that there was a general concern to raise the standards of education; however, the National Curriculum has been the subject of a great deal of controversy, particularly relating to testing at age 7 years. Only children in nursery and reception classes are exempt from activities and lessons which must give time to core curriculum subjects. Parents who are keen for their children to succeed in the tests at the age of 7 years have placed pressure upon schools to introduce National Curriculum subjects into the nursery and reception classes, and some schools have responded to these demands. Early years educationalists have expressed concern that some children will be tested before they reach their seventh birthday whilst others may be older than 7 years at the time of the test and this may prove to be a disadvantage for those in the younger age group. There has been concern about the pressures that the system places upon children and how this may be detrimental to them learning.

There has been a great deal of research on the positive effects of pre-school education and how those children who have been fortunate enough to have had this fare better when they start school. A major criticism of the National Curriculum is that it does not take into account a child's pre-school experience when carrying out the assessment tests at age 7. Thus, the results of one school may be far better than those of another school because the majority of the children at the school with the better results had experienced pre-school education. The voucher system introduced desirable learning outcomes as the basis for pre-school learning. From September 1998, children will be given baseline assessment tests when they start school in order to plan for their educational needs.

The Act places a responsibility upon schools to publish the National Curriculum test results in the school prospectus in the form of statistics (not by individual pupil name), and this inevitably results in competition between schools.

Local Management of Schools

Under section 33 of the Act each local education authority had to present schemes whereby the management of schools was devolved to the governing body and head-teacher for all secondary schools and primary schools with more than 200 pupils. Although nursery schools are exempt, nursery classes attached to primary schools are not exempt. Hand-in-hand with local management goes a number of delegated powers which were given to governing bodies in order to carry out the management role. Although this section of the Act is referring to budgeting and accounting procedures, it does have implications for staffing, resources and the maintenance of school buildings. Schools were also given the option of opting out of local authority control and obtaining their budget directly from the government. At the outset this option looked attractive as the government budget was far in excess of that being given to schools by local authorities. However, in the fullness of time, there has been a number of problems encountered by schools that have 'opted out', particularly in cases where there is a clash between governors and the headteacher.

School governors are often ill-equipped to deal with their new delegated duties and powers and in spite of numerous training courses for governors, some are still finding the situation difficult. More recently, there have been large numbers of school governors resigning because they are unable to cope with the very large workload that is now part of a governor's role. It must be remembered that being a school governor is a voluntary activity and many school governors also have full-time employment.

Where resources have been limited there have been rises in class pupil numbers in order to attract higher funding. In some cases, cost-cutting has meant the appointment of an unqualified classroom assistant to work in the nursery rather than a qualified nursery nurse. Some schools which are on very tight budgets have had to cut back on the provision of consumable goods such as books, paper and pencils.

Whilst there is a lot to be said for a school holding its own budget, if that budget is calculated in such a way as to be insufficient for the smooth running of the school, the governors then find themselves in the unenviable position of having to make decisions which may weigh one group of pupils against another.

Maintenance of school buildings has also been a bone of contention, particularly when local authorities have only calculated budgets on the basis of minor building works rather than offering larger sums for major building. Many school buildings are old and rundown and have reached the time when a major investment is required to bring them up to standard. This has been recognized by the present government which has ring-fenced large sums of money for the repair of old buildings.

As the Local Management of Schools system settles, we find more families agreeing to pay voluntary contributions for school outings, books, computers and other equipment to aid their children's learning. In schools in areas where unemployment and poverty are high and parents are unable to provide voluntary contributions, the children are likely to have to go without some of the things that children in more affluent areas may have. The Act clearly states that parents cannot be charged for their children to go on outings or for other educational services; however, many schools would have to forgo such visits if they were unable to rely on the voluntary contributions made by parents.

Education Act 1993 (now incorporated into the Education Act 1996)

This Act covers the Code of Practice on the Identification and Assessment of Special Educational Needs. The Code of Practice is one of the guiding principles of the Early Years Development Plans. (The Principles of the Code of Practice can be found in Ch. 5.) The Code lays down a five-stage assessment model towards the early identification of children with special educational needs.

Stage 1

The trigger for this stage is that a child is showing signs of having special educational needs and the evidence for that concern may come from a teacher, parent, health visitor or social services. The Special Educational Needs Co-ordinator (SENCO) then places the child on the school's Special Educational Needs Register. The child's needs are assessed, and advice and support are given to the child's teacher in order to give the child special help within the child's normal curriculum. A review date is set to monitor the child's progress. The outcome of the review may be:

- that the child's progress is satisfactory and the child is set specific targets and left at Stage 1
- that the child no longer needs special help
- that the child has had two Stage 1 reviews and is not making progress so this will trigger Stage 2.

Stage 2

The SENCO takes the lead in Stage 2 and after discussions with the child's parents/carers, teacher, and other agencies involved with the child draws up an Individual Education Plan (IEP) for the child. The child's progress is monitored and at the review the outcome may be:

- that the child is making satisfactory progress but needs to stay at Stage 2
- the child has made extremely good progress and can revert back to Stage 1 monitoring
- the child has had two Stage 2 reviews and is not making progress so moves to Stage 3.

Stage 3

It is at this stage that the school is able to get specialist external support for the child. The SENCO continues to take the leading role. The school may get help from a variety of agencies such as the behaviour support service, hearing or visually impaired unit, or educational psychologist. Another IEP is drawn up for the child which, wherever possible, can take place in the child's normal classroom setting. A review date is set to monitor the child's progress and the people giving the specialist input attend the review. The outcome of the review may be:

- the child is making satisfactory progress and can stay at Stage 3
- the child has made extremely good progress and can revert to Stage 2
- the child has made little progress and after two reviews is referred by the headteacher to the LEA for statutory assessment.

Stage 4 (Statutory Assessment of Special Educational Needs)

First, the LEA working with the child's school, parents and other agencies involved with the child carefully consider whether statutory assessment of the child's needs is necessary. If the answer is positive (Yes), then the LEA goes ahead and arranges the assessment. Before the assessment takes place, the LEA must write to the parents/carers explaining its proposal, informing them of the procedure, give them the name of the LEA officer who can give further information and the procedure for the parents to implement their rights to make representations and submit written evidence. The local authority also has to notify social services, the district health authority and the headteacher at the child's school. There must only be a total of 26 weeks between the date when the statutory assessment is first considered and the finalizing statement is issued. If a decision is made not to issue a statement, the LEA must write to inform the parents/carers and tell them that they have a right to appeal to a tribunal.

Stage 5

This is when the child's statement has been issued. The statement sets out the child's special educational needs and what special provision the child needs to help the child's future education. The statement is a legal document and commits the local authority to providing the specialized help and making the additional resources available to enable this to happen. The statement must be reviewed annually.

The Code of Practice requires each school to have a policy on children with special educational needs. This also applies to all pre-school establishments that take 4-year-olds. The policy document will usually have the establishment's intentions stated under the following headings:

- Introduction – which cites the Education Act 1993 (1996)
- Admission policy of the school – in relation to children with special educational needs
- Identification and assessment of children with special educational needs – to include the 5 stages required in the Code
- The role of the SENCO
- How the establishment will manage provision
- The resources available
- The external support the establishment can call upon
- The monitoring policy.

In the government's document *Excellence for all Children. Meeting Special Educational Needs* (DfEE, 1997), it is made very clear that the underlying principle is inclusion of children with special educational needs within mainstream schooling wherever possible. (More information on inclusion can be found in Ch. 5.)

Dickins and Denziloe (1998) make it very clear that inclusion is children being taught together in classrooms and specialist support being brought into the school and the views of children with special educational needs being valued and acted upon. The Code of Practice and the *Excellence for all Children* documents reinforce the above definition and offer ways as to how best this can be achieved.

Early years development plans and partnerships (Child care partnerships)

In May 1997 the government announced the abolition of the nursery voucher scheme and laid down its policy and plans for early years services. The target the government set was that a good quality early education place should be provided for all 4-year-olds whose parents wanted it, free of charge, by September 1998. In order to achieve this it was necessary for local authorities to establish early years development partnerships with a wide range of representatives with early years interests. The partnership and the local authority then drew up an agreed early years development plan. The plan required the involvement of a variety of services covering education, day care and out-of-school care in order to meet the needs of the children and their parents. Local education authorities had to submit their plans to the Secretary of State by February 1998 and the plans came into force on 1st April

1998. Plans needed to take into consideration parental choice and have regard to the Code of Practice for Children with Special Needs.

Early years partnerships were already well-established in the majority of local authorities which had early years forums. Where necessary these were extended to cover representation from all interested parties. The members of early years forums were able to make important contributions to the partnerships as they often acted as watchdogs on behalf of children and their families so were able to share knowledge, ideas and expertise. By April 1998 only two local authorities had been unable to provide acceptable early years development plans.

The benefits of early years development plans are clearly stated by Stone (1997):

For the children these plans offer:
- high quality learning experiences
- continuity between their experience of learning in pre-school and school
- aid to ensure a smooth and confident transition to school
- close links between pre-school and school about individual children's needs.

Benefits for the provider:
- access to resources they would not have been able to afford
- sharing knowledge, skills and expertise
- a model of a different approach to early years work
- mutual recognition of the value of different services
- assistance with planning and record keeping.

Benefits to the local authority:
- improvement in the quality and range of local services for young children and their families
- ability to develop services that are more responsive to the needs of the community
- possibility of replicating successful schemes
- more effective use of resources
- lessons to inform future developments.

Potential members of the partnerships are schools (nursery, infant, primary, special) pre-school/playgroups (statutory, voluntary, private), day nurseries and family centres (statutory, voluntary, private). Added to this list could be parents, school governors and other representatives from the users' side. The early years development plans indicate some very innovative systems for providing child care, such as schools and playgroups working together, social services and education in partnership, and voluntary agencies working together to support children with special needs. All early years development plans must also have a section on training in which providers state how they will identify staff training needs and how they will ensure that these needs are met.

Sex Discrimination Act 1975

This Act prohibits people discriminating against a person on the grounds of sex in the areas of employment, housing, education and in the provision of goods and services. The body responsible for administering the Act is the Equal Opportunities Commission which has the power to investigate alleged discrimination. The Act applies to both men and women.

There is also an Equal Pay Act 1972 which relates to equal pay being given for like work, irrespective of the sex of the worker. There is often confusion between the two Acts and even lawyers have difficulty in distinguishing them. The two Acts cannot be read together as they do not represent a cohesive body of legislation.

Both of these Acts are relevant to those who provide services, e.g. child care. As the field of child care and education is dominated by females, extra efforts need to be made to ensure that the few males working in the field do not get treated differently. Differences in treatment may not always be negative; e.g. expecting female child care workers to change nappies but allowing male child care workers to be exempt from this task would be unlawful under the Sex Discrimination Act. Men entering the field of child care should undertake the same tasks as women and have exactly the same job descriptions. Conversely, always asking the men to move furniture or undertake the heavier tasks in the nursery or playgroup would also be unlawful.

Figure 8.2
Men running a crèche.

Gender issues in child care

Gender stereotyping begins at an early age and research has shown that it is detrimental to both sexes. Girls are affected by their relatively poor development of mathematical and spatial concepts, whilst boys suffer in their emotional development by being expected to react in an emotionally different way from girls. Child care workers must make concerted efforts to ensure that gender stereotyping does not take place in their establishments and this may require them to take affirmative action to overcome the problem. Such action will involve changing their language and attitudes, providing resources and activities for children that are not gender-specific and encouraging all children to participate in *all* the activities provided.

A more detailed account of gender issues in the early years can be found in Chapter 3.

Figure 8.3
Girls must be given the chance to use all available equipment.

Sex Offenders Act 1997

The details of this Act can be found in Chapter 7.

Disability Discrimination Act 1995

This Act gives disabled people new rights in the areas of:

- *obtaining goods, services and facilities*
- *buying or renting land or property*
- *employment.*

Under the Act disability is defined as physical or mental impairment which has substantial and long-term adverse effects on a person's ability to carry out normal day-to-day activities. (The main meaning of long-term is lasting or being likely to last at least 12 months.)

Under the Act discrimination occurs when:

- a disabled person is treated less favourably than someone else
- the treatment is for a reason relating to the person's disability
- this treatment cannot be justified.

Discrimination also occurs where:

- there is failure to make a reasonable adjustment for a disabled person
- that failure cannot be justified.

Making reasonable adjustments in the provision of services is to be phased in over a number of years.

It is to be noted that in the section of the Act which covers goods, facilities and services, public vehicles and providing education are exempt from the Act. Also there may be limited circumstances when it is not always possible to give disabled people the same service as other people, e.g. if it would endanger the health and safety of any person including the disabled person. It is also possible to give disabled people more favourable treatment than others, e.g. football clubs can reserve pitch-side places for wheelchair users. In the terms of the employment aspects of the Act this only applies to those companies which have over 20 employees.

Since the implementation date of the Disability Discrimination Act 1995 (2nd December 1996) people are no longer registered as disabled under the Disabled Persons (Employment) Act 1944. Under the 1944 Act, employers were required to operate a quota scheme for employing registered disabled people; that quota scheme ceased with the implementation of the 1995 Act.

Whilst child care workers may not be directly affected by the Act in their daily work situation, parents/carers of the children may need to know about the Act and where they can get information. Anything which is able to enhance the lifestyle of the parents will have a positive spin-off on the lifestyle of their children.

Assignments

Assignment 1A

(For those working in inner city areas)
Find out which ethnic/cultural groups reside in the locality of your workplace. Write a list of the ways in which your establishment provides positive experiences for children from those ethnic groups. Suggest ways in which the provision could be enhanced.

Assignment 1B

(For those in rural areas)
It is probable that you have few, if any, children from ethnic groups in your establishment. However, it is important that the children in your care gain positive attitudes towards people from different cultures. Write down how best you could achieve this and then discuss with your manager how this could be incorporated into your day-to-day practice.

Assignment 2

Obtain a copy of your local authority guidelines for implementing the Children Act. Study this thoroughly, write down the points that you do not understand and discuss these with your line manager.

Assignment 3A

(For those working with under-5s)
Look at the desirable learning outcomes and analyse 1 week's activities and link these with the desirable learning outcomes. Devise a leaflet for parents explaining how these activities are preparing their children for baseline assessment.

Assignment 3B

(For those working within the National Curriculum key stage 1)
The children in your care will be preparing or working towards their key stage 1 assessments in the National Curriculum. Find out about the attainment targets for key stage 1 and describe how these link with the weekly timetable of activities in your classroom.

Assignment 4

Good child care practice does not discriminate between 'girls' activities' and 'boys' activities'. However, research has shown that when boys and girls play together in the home corner they fall into stereotypical societal roles, the girl cooking and the boy waiting for his meal! Carry out a series of observations of children playing in the home corner and record your findings. Do you think, as Browne and France (1986) (and see Ch. 3) advocate, that home corners perpetuate stereotypical roles? If your observations show that Browne and France are correct, how can you change the situation?

REFERENCES AND FURTHER READING

Race relations

Brown, B. (1990) *All our Children.* London: BBC Education.

Brown, B. (1998) *Unlearning Discrimination in the Early Years* Stoke: Trentham Books.

Cellestin, N. (1986) *A Guide to Anti-Racist Childcare Practice.* London: VOLCUF.

Coard, B. (1971) *How the West Indian Child is made Educationally Subnormal in the British School System.* London: New Beacon Books.

Cohen, P. (1997) *Forbidden Games.* Working Paper 5. London: Centre for New Ethnicities Research University of East London.

Commission for Racial Equality. (1996) *From Cradle to School: A Practical Guide to Race Equality in Early Childhood Education and Care.* London: CRE.

Derman-Sparks and the ABC Task Force. (1989) *Anti-bias Curriculum: Tools for Empowering Young Children.* National Association for the Education of Young Children. Washington DC: (UK Distributor: National Early Years Network.)

Elfer, P. (Ed.) (1995) *With Equal Concern.* London: National Children's Bureau.

Hazareesingh, S., Simms, K. and Anderson, P. (1989) *Educating the Whole Child.* London: Building Blocks.

Maxime, J. E. (1987) *Black Like Me: Black Identity.* Emani Publications

Milner, D. (1983) *Children and Race: Ten Years On.* London: Ward Lock Educational.

National Early Years Network. (1995) *Playing Fair: a parents guide to tackling discrimination.* London: National Early Years Network.

Race Relations Act. (1976) London: HMSO.

Siraj-Blatchford, I. (1994) *The Early Years: Laying the foundations for racial equality.* Stoke: Trentham Books.

Smith, P. and Berridge, D. (1993) *Ethnicity and Childcare Placements.* London: National Children's Bureau.

Children Act

Allen, N. (1991) *Making Sense of the Children Act 1989.* Harlow: Longman.

Children Act 1989 London: HMSO.

Cowley, L. (1993) *Registration and Inspection of Daycare for Young Children.* London: National Children's Bureau.

Department of Health. (1989) *An Introduction to the Children Act 1989.* London: HMSO.

Department of Health. (1989) *Working Together: Under the Children Act 1989.* London: HMSO.

Department of Health (1991) The Children Act Guidance and Regulations. Volume 2: *Family Support, Day Care and Educational Provision for Young Children.* Volume 3: *Family Placements.* Volume 6: *Children with Disabilities.* London: HMSO.

Department of Health. (1998) *Working Together to Safeguard Children: New government proposals for inter-agency co-operation.* Consultation Paper. London: HMSO.

Gunner, A. (1997) *The Children (Scotland) Act 1995.* Highlight No. 152. London: National Children's Bureau.

National Children's Bureau *Working with the Children Act 1989.* London: National Children's Bureau.

Smith, F. and Lyon, T. (1991) *Personal Guide to the Children Act 1989.* London: Children Act Enterprises.

Sutton, P. (1995) *Crossing the Boundaries. A*

discussion of Children's Service Plans. London: National Children's Bureau.

N. Ireland

Commission for Racial Equality for Northern Ireland. (1997) *Advice and Assistance from the Commission*. Belfast: Commission for Racial Equality Northern Ireland.

Department of Economic Development. (1989) *Fair Employment in Northern Ireland: Key Details of the Act*. Belfast: Department of Economic Development.

Fair Employment (Northern Ireland) Act. (1989) London: HMSO.

Horgan, G. (1997) *The Children (Northern Ireland) Order*. Highlight No. 153. London: National Children's Bureau.

Northern Ireland Council for Educational Development. (1988) *Education for Mutual Understanding*. Belfast: NICED.

Education Reform Act

Davies B. and Braund, C. (1989) *Local Management of Schools*. Plymouth: Northcote House.

Department for Education and Employment. (1997) *Early Years Development Partnerships and Plans. Guidance 1998/1999*. London: DfEE.

Department for Education and Employment/Department of Health. (1996) *Children's Services Planning: Guidance*. London: DfEE.

Department for Education and Employment. (1998) *Education Development Plans. Local Education Authorities Plans to Promote Improved Standards of Pupil Performance. Draft Guidance for Consultation*. London: DfEE.

Department of Education and Science. (1988) *Education Reform Act*. London: HMSO.

Department of Education and Science. (1988) *Education Reform Act: Local Management of Schools*. DES Circular 7/88. London: DES.

Stone, J. (1997) *Progress with Partnerships. How partnerships contribute to Early Years Services*. London: DfEE/National Early Years Network.

Sex Discrimination

Adams, C. and Laurikietis, R. (1980) *The Gender Trap: Book 3 Messages and Images*. London: Virago.

Aspinwall, K. (1984) *What are Little Girls Made of? What are Little Boys Made of?* London: National Nursery Examination Board.

Belotti, G. (1975) *Little Girls*. Aylesbury: Writers and Readers Publishing Co-Operative.

Browne, N. and France, P. (1986) *Untying the Apron Strings: Anti-sexist Provision for the Under Fives*. Milton Keynes: Open University Press.

Equal Pay Act. (1972). London: HMSO.

First Reflections. (1986) *Equal Opportunities in the Early Years*. London: ILEA.

Grabrucker, M. (1988) *There's a Good Girl: Gender Stereotyping in the First Three Years of Life*. London: Women's Press.

Mullin, B. Morgan, V. and Dunn, S. (1986) *Gender Differentiation in Infant Classes*. Coleraine: Equal Opportunities Commission N.Ireland.

Sex Discrimination Act. (1975) London: HMSO.

Sharpe, S. (1987) 'Just Like a Girl.' Harmondsworth: Pelican.

Spender, D. (1982) *Invisible Women: the Schooling Scandal*. London: Writers and Readers Publishing.

Walkerdine, V. (1989) *Counting Girls Out:*

Girls and Mathematics Unit Institute of Education. London: Virago.

Whyte, J. (1983) *Beyond the Wendy House: Sex Role Stereotyping in Primary Schools.* Harlow: Longman.

Special Educational Needs

Dare, A. and O' Donovan, M. (1997) *Good Practice in Caring for Young Children with Special Needs.* Cheltenham: Stanley Thornes.

Department for Education and Employment. (1994) *Code of Practice on the Identification and Assessment of Special Educational Needs.* London: DfEE.

Department for Education and Employment. (1997) *Excellence for all Children. Meeting Special Educational Needs.* London: The Stationery Office.

Dickins, M. and Denziloe, J. (1998) *All Together – how to create inclusive services for disabled children and their families.* London: National Early Years Network.

Mason, M. and Davies, A. (1993) *Inclusion: the way forward: a guide to integration for young disabled children.* Starting Points

Series No. 15. London: National Early Years Network.

Wilson, R. (1998) *Special Educational Needs in the Early Years.* London: Routledge.

Wolfendale, S. (Ed.) (1997) *Meeting Special Needs in the Early Years.* London: David Foulton.

Disability Discrimination Act

Department for Education and Employment. (1996) *Disability on the agenda. The Disability Discrimination Act 1995 – a guide for everybody.* (DL160) *What Service Providers Need to Know.* (DL150) *What Employers Need to Know.* (DL170) London: DfEE.

General

Newell, P. (1991) *The UN Convention and Children's Rights in the UK.* London: National Children's Bureau

9: Aspects of Children's Behaviour

Objectives	• Behaviour policies	• Play tutoring
	• Positive and negative behaviour	• Play therapy
	• Discipline, goals and boundary setting	• Empowering children
	• Promoting positive behaviour	• Specific behaviours
	• Techniques for problem behaviour	

Links

This chapter has links with:
- NVQ (EYCE) Units: C7, C4.
- CACHE Diploma Module E.

Introduction

The *Concise Oxford Dictionary* defines behaviour as 'manners, moral conduct, treatment shown to or towards others'. This implies that there is an element of judgement that we use when talking of a person's behaviour, based on our own standards, attitudes and values as well as our training and experience. When dealing with children this is particularly so, and workers continually make judgements regarding children based on the child's observable behaviour. Everyone who works with children has to learn to cope with all sorts of difficult and damaging behaviour which can range from children who are tired or having an 'off' day to very serious self-destructive behaviour with a variety of potentially worrying root causes. Most settings have a 'behaviour policy' and this helps workers to know what is acceptable and how to respond.

'Behaviour' covers everything children do and is one of the principal means by which we can recognize what they are thinking, feeling and experiencing. Behaviour is linked to their stage of development, personality and capacity to cope. Generally we have to be tolerant of many different types of behaviour and usually only become concerned when we see extremes or damaging behaviour. Children who are happy, loved, healthy and well adjusted will sometimes display difficult behaviour temporarily in response to specific situations but more often they will relate well to others and behave in a positive manner. Other children with a different life experience or who may have particular problems, e.g. learning difficulties or food sensitivity, can sometimes behave in very negative ways and where this is the dominant behaviour over time, workers are alerted and concerned.

Although some behaviour in the newborn is innate, e.g. searching for the nipple and sucking, the vast majority of human behaviour is learned in the same way as any other activity. Children learn through their senses and through exploring and experimenting with their world. They also learn through modelling (copying) the behaviour of adults and others who are important to them (see Ch. 1). Children learn that certain types of behaviour are usually rewarded in some way, e.g. with a smile or hug. Conversely, they learn that other forms of behaviour receive a frown or result in cross words or in some cases a smack. Children usually want to please those who care for them, especially if they have a good relationship, and over a period of time they learn how to behave in ways which adults will reward. If adults are inconsistent and change from day to day, children become confused and uncertain of how to behave and what will be acceptable.

Adults' expectations of children's behaviour have to be realistic and linked to the child's stage of development and particular needs. As an example, it is rare for toddlers willingly to share their toys as they are more concerned with what they themselves want and are naturally 'self-centred' at this age. Expecting toddlers to share is unrealistic, but adults should model sharing behaviour and encourage young children when they begin to learn to share. Adults sometimes worry that they are spoiling their baby when they attend promptly to its needs even though it is unlikely that a baby less than 1 year can be spoilt in the usual sense of the word. Young babies should not be punished as if they have been deliberately naughty when, at this age, intense curiosity and attention-seeking behaviour are reasonable and normal. Judgements concerning behavioural issues must always be based on a sound knowledge and understanding of child development, on careful observations and assessments of the child, and in consultation with parents and other professionals.

Behaviour policies

Behaviour policies are now common and provide a useful framework for workers to interpret what is acceptable and when action needs to be taken. The National Children's Bureau (1991) states:

A policy should be drawn up which clearly identifies the types of behaviour which are regarded as unacceptable from a child, and how staff will respond if this occurs.

A behaviour policy protects both children and staff as it should clearly state not only when action will be taken but also the type of action, e.g. it will exclude the use of physical punishment, depriving or forcing children to take in food or drink, and frightening or humiliating children

Scenario 9.1

You are a new nursery manager and have been asked by the management committee to draw up a behaviour policy.

- Draw up a draft behaviour policy.
- Discuss its contents with colleagues, parents and children.
- Record their views and how you incorporated these into the policy.
- Evaluate the effect of the policy after 3 months of use.

Positive behaviour

Deciding what is positive behaviour for a child can be very subjective. In general, our society values independent, individualistic and self-assertive people who are able to exercise personal autonomy and decision-making. However, there are cultural groups within society who are more likely to stress co-operation and interdependence. It is important, therefore, that workers consider the social and cultural background of the families of the children in their care and do not impose a set of behavioural expectations and values which may be inappropriate and out of context for today's pluralist society. This means that all workers should be aware of their own values and attitudes. There are, however, many universally-accepted, positive aspects of behaviour and these should be encouraged, e.g. sharing, turn-taking, considering others and showing caring and empathetic behaviour. It is important that children should be able to negotiate and see other points of view. Another goal for our children is that they should learn to handle their emotions and cope with difficulties and stresses. This can be encouraged by adults modelling such behaviour in day-to-day activity and rewarding children through praise and encouragement when they follow suit. Some nurseries play games designed to encourage co-operation and pro-social behaviour and provide toys and equipment that are not likely to encourage aggressive play.

Figure 9.1
Strong emotion.

Negative behaviour

Negative behaviour is that which affects others negatively or is personally uncon-structive for the child concerned. Children who withdraw, seek attention inappro-priately, are self-damaging and anti-social are exhibiting negative behaviour. Negative behaviour includes verbal and physical aggression, tantrums, urinating or soiling clothes, self-mutilation such as biting or head banging, running around out of control, breath holding and ignoring instructions.

Treating all children equally is a mistake as children vary and should be treated dif-ferently according to their individual needs. This is not the same as preferential treat-ment. Workers should be calm and controlled themselves as this helps the child to gain control.

This chapter looks at some common aspects of behaviour, which can be worrying, and the techniques that are sometimes used to deal with them. It does not consider deep-seated and intransigent behavioural disorders that require specialized help. It is sometimes very difficult to know when particular behaviour has gone beyond the point at which staff can cope with it and when specialized help is needed. With all the forms of behaviour discussed below, it is possible they may become so extreme and so bizarre that outside help is needed.

Outside agencies

There are a variety of statutory or voluntary agencies that can be involved in helping the child and family. These will vary according to local availability, the age of the child and the severity and nature of the problem. They may include the following:

- *Child and family guidance*
- *Family therapy clinics*
- *Educational psychologists*
- *Social services*
- *Health visitors*
- *Hospital psychiatric departments*
- *Speech therapists*
- *Child and family assessment centres.*

Factors linked to problem behaviour

Behavioural problems are not usually related to one factor only but to several, of which the following constitute a sample.

Physical

- Reactions to additives and foods which may lead to hyperactive and aggressive behaviour.
- Poor diet.
- Tiredness or hunger exacerbate difficult behaviour.
- Physical illness may be linked to regressive behaviour where the child behaves as if at an earlier stage of development.
- Lack of exercise and fresh air.
- Sensory impairment may contribute to frustration and lead to problem behaviour.
- Problems and frustrations associated with poor physical skills.
- Physical or sexual abuse or neglect.

Socio-emotional

- Children who lack love, care and acceptance.
- Children under stress of all kinds may regress and/or show behavioural symptoms such as withdrawing or becoming aggressive.

- Family difficulties such as parents' separation or arrival of a new sibling.
- Poor self-esteem or lack of confidence.
- Excessive fears, phobias or anxieties.
- Poverty and deprivation may exacerbate existing behavioural problems but are unlikely to be the sole cause.
- Poor social skills.
- Emotional abuse or neglect.

Cognitive and language

- *Poor language skills to express feelings and anger.*
- *Restricted vocabulary.*
- *Learning difficulties.*
- *Lack of concentration.*
- *Boredom.*
- *Over-stimulation.*
- *Constant failures.*

Environmental

- *Lack of play opportunities.*
- *Lack of space.*
- *Noise and no opportunity for quiet play.*
- *No privacy.*

Discipline, goals for behaviour and boundary-setting

Discipline, goals for behaviour and boundary-setting are necessary to provide children with a secure framework of rules, which they can understand and which are necessary to ensure that they learn consideration for others, and how to behave in a constructive manner for themselves. Rules and breaches of rules should be discussed calmly with children as appropriate to their level of understanding. A child learns rules and is most likely to accept them if they are applied fairly and consistently and in a caring context where the child is loved and accepted for itself not just for good behaviour. Also behaviour is learned and children will copy adults who are important to them. Goals for behaviour must take into account children's memory and understanding which vary with their age. The goal for children is to learn self-discipline without the need to have external discipline imposed upon them. How long this takes varies from child to child according to their level of maturity and life experiences. In a few tragic cases, children never seem to learn and become disturbed, anti-social adults.

Most children learn right from wrong very early and around the age of 3 years may experience guilt when they disobey the rules. For the majority of children, by the time they are in school their conscience is well and truly in place. They may not always understand why rules are there but they feel bad when they break them. Some children who have particular problems, either developmental or environmental, take longer to reach this stage, especially if they have poor attachments to adults. Some children are used as scapegoats because they always seem to feel guilty and take the blame even when they are not in the wrong. This can derive from the home or other setting when adults tend to blame one child constantly for the family ills until that child actually believes it is always in the wrong. This is very damaging, and children who are scapegoats will suffer until the situation is dealt with.

Forms of discipline

The form that discipline should take depends on the stage of development of the child, its personality and level of maturity. Adults may have a variety of styles of discipline and different tolerance levels but should not be extreme. Adults who are warm and caring towards a child may be either permissive or authoritarian in their style of discipline, but usually the child is responsive and wanting to please. Where adults are negative and uncaring towards children, the child will be confused and often aggressive and uncontrolled. If children are too strictly disciplined in a home where there is little warmth, they may repress their anger and frustration and become withdrawn and unco-operative.

All discipline should be consistently applied and directly related to the unwanted behaviour and should be applied at the time of the behaviour, not much later when the child cannot remember the incident. The discipline should focus on the unwanted behaviour not on the child, e.g. it is better to say 'I don't like what you have done', rather than 'You're a very naughty girl.'

Physical

Physical discipline can take many forms and varies in severity from a beating with a strap or other instrument to a light tap on the hand. At present there is no legislation in this country to stop parents physically punishing their children, but recent cases taken to international courts indicate a slow change of attitude which may eventually lead to a change in the law. In many group settings the law bans physical punishment. Many workers feel that to punish a child physically is a violation of human rights and no better than common assault. As a result of this, other forms of non-physical discipline and boundary-setting are more widely used and are very effective when applied consistently, fairly and with the child's full understanding, taking into account stage of development.

Children who are consistently smacked for various reasons are often driven to worse forms of behaviour and can become very skilled at hiding their behaviour; e.g. if they are smacked for stealing, they learn quickly how not to get caught. Children are also thought to learn how to be physically violent and aggressive by watching adults who act in this way.

Non-physical

Children are all different and there are no hard and fast rules regarding discipline. For most children being deprived of a favourite television programme, toys or foods, or being sent to bed early can work, and sometimes these are useful. They are more effective if the child concerned has a clear understanding of the rules and is used to being praised and rewarded for good behaviour at other times. Children who are secure and loved will generally accept these forms of discipline as being fair although they will grumble at the time.

Scenario 9.2

Luke is 3 years old and attends nursery part-time. His behaviour is erratic and changeable and he often appears out of control. Luke's parents say that he gets a good telling off or a smack when he is naughty and that nursery staff should smack him too as it is the only time he takes any notice.

Role play an interview between Luke's parents and nursery staff to try to discuss the ways in which his behaviour can be managed both at home and in the nursery.

Write a letter to new parents explaining the nursery's policy on physical punishment.

General principles when promoting positive behaviour

If children are well treated, loved and cared for and have all their basic needs met, it is unlikely they will exhibit serious problem behaviour except on a temporary basis. There are, of course, exceptions and it is a mistake to assume that all children who display challenging behaviour are unloved or not cared for.

The following general principles underpin much work with children and are guidelines for good practice. They are often common sense and used in many therapeutic approaches and different situations.

- *Praising and rewarding positive behaviour.*
- *Playing down negative behaviour within a framework of safety and consideration for others.*
- *Providing safe and consistently applied boundaries.*
- *Remaining calm and controlled, i.e. adults acting as positive role models.*
- *Modelling positive ways of behaving back to the child or within the group.*
- *Discussing issues with older children.*
- *Distracting, not confronting, young children.*
- *Giving children the language to use to express themselves.*
- *Providing a caring and safe environment where a child is accepted for itself.*
- *Providing a stimulating and developmentally appropriate curriculum.*
- *Providing equipment and materials through which children can 'play out' their strong feelings.*
- *Giving attention on a one-to-one basis wherever possible.*
- *Meeting basic needs for love, care and personal attention.*

Specific techniques for problem behaviour

Children's hours/timeout

Children's hours are special times given to individual children, usually on a one-to-one basis. They are based on the writings of Dr Rachel Pinney and have been further developed by Bray (1989) and others. They are now used in the management of difficult behaviour, sometimes with abused children, and take the view that all children need attention and if they do not have their emotional needs met, they will devise other strategies for gaining adult attention.

The original children's hours took place with one adult and one child. During that time the child was allowed to do whatever it wished and make its own decisions and choices in order to prevent the adult imposing limits.

The 'hour' can be a shorter or longer period according to circumstances but children should know in advance how much time they will be getting. During this time the adult focuses on the child and comments on the child's activity without judging or interpreting. Within this framework the adult decides on what is unacceptable behaviour, usually on the basis of safety and what individual adults can tolerate. The process is therapeutic and enriching for the child as the child is allowed to be itself with an adult's full attention. There is no need, therefore, for attention-seeking strategies.

Workers using this technique have found that children work through aspects of their difficulties in these sessions and become more secure. As a result, the difficult and demanding behaviour often improves.

Positive reinforcement programmes

Positive reinforcement is based on the work of Skinner and other behaviourists who state that punishments become unnecessary if rewards are carefully and appropriately applied. This is not the same as bribing a child with sweets or outings, and concentrates on reinforcing only those aspects of behaviour which are wanted. Behaviourists such as Skinner suggest that the unwanted behaviour, if not rewarded, will diminish and eventually disappear.

Positive reinforcement techniques can be very effective and vary from carefully worked out regimes of rewards organized by psychologists and other specialists to simple techniques such as rewarding good behaviour by ordinary staff working with young children. Rewards may consist of praise, a hug or expression of pleasure from the parent or worker (see Ch. 1).

Many settings will take a positive approach across the whole class or group and consistently apply the principles of praise for wanted behaviour as a matter of routine. This can be very effective at preventing unwanted behaviour. An effective programme may use the following sequence:

- *Give clear and unambiguous directions to the group.*
- *Look for a child who is following the directions.*
- *Say the child's name and repeat the directions.*
- *Give positive comment back to the child, e.g. 'Liam, you're clearing up the sand. That's really helpful.'*

When applying this strategy, staff have to be pro-active and to look for the behaviour they want; they have to move about the room, and immediately and frequently make positive comments. There will still be individual children who need additional attention and this should be built into their programme.

Play tutoring

Play tutoring is where adults become involved with children's play (see Ch. 2). The aim is to extend and to enrich the play in order that the child should develop healthy and socially acceptable ways of dealing with feelings. Play tutoring can take several

| Scenario 9.3 |

Kirsten is 3 years of age and has been at nursery since she was a baby. You are her key worker and are aware she is a poor eater, will not eat her meals except for dessert and will not use cutlery. During meal-times, Kirsten gets a good deal of negative staff attention and is obviously tense.

How could you use positive rewards to help Kirsten and encourage her to relax at meal-times and enjoy her food?

forms. Sometimes it is useful to assist in the development and extension of imaginative play: here adults can take on a role in the play scenario or can provide ideas and props without taking on a role in the dramatic sequence.

Adults may accompany a child at play or through a period of time when they may be involved in non-play activity. During this time the adult comments on the activity and acts as the child's externalized conscience. Using simple comment and offering insights to the child as well as praise and reward can have a positive effect, even on deeply disturbed children. Play tutoring gives the child a good deal of personal attention as the member of staff usually works with the child on a one-to-one basis.

Play therapy

There are many forms of play therapy. It is a form of therapy widely used in hospital and other therapeutic settings and is based on the idea that children can 'play out' their hidden fears, anxieties and aggressions (see Ch. 6). Play therapists in these settings often have post-basic training and a deep knowledge and understanding of child development and behaviour. They usually work as part of a multi-disciplinary team and have their own area of expertise.

Play therapy can draw on many of the techniques mentioned in this chapter and will modify them appropriately. It relies, as its name suggests, primarily on play, and therapists will supply a wide range of play experience for children; e.g. children in hospital may be given 'medical' props such as masks, gowns, stethoscopes, syringes and dolls to help their imaginative play and the play therapist might act as a play tutor in this case.

Empowering children

Empowering children is an important part of the therapeutic process as well as being a positive goal for all children. Children should be given a sense of control over their lives and ownership of their environment. This can be done by allowing them freedom and choice within firm boundaries of safety and consideration for others.

Empowering children through positive action programmes is also an effective technique. This is useful for many children but can be used to help victims of discrimination or abuse to become more assertive through raising their self-esteem and self-confidence. Examples of this technique are valuing cultural diversity and countering children's racial and gender stereotypes through activities which show positive acceptance of difference, and encouraging activities, e.g., which allow girls to be seen as strong and active and boys to be serious and reflective.

Teaching children basic social skills and ways of dealing with their feelings which are socially acceptable is very important. This means showing children, by example, different ways in which conflicts and squabbles can be resolved without resorting to physical violence. It also involves giving children the words and language to use to defend themselves, and techniques of assertiveness, not aggression. It should include other forms of representation such as drama. The provision of playthings that can facilitate the release of tension and aggression is also helpful.

Encouraging children to talk through difficulties and to express themselves through play and creative activities is useful. Adults should create an environment where children can be themselves and know they are loved and accepted even when their behaviour is less than perfect. Children are then more able to take risks and experiment by breaking old habits and learning new forms of relating to others; this will build their self-esteem and help to reduce self-destructive behaviour.

Specific behaviours

Spoilt children

The term 'spoilt children' is very emotive and frequently leads to judgemental attitudes concerning the child. The usual meaning of the term is a child who is used to having its own way in the home and to having toys and playthings on demand. Often these children cannot tolerate any delay in having their demands attended to, and will behave in an anti-social manner if they do have to wait. In general it is better to avoid labelling a child using this destructive term and to concentrate on any specific problems they may have. Such children often have to learn how to share and to take their turn; this can be a painful experience for them, and their behaviour often makes them unpopular with others. Spoilt children are often fearful of the power they appear to wield over the parents and become insecure as a result. Some 'spoilt' children are 'hurried' children who are encouraged to grow up too quickly and are pressured to succeed. These children are fearful of failure and may develop problems in coping with the adult world.

Coping with spoilt children

Staff should avoid punitive attitudes towards children they consider spoilt. They should explain why the answer has to be 'no' on occasions and should attempt to get the child to understand the effect that self-centred behaviour has on others. As well as being firm, consistent and fair, staff should concentrate on positive features and praise the child when it shows consideration for others or is willing to share. These children should be encouraged to make small decisions for themselves to increase their feelings of autonomy. In attempting to teach them to share, adults should not be extreme but should allow the children some (not all!) of what they ask for.

Disruptive/attention-seeking behaviour

Some children are disruptive in school or nursery, constantly seek attention and cause difficulty with other children using many different strategies. Many disruptive children cannot concentrate even for short periods and their attention is easily diverted.

Coping with disruptive/attention-seeking behaviour

Early years workers have to make sure that such children are not given undue attention at the expense of other children, but at the same time that their basic needs for care and adult attention are met. Sometimes the children are simply bored and understimulated and find their daily routine and curriculum are not relevant to them or do not offer any challenge. Simple organizational changes within the setting might help such as allowing more play choices or encouraging more use of the outdoor areas. Staff should be aware of changes at home, which might affect behaviour and work with parents to improve things for the child, wherever possible. If children are anxious, providing play activities which allow them to express themselves in a safe environment is very helpful; e.g. a child who has a new sibling can find domestic play helpful, especially as the child can get angry with dolls in a way that is not possible with the sibling. Some staff use the technique of 'time out' or 'children's hours' very effectively. Others find simple positive reinforcement techniques are useful. At other times 'play tutoring' techniques have been used successfully.

Children whose disruptive behaviour continues with no apparent external cause which can be dealt with and who respond neither to the use of commonsense approaches nor to the techniques mentioned in this chapter, should be monitored carefully and assessments should be made to decide whether the children need specialist help.

Withdrawn/shy children

Young children are often shy and seem overwhelmed by new situations or when attention is drawn to them. A baby of around 9 months onwards who has become attached to significant adults will become shy with strangers. However, most children overcome their early shyness and learn to interact in a positive and social manner with others. There are certain situations that may arise through which children learn to be shy, e.g. if parents are pressurizing them to measure up to their peers or siblings. They may also respond in this way after being labelled 'stupid' or 'slow', or in response to external pressures or abuse.

Coping with withdrawn/shy children

It is important that all children are allowed their privacy but this is not the same as persistent and painful shyness. The very shy or isolated child may not develop the necessary social skills or choose not to use them and prefer to remain alone. Although this natural shyness which is part of personality should be respected, it is also important that the child should interact successfully and make good relationships with other children and with adults when they wish to do so.

It is of particular concern when a previously outgoing and sociable child suddenly becomes shy and/or withdrawn. This can be linked to a significant change in the child's life that may put the child under stress or pressure. See 'Helping the shy/unpopular child' below.

Scenario 9.4

Darren is a 4-year-old boy in a workplace crèche. He is part of the pre-school group which is beginning to take on more formal activities to prepare the children for school. As Darren's key worker, you have noticed that although he has always been a quiet, shy boy, he now appears withdrawn and unhappy. Furthermore, none of his peer group wants to sit with him and work with him during these more formal activities. He is due to start school in 3 months' time and you are concerned about his behaviour.

(a) What immediate steps could you take to help Darren?
(b) How could you involve his parents?
(c) How could you assess his state of mind and behaviour?
(d) If necessary, what agencies could you call upon?

Unpopular children

Relationships amongst pre-schoolers are often tenuous and fleeting. It is an everyday occurrence to see a child upset because 'X won't be my friend'. This rough and tumble and establishing a pecking order are normal amongst groups of children but it is important that adults do note the child who may be persistently unpopular and has few or no friends. It is possible to detect these children through looking at patterns of interaction and friendship, perhaps using tools such as the sociogram where friendships can be mapped out. If you ask children with whom they like best to play and check this over the next few days it is usually possible to see a pattern emerging with some children at the hub of the interactions and others marginalized and on the fringe.

Children may be unpopular for many reasons. Some are unpopular because they behave in an inappropriate way with their peers. They may be bossy and demanding or aggressive and rude; they may cry, whine or beg which other children ignore. In these cases it is possible to work with them and their families to try to enable them to see life from others' points of view. Positive reinforcement of their efforts should be given.

In some cases children are unpopular because of reasons over which they have little or no control. Children with disabilities or those from different cultural or ethnic groups may fall into this category because they do not conform to the norm. Other children may be unpopular and teased because they are fat or wear glasses or their families are poor and cannot afford to dress them fashionably. It is important that these situations are addressed and not ignored. Children must not be allowed to create a rejecting or discriminatory atmosphere for other children. Discussion with the perpetrators and making sure that standards are consistently maintained are vital. Parents often have to be involved where their child is a persistent offender and this can lead to a clash of values which makes life very difficult for the children concerned.

Unpopular children will often be sad and withdrawn but they can also be hostile and aggressive. When you suspect that children have no friends and may be targets for discrimination or teasing you must step in and deal with the situation.

Helping the shy/unpopular child

Shy or unpopular children need encouragement to mix and adults should allow the child to stay alongside them in new or strange situations until their confidence grows. The organization of the nursery can have significant effects on children's attitudes to one another. Their individual security should be encouraged and popular, confident children should be allowed to do the more public jobs such as giving out drinks and taking responsibility for small tasks. This encourages shy or unpopular children to model this behaviour and to take small steps forward in confidence and makes for a more tolerant and accepting attitude in the group of children. Sometimes it is useful to pair shy or unpopular children with popular children at certain times of day or to encourage their interaction with younger children who are less of a threat. Allowing the children to stay within any loose friendship groups they may have can also be very positive.

In group situations it is possible to work using positive action programmes and anti-discriminatory practice which can assist in removing stereotypes and encouraging children to be more reflective and caring. It is important to ensure that the nursery presents positive images for all children and the caring ethos ensures no child is isolated. This requires a non-judgemental attitude from staff as children will soon tune in wherever wrong attitudes exist.

Many unpopular children have poor social skills and seem to be their own worst enemies. They can be helped with social skills not only in everyday situations but in structured programmes that are designed to encourage communication, participation, co-operation and skills for supporting other people.

Temper tantrums

Many children around the age of 2 years are prone to temper tantrums. Children of this age can become very frustrated when they do not get their own way and will express their rage violently, sometimes in self-destructive ways. This is an attempt to assert themselves in a world that is full of interesting and exciting opportunities of which they would like to take part regardless of safety or consideration for others. This phase is commonly called the 'terrible two's'. Children in the throes of a tantrum are often very frightened and feel out of control. Most tantrums follow broadly the same pattern. Some children will throw themselves to the ground often in a public place and scream loudly and furiously. Others are less noisy and will include a breath-holding session until they are blue in the face. However they manifest themselves, temper tantrums are often embarrassing for parents and carers and leave behind feelings of inadequacy and inability to cope.

Most children grow out of this phase quite soon, but some children are still having tantrums at the age of 5 or 6 years. When this happens the physical size of the child is in itself a problem.

Coping with temper tantrums

There is no right way of coping with temper tantrums as situations vary. It is always better to try to avoid creating circumstances when they are likely to occur. With very young children it is important to avoid confrontations, especially in public places or when children are tired. As well as this it is important to encourage young children's sense of ownership of their environment by allowing as many choices and as much freedom as possible, e.g. homes for toddlers and young children should be geared to their needs and made safe for them to play without damaging themselves or precious possessions. They should be given opportunity for vigorous physical activity that helps them to cope with frustration. A variety of play materials and types of play are also useful such as pummelling clay or dough or acting out worrying situations through dramatic play. Children at this developmental stage and older children still prone to tantrums should be given appropriate play and learning materials with which they can succeed and not given tasks or playthings that cause them to fail and ultimately create powerful feelings based on loss of confidence and self-esteem.

No matter how careful you are, young children will still have occasional tantrums. Some people find that ignoring the situation works but this is often very difficult. Others will touch the child and talk soothingly to help the child feel safe and in control again. As children get older, the development of language and understanding gives them another vehicle to express their strong feelings and this should be encouraged. They will also become aware of their feelings building up and may regret the incident afterwards. Talking about angry feelings is often a good way of diffusing situations that are getting out of control.

Relaxation techniques can be especially useful for young children between 4 and 7 years who are easily frustrated and prone to temper tantrums. Workers can use standard relaxation techniques suitably modified for young children.

Scenario 9.5

You are working in a family centre with a group of parents and children aged 6 months to 2½ years. One mother with a baby of 1 year and a toddler of 2 years 3 months is under a good deal of stress as the baby is very active and 'into everything' and the toddler has frequent temper tantrums, sometimes several in one day. These leave the young mother exhausted and tearful. You have noticed that the mother sometimes smacks the baby's hand when the baby explores and tells her not to be naughty. She often stops her partner picking the baby up when she cries for fear of spoiling her. The mother is very dependent on her own mother and sister for help and advice.

(a) What is the best way to help this mother to understand: her baby's needs and the toddler's behaviour?
(b) What strategies would you suggest to her concerning the temper tantrums?

Angry and aggressive outbursts

Angry and aggressive outbursts are common at around age 2 years and involve wild, undirected activity closely linked to temper tantrums. After around age 3, children may become aggressive concerning playthings, privileges or territory. Older children who cannot control their angry feelings may exhibit anti-social behaviour that is more likely to be directed against other children or adults such as hair-pulling, hitting or biting. Older children may also use verbal abuse very effectively either to adults or other children. Such children do not seem able to tolerate being thwarted or have any of the usual range of strategies or social skills available to deal with difficult situations. This has to be dealt with and the child has to learn other ways of controlling the rage.

Angry outbursts may take the form of destructiveness when a child deliberately breaks objects and destroys other children's toys and constructions. Often their rage will lead them to throw things around in a furious and potentially dangerous manner. In other circumstances anger and frustration may be much more hidden, e.g. a child who plays with matches and sets things ablaze or bites and pinches when not being observed by an adult.

Coping with angry and aggressive outbursts

Dealing with angry and aggressive outbursts might be done through encouraging talk and discussion if the child is old enough and enabling the child to ask adults to help in disputes. This is far more effective if it takes place after the child calms down.

Staff should attempt to distract and avoid confrontation in similar ways to those used to deal with temper tantrums. Occasionally, when workers see a child who is about to behave aggressively, a sharp 'no' is necessary and physical removal of the child or any weapon the child is about to use. It is important that children understand that their behaviour is unacceptable, so making eye contact and a short reprimand may be effective. Giving too much time and disrupting a whole group of children to deal with the issue may become a reinforcement for the behaviour as the child will have gained a good deal of attention. For some children in this category, negative attention is better than no attention. It is also worthwhile noting what toys and playthings are around which are basically hostile in purpose and attempting to remove these. Children may also model hostile behaviour they see in adults or in the media, and care should be taken that they are not exposed to this.

Persuading children to apologize to those they have wronged has limited effect. Many children are very good at saying 'sorry' and then proceeding as if nothing has changed. However, they should see this being modelled amongst adults and should be encouraged to apologize if they seem genuinely repentant.

Scenario 9.6

You are a student nursery nurse on placement in a reception class in a primary school. At the beginning of term, 12 new children started school all aged 4 years. Alice is an only child of caring, but overprotective, parents who have very high expectations for her. Alice is not used to coping with the rough and tumble of large groups of children and is becoming increasingly upset and angry at having to share and wait her turn. She insists on being at the head of the line for playtime and pushes the other children out of the way.

- What would be the best method of dealing with Alice?
- What immediate, practical steps could you take?

Jealousy

Children can be jealous and resentful of those who they perceive as taking what is rightfully theirs or who have things they themselves want. Many children feel strong feelings of jealousy when new siblings arrive in the family: they quite accurately perceive that their own relationship with their parents will be changed. Children usually have very strong bonds with their primary carers and can resent any change in their special relationships. They may also fear that they will no longer be loved and cared for. Changing family patterns may mean that children have to cope with step-parents and their children moving in together. This can cause intense jealousies and insecurity.

Children today are bombarded with messages from a consumer society concerned with selling to them and their families. Toys and 'educational' products are a multi-million pound industry, and advertising and marketing strategies are aimed at children. Parents are pressured to feel that they are letting their child down if they do not provide the child with all these latest toys and 'educational' items. Such pressures on children and their families can lead to conflicts and jealousies that can be difficult to deal with.

Coping with jealous feelings

Specific ways of coping with jealousy depend on the source. If a child is intensely jealous of a new sibling, it will take time and patience to work with the child and their parents to overcome this. Some situations are very difficult to deal with and require careful analysis of the problem and individualized strategies. Children experiencing jealous feelings may be insecure and lacking in self-esteem and need to build up their confidence and self-worth.

It is important that children are not made to feel guilty because they are experiencing jealous feelings. Jealousy is a universal emotion and children can understand that everyone feels this way sometimes. It is also true that some children are less able to cope than others, and adults should be sensitive to this.

When the jealousy concerns objects, attempt to explain at the child's level that there are benefits in sharing and that many children have less than they have.

Bed-wetting (nocturnal enuresis)

Most children develop night-time bladder control before they start primary school although it is common for the occasional accident to occur for some years after. However, many children, especially boys, go through difficulties with bed-wetting and this can cause great embarrassment to them and feelings of guilt in their parents. As well as this there is stress on the families through the extra washing and fear of staying away from home.

It is difficult for families to seek help for this sensitive matter and sometimes they receive unhelpful advice such as 'He'll soon grow out of it' which only worsens the problem, and dismissive attitudes such as 'What do you expect?' When parents seek help they should be taken seriously and given adequate support. A visit to the GP is necessary in the first instance to exclude physical causes.

There are some simple measures that those caring for children, particularly those between 5 and 7 years, can take before referring the children to other professionals.

- Avoid fizzy drinks, tea and coffee which can have a diuretic effect around bed-time.
- Make sure the child is fully awake when 'lifted' last thing at night to enable the child to recognize the sensation of a full bladder.
- Keep records of dry or wet nights: using some kind of reward chart can help.
- Praise and encouragement for success.
- Avoid nappies or pads for older children.
- Have a potty nearby if the toilet is inaccessible.
- Keep the light on in the toilet or hall.
- Make sure the child can get to the toilet as quickly as possible.
- Reassure the child that others have this problem and that it will improve.

Persistent bed-wetting

The reasons for bed-wetting are many and varied and range from simple urinary infections to severe cases of sexual or other forms of abuse. When physical causes have been excluded (which happens in most cases), the most likely cause is some form of stress affecting the child, e.g. a child who has been dry for some time may regress and become wet after a stay in hospital or if there is tension in the family. If there are obvious stresses and the child is showing other signs of distress, this can form part of an overall picture of a child with serious problems and who needs specialist help. Sometimes there is apparently nothing to cause this problem and it clears up in time of its own accord.

Masturbation and inappropriate sexual behaviour

Most young children can be found at some time handling their genitals. Adults who care for them sometimes find this very natural act embarrassing and tell the child not to be 'dirty'. By doing this they draw attention to something that is not important and gives the child comfort not sexual relief. As a result many children will associate touching their genitals with guilty feelings which can lead to problems for them in the future.

In some situations it is not appropriate for young children to masturbate in this way and rather than drawing attention to the behaviour it is always better to distract them. As they become able to understand, explain in a simple manner that some people do not like seeing this sort of behaviour and that those people have a right to their viewpoint.

Children who masturbate excessively and over a long period may have some underlying anxiety or fear and may do this to obtain emotional comfort and security. Where this happens specialist help may be required. Some children may have experienced sexual abuse and workers should be sensitive to this possibility.

Young children are intensely interested in their bodies and those of adults and other children. They can often be found exploring their own bodies and those of other children and commenting on the differences. This is perfectly healthy, normal curiosity and should not be punished. However, children should realize that privacy is important, and this can often lead on to talking about 'good' or 'bad' touching. It is sometimes necessary to stop children playing together who persistently engage in sexual behaviour and the reasons for this should be given at the child's level. Overt sexual behaviour which mimics adult sexuality should be taken very seriously, and the policies and procedures of the work setting for suspected sexual abuse may need to be used.

Stealing

Children often take things that do not belong to them, and this has to be dealt with as part of their social development. For most young children these are isolated occurrences and they soon learn that it is unacceptable, anti-social behaviour. Young children tend to judge stealing in terms of the amount or value of what is stolen rather than the motive behind it. It is important that the child returns the stolen object, and, if the child refuses, the parent or worker can model the behaviour, verbalizing the reasons why the object is being returned.

Children who steal over a period of time are often insecure and feel deprived. They are usually looking for emotional comfort and love or can be seeking attention for a variety of reasons. Adults should not condone this behaviour but should try to look at possible reasons and underlying causes. Change and stress in the family can often be a key, and with extra love and attention the problem goes away. As with all forms of difficult behaviour, persistent stealing may need specialist help.

Scenario 9.7

You are a childminder caring for 7-year-old Katie after school and during school holidays. Katie has been with you since she was 2 and you know her and her family well. Recently you have noticed that Katie is taking sweets and snacks from your home and hiding them in her school bag. You are concerned that money may have gone missing from the kitchen where it is displayed openly. You suspect that Katie may be responsible.

(a) What are the first steps you would take?
(b) How would you deal with Katie and her family?
(c) What do you feel may be some of the underlying causes of Katie's behaviour?

Bullying

Bullying is the unprovoked, intentional and repeated act of inflicting either physical or psychological pain directly or indirectly on to an individual by another person or group of people who are thought to be more powerful or stronger. Bullying can occur at any age, and it is only in recent years that serious attention has been paid to the problem. There are now special telephone helplines for children to use who are being bullied and many schools and early years settings have anti-bullying policies and take positive action against bullying.

Bullying can take many forms and it is sometimes difficult to distinguish between children who are rough and unthinking and those who are calculating and malicious. *Bullying is often covert and both victims and bullies hide the behaviour from adults*. It can consist of verbal abuse such as name-calling, teasing or racial and other insults, or physical abuse which can be punching, kicking, jostling, pinching, or extortion and threats.

Bullying varies in severity and in the response that it evokes. There is less recorded evidence in pre-school children, but workers with young children have usually come across children who are beginning to bully and others who seem potential victims. Tattum and Herbert (1990) note that some children as young as 3 or 4 have already learned that being aggressive helps them to get what they want, and that making other children frightened of them is a rewarding experience.

Figure 9.2
Child bullying.

Madsen (1996) describes how she interviewed children in various age groups including 5- to 6-year-olds about bullying. These children were found to have a comprehensive understanding of the term bullying but tended to focus on specific examples they had seen or experienced and were less concerned about the bully's intention or power relationship with the child being bullied.

Coping with bullying

Workers with young children have to deal with both the bully and the victim and will be looking for a pattern of behaviour that may be emerging. Bullies may be frustrated children who themselves are bullied at home and who need attention and help. Children who are victims need to have their security, self-esteem and self-worth increased. Children who are easily bullied can be helped to be assertive (Penn Green Family Centre, 1990), and in many cases careful handling in the nursery and at home can do this. In some instance, though, children will be referred for specialist help.

Swearing

There are various degrees of bad language and different levels of tolerance. Children may have been brought up in a home where swearing is commonplace and not considered shocking or unusual. Most children in those circumstances will swear at an appropriate juncture without realizing that they are using bad language. Children may have learned to swear as a form of aggression or a part of name-calling, and it is very confusing for them when they are told not to say particular words. Other children or their parents may ostracize children who regularly use bad language and we do them no favours by allowing the swearing to continue unchecked.

Scenario 9.8

You are working in a day-care setting in an inner city environment. Most of the children are between 18 months and 4 years of age and come from a variety of cultures and backgrounds. Not all speak English as a first language. Two of the 4-year-old boys in a small group of mixed ages can behave in a very disruptive manner and occasionally use racist and sexist insults, swearing and other verbal abuse towards staff and other children. The younger children admire the boys and are beginning to mimic their behaviour.

One member of the staff seems not to see this as a problem and laughs when it occurs. Her attitude is that 'boys must be boys' and children have to learn to take the rough with the smooth. You find yourself becoming increasingly upset and angry both with her and the children after a recent spate of insults.

(a) What should you do concerning your own angry feelings?
(b) How could you deal with your colleague's attitude?
(c) How should the racist and sexist language be dealt with?
(d) What immediate steps could you take to improve the situation in the group?

Coping with swearing

It is important that workers explain to children just what is acceptable in the nursery and the effects on other people of using bad language. It is important that children are given time to fully understand and adjust. Sometimes continuous swearing is simple attention-seeking or may be due to the child's limited vocabulary. The child may be helped to find more appropriate words as part of a general programme to develop language skills.

Workers use a variety of means to encourage the child to stop swearing. A favourite ploy is to use a nonsense word or phrase yourself in circumstances where a child may have been used to hearing swearing. So if you drop something or bang your head, you would use this phrase and model something less offensive. Also encourage children to express their frustration in a less self-destructive manner such as vigorous physical play or pounding clay and dough.

Comfort habits

Comfort habits such as thumb-/finger-sucking or nail-biting are usually temporary and may be in response to stress or appear to have no particular underlying cause. They seem to be a form of emotional comfort to the child, and sucking may be regression in behaviour to pre-weaning. Children do sometimes find it difficult to break these habits and may need help. They are usually only of concern when persistent and excessive, and in these cases it is worth attempting to discover any underlying cause.

Figure 9.3
Toddler comfort.

Children who rock themselves to and for or head bang for long periods may be suffering from emotional or sensory deprivation. These sorts of behaviour have been observed amongst babies and children of normal intelligence who are isolated and receive little love, individual attention or sensory and cognitive stimulation. Such comfort habits are more commonly noticed amongst children with learning difficulties or other special needs. Meeting a child's basic needs will go some way to helping with these problems but specialized therapy is usually required.

Assignments

Assignment 1

Observe a child having a temper tantrum or other angry outburst
Either:

1. Undertake an event sample, in this case, over a period of days, recording every incident that involves temper tantrums or angry outbursts for your target child

Or:

2. Observe one such occasion in depth. Record accurately what happened.

Questions to ask yourself:
(a) What were the antecedents of the behaviour?
(b) How was it dealt with?
(c) Does it link with past behaviour?
(d) Are there any predisposing factors that you are aware of?
(e) How were other children/staff/parents affected?
(f) What lessons can be learned?

Assignment 2

Plan/implement/evaluate a programme for a child who is exhibiting problem behaviour
Provide a brief history and the rationale for your programme.

Record accurately what happened on implementing your programme and details of your evaluation.

What other actions need to be taken to help the child?

Assignment 3

Choose a child you know who is either very withdrawn or is attention-seeking and disruptive. Plan a structured programme of work with the child:

1. To involve parents or carers
2. To include use of structured/guided play and/or free play.

How would you evaluate this programme?

Assignment 4

Prepare a brief set of guidelines for parents and other carers concerning the possible effects on a 2-year-old of a new baby in the family.

Assignment 5

Write an essay on the management of unwanted behaviour:
Either:

In a home-based setting

Or:

In a group care and education setting.

Assignment 6

Prepare a case study to use with students or NVQ candidates based on the problems and management of challenging behaviour
Devise a set of questions for the student/candidate to test:

(a) their understanding of the principles of behaviour management
(b) whether they could apply their knowledge in different circumstances, e.g. different age ranges.

REFERENCES AND FURTHER READING

Atkinson, C. (1997) *Screen Violence.* London: National Society for the Prevention of Cruelty to Children.

Axline, V. (1971) *'Dibs' In Search of Self.* Harmondsworth: Pelican.

Bray, M. (1989) *Children's Hour: A Special Listen.* Nightingale Books.

Hennessy, E. (1992) *Children and Day Care.* London: Paul Chapman.

Herbert, M. (1988) *Working with Children and their Families.* London: Routledge/BPS Books.

Laishley, J. (Lindon). (1987) *Working with Young Children.* London: Arnold.

Madsen, K. (1996) *Bullying in Schools: Prevention is Better than Cure.* OMEP Update 93.

Millar, J. *Never too Young.* London: The National Early Years Network and Save the Children.

National Children's Bureau. (1991) *Young Children in Group Care; Guidelines for Good Practice.* London: NCB.

Penn Green Family Centre. (1990) *Learning to be Strong: Developing Assertiveness in Young Children.* Changing Perspectives.

Stevensen, H. (1990). Tom! Using play tutoring to integrate a difficult child in a nursery school. *In TOPIC: Practical Applications of Research in Education* (Resource pack) Spring 1990. Windsor: NFER/Nelson.

Tattum, D. and Herbert, G. (1990) *Bullying: A Positive Response. Advice for Parents, Governors and Staff in Schools.* Cardiff: South Glamorgan Institute of Higher Education.

Tattum, D. and Herbert, G. (1997) *Bullying: Home, School and Community.* London: David Fulton.

Treseder, P. (1997) *Empowering Young Children.* London: Save the Children.

Woolfson, R. (1989) *Understanding Your Child: A Parent's Guide to Child Psychology.* London: Faber and Faber.

10: ORGANIZATION AND MANAGEMENT SKILLS

Objectives

- Child care and education as a business
- The organization
- Aims and structures of the organization
- Staffing
- Working as a member of a staff team
- Aims and objectives of team work
- Confidentiality
- Individual contributions to the team
- Styles of team leadership
- The team meeting

- Working under the direction of others
- Delegated tasks
- Working to a management committee
- Organizing the budget and handling money
- Dealing with conflict situations
- Assertiveness
- Supervising learners
- Assessments processes
- Staff appraisal
- Dealing with unsatisfactory performance

Links

This chapter has links with:
- NVQ (EYCE) Units: M2, M6, M20, MCI/CI, MCI/C4.
- CACHE Diploma Module P.

Whatever the work setting, child care workers will need a knowledge of what management is all about and which skills are needed to be a good manager. By and large most establishments for the under-5s are small-scale settings which result in the greater involvement of all staff in the day-to-day management. Most settings do not have on-site secretarial help and most workers may be expected to be involved in some, if not all, of the following tasks: collecting and banking money, ordering equipment, managing budgets, supervising qualified staff and professionals, devising and implementing policies, liaising with parents/carers, ensuring that the curriculum enables the children to achieve desirable learning outcomes, fundraising, organizing fêtes and jumble sales, and writing papers for and attending management committee meetings. All these diverse activities can be encompassed under the broader heading of 'organization and management'. These are areas which college-based courses may fail to include in their training packages as it is often thought that new recruits will be given in-service training in these skills once they are employed.

The importance of organization and management skills has been recognized in the new Early Years Care and Education NVQs and there are new units to cover these skills, some of which have been imported from the Management Charter Initiative NVQs. Most people would have difficulty in coping in our present world if they did not have the skills to answer the telephone or use a photocopier. However, not all people are familiar with the other aspects of management, some of which are listed above.

In the present climate of 'purchaser/provider' relationships, the importance and needs of the stakeholders and emphasis upon the quality of the service received, no child care worker can afford to ignore the organizational and managerial aspects of the work. All those who work in an establishment, whatever the setting, have a responsibility to the organization (however small) in order to ensure that the relevant laws are implemented and a high quality of care and education is available to the children at all times. Good management is both an 'art' and a 'science'; the 'art' of management refers to those aspects which deal with people, whereas the 'science' of management deals with paperwork and organization.

There are many books written on management but very few are written specifically for those working in the child care and education field. This chapter will offer an outline of some of the skills which are specifically needed by child care workers.

Child care and education as a business

Whether you are running a nursery, playgroup or are a self-employed childminder, for the provider it is exactly the same as running a small business. If the business is also a registered charity, e.g. a pre-school learning group or a voluntary sector day nursery, it must have a Board of Trustees and all profits must be re-invested back into the business. It is responsible to the Charity Commissioners and all its activities must conform to the requirements of the Charities Acts 1992 and 1993.

If the business is a nursery class or a school or a local authority family centre, then it may have a delegated budget which may be the responsibility of a Board of Governors or the senior managers.

As a business, the setting will need to conform to the same laws as any other business:

- *Offices, Shops and Railway Premises Act 1963*

- *Health and Safety at Work Act 1974*
- *Sex Discrimination Act 1975*
- *Equal Pay Act 1970*
- *Race Relations Act 1976*
- *Food Safety Act 1990*
- *Disability Discrimination Act 1995.*

In addition, there are Acts which specifically apply to child care and education:

- *Children Act 1989*
- *Education Acts 1981, 1990, 1993.*

Hay (1997) refers to a piece of research undertaken by Coopers and Lybrand which looked at the factors which motivated people to start a small business. Of those people interviewed, 82% regarded the quality of the service as the most important factor whereas only 64% saw financial gain as important. This is probably the case for child care and education as there is a very low profit, if any, made from providing child care. Like any other small business there will be 'clients' for whom the business provides a service and there will be 'stakeholders' who are those people who have an interest in the business. The two groups are not necessarily the same: the 'client' is likely to be the person who is actively seeking day care/sessional care for a child whereas the 'stakeholder' may be a local authority that is purchasing places in the facility, local employers who know the facility is used by a number of their employees or a local activist group who were instrumental in getting the facility set up. All these people may want a voice in how the facility is managed and what it is able to provide. Then we must not forget the children (the customers) whose needs will be met by the facility. All of these groups will expect a high quality service from the business.

The organization

The mission statement

The mission statement is an idea which originated in the USA and was adopted by large corporate businesses. It has now been used by numerous organizations as a way of telling customers what the business is about and giving employees a 'sense of mission'. Hay (1997) gives five points that could be incorporated into a mission statement:

- *For **what** reason are you doing this?*
- ***Who** are you trying to satisfy?*
- *With **what** services will you meet that demand?*
- ***How** will you deliver the services?*
- ***Where** will you be in the future?*

o points out that mission statements should be realistic, achievable and brief.
ission statement is a philosophical statement which tells the reader about the
of the establishment.

s and structures of the organization

Policies and procedures

All organizations relating to children need policies in order to ensure the smooth running of the establishment and to provide consistency for children, parents and staff. Policies must be written down and kept in a manual which can easily be updated. The manual should be kept in a place easily available to all staff. When new staff/students/volunteers join the establishment they need to be shown the location of the policy manual, it should be clearly explained why there is a manual and they should be encouraged to make themselves familiar with its contents.

Policies are usually generated by managers and staff working together as it is important that all staff feel that they have ownership of the policies. Once all the staff have agreed a policy it is then presented to the management committee or governing body or proprietor for ratification. Organizations such as the Pre-school Learning Alliance (PLA) and the National Child Minding Association (NCMA) are often able to supply copies of model policies which establishments are able to adapt to their own needs. There is also a demand from outside organizations that establishments should have policies; it is a requirement of many social services departments that are entering into service provider contracts with a facility, and OFSTED requires their inspectors to check on policies when they visit.

The types of policies which are frequently found are:

> Administration of medicines
> Admissions
> Behaviour management
> Child protection
> Confidentiality
> Equal opportunities/anti-discriminatory
> Health and safety
> Monitoring and analysing
> Special needs code of practice.

With policies go procedures for implementation, roles and responsibilities and monitoring. Alongside a policy document there should be a procedures document. In some cases there are procedures for areas that are not aligned with a policy, e.g.

Financial procedures – who is responsible for signing cheques, banking money and handling petty cash.

Record keeping – which records are mandatory and who is able to instigate additional records being kept, who the records can be made available to and frequency of updating.

Roles and responsibilities of staff – who attends committees, who are line managers, who are responsible for students, who are responsible for volunteers and job descriptions of all posts.

Appraisal and professional development – how long do you have to be in post to apply for in-service training, how the centre's appraisal system works and how training/development needs are identified.

Children's outings – who is responsible for organizing these, number of staff that need to attend in proportion to number of children going, whether parents/carers are invited to attend, how the costs are calculated and what proportion of costs are paid by child's family.

Children who are sick – who is responsible for informing the parent/carer, who makes the initial decision as to whether a doctor should be called, who is responsible for first aid and who takes the decision to call an ambulance.

Quality indicators – what these are, who monitors them and who reports to the staff on how well they are achieving the indicators or where they are failing to reach the required standards.

Staffing

The minimum number of trained staff employed in proportion to the number of children being cared for is clearly laid down in the Guidelines to the Children Act. It is important that all staff are aware of their role and areas of responsibility and these should be clearly stated in the job description. Staff also need to know what their terms and conditions of employment are.

All employees who work for at least 16 hours per week, unless they are self-employed or volunteers, should have a document which clearly states their terms and conditions of employment. This is a legal requirement under the Employment Protection Act 1978 and the Employment Acts 1980 and 1982. The statement must contain the following:

- *The names of the employer and employee.*
- *The title of the job.*
- *The date when the employment commenced.*
- *The scale of pay.*
- *The hours of work.*
- *Entitlement to holidays.*

- *Provision for sick pay.*
- *Pensions and pension schemes.*
- *The length of notice that is required and that the employee is entitled to receive.*

The statement should also lay down the procedures for any disciplinary action and/or grievance procedures. These are all minimal requirements under the law and some conditions of employment may be written in much greater detail.

Under the Employment Acts employees have certain rights available to them but these may depend upon the length of service, e.g. the higher rate of maternity pay and the right to return after maternity leave are only available to those who have completed the minimum of 2 years' service. The rights which are available to everyone regardless of the period of service are:

- *Protection from discrimination on the grounds of race or sex.*
- *Right to be a member of a trade union and to take part in union activities.*
- *Time off work to be the safety representative.*
- *Time off work for ante-natal care.*
- *The right to an itemized statement of pay.*

Even in very small-scale settings it is important that workers know who their line manager is and what procedures exist if they have a grievance complaint. This is particularly important information for volunteers, learners or other people who are coming into the establishment for odd hours or days. In order for people to feel secure in the workplace they need reference points, the main ones being, knowing the layout of the building and who is their mentor or line manager.

Whilst this section makes clear the responsibilities of employers to employees, there is also a commitment on the part of the employee to perform to a reasonable standard and to act in a reasonable manner towards the work role.

Working as a member of a staff team

Most child care and education settings require people to work as a member of a team. Teams can be multi-disciplinary, e.g. they may include managers, volunteers, students, qualified staff, unqualified helpers or parents. All people working with children should work as a team to ensure that there is an overall child care policy for the establishment and an atmosphere of consistency for the children. The overarching principle of all teams must be the welfare of the children and families in their care. Decisions made by teams must be made in the light of the team's knowledge of the children.

Good teams do not just arise but are the result of hard work on the part of the team members. The people who are required to work within a team cannot always be specially chosen, therefore they have to learn to work together. It is important that you know your own strengths and weaknesses and the skills that you are able to bring to a team. Joining an existing team which has developed strong working relationships is difficult and it may take a while to fit in.

Young (1987) lists three requirements for a successful team:

1. *Shared aims.*
2. *A common working language.*
3. *The ability to manage relationships as well as tasks.*

Teams may be set up as part of the normal work situation, e.g. all staff working in the same room in a nursery; or they may be set up for a specific purpose such as to organize the summer fair. When choosing teams for a specific purpose, it is useful to weigh up the skills that may be required to undertake the task and then to look for participants. This may require you to look at the weaknesses and strengths of those who have volunteered their services. People with over-dominant personalities do not always make good team members as they are likely to prevent the weaker team members participating.

Teams may be formal or informal entities, e.g. they may be a staff grouping which meets regularly to discuss the children in the team's care and the plans for the forthcoming week or they may be an ad hoc group which meets together as a mutual support group. Whatever the purpose, they will need to adopt a consistent approach to dealing with problems, to allow time for all members to participate and to have a system for evaluating their progress in dealing with the tasks.

Aims and objectives of team work

The first task for any team is to clarify its aims and how these fit in with the mission statement. This can be done by answering questions such as 'What is our objective?' and 'How best can we meet that objective?' From the answer to the second question a plan should emerge and this will point the team towards the way forward. When working as a member of a team, it is important to remember that there is a collective responsibility for the decisions that the team make; you cannot be a member of a team and then abdicate responsibility if a wrong decision is made.

The case conference is a special multi-disciplinary team meeting called to discuss a specific child or family. More details regarding case conferences can be found in Chapter 7.

Confidentiality

Team members must share their information whilst at the same time maintaining the establishment's policy on confidentiality. This is not always easy and it is best only to divulge information on a 'need to know basis'. This means that you first need to examine the situation and decide whether anyone else needs to know the confidential information that you hold in order to effectively care for the child. This is particularly pertinent in cases where children or members of their family may have a stigmatizing condition such as being HIV positive, have AIDS or be a carrier for hepatitis B. In most cases there is no need for all the workers to know the medical status of a child as rules on protective hygiene should be part of the normal routine and applied by the staff when they are dealing with all children.

Individual contributions to the team

Teams cannot operate if their members do not contribute to the proceedings. This means bringing information, sharing expertise and volunteering an opinion or relevant information. It also entails undertaking some of the administrative duties such as taking a turn at writing the agenda, being the minute/note-taker or being the chairperson. Once a decision has been made at a team meeting, it is necessary for all the team members to work towards implementing the decision, whatever their personal feelings are about the decision. Sometimes teams are unable to make a decision without the assistance of outside expertise; it is important for team members to acknowledge this rather than trying to struggle along alone.

Styles of team leadership

There are two major leadership styles: the autocratic and the democratic. The autocratic leader will issue orders and have little time for the contributions of others; these people do not make good team leaders. The democratic leadership style is one whereby the contributions of team members are taken into consideration and decisions are made on a collective basis; e.g. the team is given a task and then works together to devise a strategy for dealing with it. This style of leadership is conducive to effective teamwork.

A good team leader will have the ability to:

- *Respond to the team members.*
- *Promote a team spirit.*
- *Motivate the team members to carry out tasks.*
- *Allow team members to express their ideas.*
- *Enable the team to devise action plans and strategies.*
- *Direct the team towards making decisions.*

- *Use the skills of all team members effectively.*
- *Be supportive to fellow team members.*
- *Give positive feedback to team members.*

Scenario 10.1

Jill is a new senior nursery officer who has just joined your establishment. She is in charge of the Blue room and is your immediate line manager. The staff in the Blue room have always been a cohesive team and the previous senior nursery officer, Mary, was respected by them all.

At Jill's first team meeting, she says very little but makes a lot of notes. Two days before the next team meeting Jill issues everyone with an agenda for the meeting. At the meeting the staff are resentful and angry and tell Jill that they worked very well with Mary and never needed an agenda. The meeting progresses, working to Jill's agenda but there is much suppressed mumbling and a general feeling of discontent.

At the third team meeting, Jill tells the group that she has decided to change the staff shift working pattern and proceeds to tell them the new roster. Two members of the team leave the meeting in protest.

None of the team attends Jill's fourth team meeting.

(a) What has Jill done wrong?
(b) What did the team do wrong?

The team meeting

Team meetings are usually held on a regular basis. Meetings can be informal or formal. Meetings should always have an agenda that acts as the discussion basis for the meeting. All the team should be able to contribute items to the agenda. Participants should listen to what fellow team members have to say, consider other people's ideas and offer ideas of their own. All proposals should be carefully considered before making a final decision. Participants should be objective, concentrate on the business at hand and not allow the personal attributes of a proposer to sway a decision. Decisions should be taken on the basis that they are of benefit to the child and the child's family, the establishment as a whole or the smooth running of the establishment. Ideas should be pooled, participants' particular skills or expertise should be called upon and clear lines for action drawn up. Team meetings should be opportunities to air difficulties in a healthy, open climate. Once the team has made a decision all members must work towards the implementation of that decision.

Figure 10.1
Team meeting.

Working under the direction of others

Most people work under the direction of others, whether this be working to a management committee or to a direct line manager. A major part of working in this way is to be able to carry out tasks which you have been requested to undertake by a colleague or a superior. Even the smallest organizations distribute and delegate work in this way. Staff need to be clear about their own role and that of their colleagues, as well as how these fit together within the management structure.

In most instances instructions will be given verbally. It is important to listen carefully to what is being asked of you (write notes if the task is complex) and to be certain as to what is required of you. Clarification should be sought when anything is unclear or ambiguous.

Most people report directly to their line manager, but in some establishments certain people may have responsibility for policy areas such as child protection, equal opportunities and health and safety. In these circumstances it may be necessary to take instructions and report back to these people and not the direct line manager.

Delegated tasks

When a number of different people give instructions to the same person, that person may need to draw up a list of priorities in order to carry out the tasks methodically. If a person is delegated too many tasks and is unable to cope, then the advice of the line manager should be sought.

Some tasks may require the delegate to report back to the originator; this may be a verbal report on how well a task has progressed or a written report on information that has been requested. In other cases, the report may be required by someone other than the originator; e.g. if a line manager asks for a safety check on the outdoor equipment, any faults or other dangers that are found may need to be reported to the person responsible for health and safety.

When dealing with children there are a number of tasks which may require the results to be filled in on a record sheet or written up in a report book. All such reports should be done clearly, concisely and must give an objective, accurate account of the situation. A child is not helped by a report that states that, 'Tommy is now able to go to the toilet unaided' if in fact Tommy still requires adult help in carrying out this task. The confidentiality policy of the establishment must always be maintained; information must only be passed to the senior person making the request. All information in a child's records must be treated as confidential even if it does not appear to be significant.

Carrying out a task will need planning and may require decisions to be made, and ideas to be modified. Standards of good practice must be maintained when carrying out tasks and if extra help is needed to ensure this, then it is important to make this need known.

Working to a management committee

Most playgroups and community nurseries have management committees which have an overall responsibility for the way that the establishment is run. Management committees determine the policy of an establishment and they delegate the responsibility for the implementation of that policy to the workers. It is likely that the chairperson of the management committee will act as the direct line manager to the head of the nursery or playgroup.

Management committee meetings are likely to be fairly formal affairs with a chairperson, secretary, treasurer and other officials. The actual committee members may be representatives from the local Under-Fives/Under-Eights Forum, local councillors, representatives from funding bodies and parent representatives.

The agenda

An agenda states the business to be dealt with at a meeting; the secretary will be responsible for taking minutes of the meeting. A typical agenda is as follows:

Rainbow Nursery/Playgroup Management Committee Meeting
AGENDA
1. Minutes of the meeting held on 25/10/99
2. Matters arising
3. Play group/nursery leader/manager's report
4. Treasurer's report

5. Discussion document on admissions criteria
6. Plans for the Spring Fair
7. Any other business
8. Date of next meeting

The preparation of the discussion document (Agenda item 5) may have been the responsibility of the nursery/playgroup leader/manager. It is likely that the management committee will decide upon the admissions policy for the establishment on the strength of the proposals put forward in the document. The document may have taken some time to prepare and had probably been compiled in conjunction with all the staff working in the establishment. The financial aspects of running the nursery/playgroup will be discussed under the treasurer's report, and policy decisions may be made about spending levels and future fund raising.

Sub-committees

Management committees may have a second tier or sub-committees to deal with specific matters such as equal opportunities, fundraising, building maintenance and Parents' Association. Each sub-committee has a slot on the agenda when it can report its progress to the management committee. The agenda for the committee is usually set by the secretary in conjunction with the chairperson. The secretary also sets the deadline for items to be included in the agenda.

Organizing the budget and handling money

The budget is a fixed amount of money that is allocated to an establishment in order to finance the day-to-day running. This money may come from the local authority as a delegated budget, or partial finance may come from the local authority and the fees charged to the families using the facility making up the difference, or all the finance may come from fees. The nursery manager/playgroup leader will be given a budget allocation by the treasurer. Sometimes budgets are given as lump sums of money or they may be specific sums of money under distinct headings (a virement system), e.g.

Rainbow Nursery/Playgroup Budget for the period 1/4/98–31/3/99

Consumable	£2000
Furniture	£2500
Visits	£400
Computer	£1000
Toys/equipment	£2000
Staff salaries	£6000
Total budget	£13900

It is not always possible to move money between the different categories of a vied budget. A non-vied budget is one where the manager/leader is given a fixed sum, e.g. £13 900, to spend but the ratios are unspecified: the only proviso is that the needs of the establishment are met. Some budgets are tied to virement headings to enable the management committee to decide on the priority areas for the money or because certain amounts of money have been donated or raised for specific items or budget headings.

Part of the responsibility for the budget covers the way that money is received and dispersed and keeping accurate records of these transactions. On a daily basis, these duties may be delegated to all the members of the working team. Most establishments keep petty cash available for incidental expenses. All monies received must be signed for by a person who will take responsibility for distributing the money and ensuring that receipts are presented for any money spent. All child care establishments are subject to their financial books being examined during the annual audit.

The basic rule for dealing with money is that no money should be issued without a receipt being obtained, and all money spent must have a receipt for the goods. All receipts must be kept and transactions recorded in a book or on a form which is specifically designed for the purpose. All cheques should require two signatures and cheques must only be signed against invoices and never signed in advance. For every cheque signed there must be an invoice; a cheque should not be signed without an invoice. Some organizations set a ceiling on the amount of money written on a cheque, and large cheques may need to be countersigned by the treasurer or chairperson of the management committee.

All these rules prevent the misappropriation of funds. Money going astray, even unintentionally, is a serious matter and could lead to dismissal for the person responsible.

Dealing with conflict situations

Conflict can arise in what appears to be the best of situations and may be between employers and employees, employee and employee, staff and management committee, staff and parents or an establishment and the local authority. The most common form of conflict arises between employees, particularly when there is a breakdown in relationships between two or more members of a team.

Young (1987) has identified the following as signs that something is wrong within a team:

- People begin to perform poorly, miss deadlines, produce substandard work.
- People expect others to solve their problems.
- People do not take responsibility for their actions.
- People break into sub-groups instead of sharing work.

- People show destructive criticism or dismissive behaviour towards others.
- People get involved in serious and unresolved conflicts.
- People show no interest in team activity.

Resolution of such conflicts requires the team leader to work with the team, but it is always better for the team to find the solution and for the leader to act as facilitator.

Personal problems may affect a person's performance and relationships with others, and in such cases the team leader needs to talk to that person on a one-to-one basis and wherever possible offer the person help or suggest where help might be obtained. Where conflicts arise between a worker and a parent they need to be resolved quickly as they affect the child. Quite often, such conflicts arise because the member of staff does not understand or make allowances for the parent's problems. In situations where a manager is maintaining confidentiality about a parent's problems the member of staff may have no idea that the parent has problems. It is possible to warn staff that a parent is going through a stressful time and therefore needs extra sensitive handling without revealing the actual problem.

Conflict will never be resolved if it is managed with aggression or ignored, or if people are not consulted about their feelings. What is likely then to happen is that the conflict becomes even more embroiled and complicated, more aggressive or may get hidden away so that it is bubbling under the surface of all other activities that the person or the team is carrying out. Managers are responsible for the smooth run-

Scenario 10.2

Janice is a playgroup worker and has always had a very good relationship with Toby's mother, Mrs James. However, during the past 2 weeks, Mrs James has been arriving late to collect Toby and Janice is getting annoyed with her about this. When Janice has broached the subject with Mrs James she has just shrugged her shoulders and not offered any reason for her lateness. As one of the rules of the playgroup is that children must be collected on time, she decides that she must give Mrs James an ultimatum.

When Mrs James arrives to collect Toby, late again, Janice tells her that she has broken the rules of the playgroup, has no genuine reason for this so Toby no longer has a place at the playgroup. Mrs James bursts into tears. The playgroup leader comes into the room and takes Mrs James aside. Janice feels that Mrs James will manipulate the playgroup leader and feels cross that her opinion on the matter is not being sought.

(a) What do you think could be happening here?
(b) How do you think Janice should have handled the situation?

ning of their establishments and this means that they must deal with conflict when it arises.

Children are very sensitive and very quickly realize that there is a problem amongst the staff or between the staff and their parent or carer; therefore, to allow conflict situations to simmer is detrimental to the welfare of the children.

Assertiveness

Resolving a conflict may require a manager or an employee to be assertive. Assertion should not be confused with aggression: assertion is having control over the situation by ensuring that you respect people's feelings and they have respect for your feelings.

Dickson (1984) put forward the following 11 basic human rights as the basis for assertiveness:

1. The right to state my own needs and set my own priorities as a person, independent of any roles that I may assume in my life.
2. The right to be treated with respect as an intelligent, capable and equal human being.
3. The right to express my feelings.
4. The right to express my opinions and values.
5. The right to say 'yes' or 'no' for myself.
6. The right to make mistakes.
7. The right to change my mind.
8. The right to say I do not understand.
9. The right to ask for what I want.
10. The right to decline responsibility for other people's problems.
11. The right to deal with others without being dependent upon them for approval.

The field of child care is one where the majority of workers are female and it is women who are poor at asserting themselves and ensuring that they are listened to when exerting their rights. In being assertive, people need to speak out firmly and clearly and 'stick to their guns' in the face of opposition. However, this does not require you to shout, be aggressive or use indirect aggression such as sarcasm. There are now many assertiveness training courses available and they are particularly useful for child care workers.

Being assertive does not mean always winning in a conflict situation. It means being able to put forward your personal feelings on the matter in such a way that people listen. Having gained a fair hearing, people are more inclined to abide by the final decision.

Supervising learners

Most child care and education establishments have learners visiting for different periods of time in order to gain practical experience. Some establishments may be involved in modern apprenticeships, national traineeships or have trainees who are on other government schemes, and who are based in the nursery/playgroup for part of the week. They may also have students from local colleges or schools. With the advent of NVQs employees may become learners and put themselves forward for assessment.

It is important that learners are made to feel confident in the new situation. This can be achieved by assigning each learner a mentor who is a member of the full-time staff. The role of the mentor is to guide the learner through the pre-assessment work to ensure that the learner is adhering to good practices, to help the learner evaluate the work undertaken and to advise the learner on compiling portfolios of evidence, child observations and children's records. The mentor may also need to direct the learner towards suitable textbooks, journals and other resources.

The person assigned as the mentor may not necessarily be the person who is supervising or assessing the learner. In some establishments the student supervisor is a post which carries extra responsibility and may be paid accordingly. A lot of good practice in child care and education is achieved by working alongside experienced practitioners and these are often the people who are best suited to the important role of mentor.

Not all people find the learning process easy and often tasks need to be broken down into small units in order for the learner to understand the whole. It must be remembered that individuals learn at different speeds and it may take some people longer than others to reach the point of understanding. It is useful if the learner is given a programme with their learning aims and objectives clearly stated. Now that there are National Standards in Early Years Care and Education, it is possible to devise programmes which reflect these standards of competence.

Scenario 10.3

Sunita is the student supervisor in a family centre. She has four students from the local college and has assigned each of them a mentor. One of the students, Cathy, does not seem to be committed to the work and her mentor, Mavis, has given Sunita a long list of complaints. Sunita decides the time has come to have a serious chat with Cathy and she goes to fetch her. On entering the playroom, she finds Mavis in tears, the children looking terrified and Cathy throwing Lego pieces at Mavis.

How does Sunita handle this situation?

Assessment processes

Learners who are registered to be assessed for NVQs will have copies of the National Standards for the qualifications which they are working towards. Once they feel confident that they are able to perform to the National Standards and are in possession of the relevant underpinning knowledge, they will be able to request an assessment to take place. The assessment may be carried out by a member of the establishment staff who is a trained assessor and attached to the local assessment centre or the assessment centre may send a peripatetic assessor to the candidate. The candidate will know who has been assigned as the assessor and will have contacted the assessor at an earlier date to discuss the types of evidence that will be required for the assessment.

Learners who are on college-based courses may have different assessment requirements and the staff they are working with should be aware of exactly how much and what level of work learners will need to produce. Colleges and awarding bodies may have a variety of assessment forms which need to be filled in and the supervisory staff need to have contact with the college tutors to clarify the requirements.

Induction of learners

All learners who are not employees should spend their first visits getting to know the setting, the people, the children and familiarizing themselves with the layout of the building. They will need to be introduced to the relevant procedures and policies relating to the establishment, and know who their line manager is and the regular time that has been set aside for their supervision feedback session.

Learners should be treated as team members and should attend team meetings that are involved with planning matters. They should be encouraged to make a contribution at these meetings and it is useful if they are given a specific topic to report on. In that respect, learners should be encouraged to keep a notebook in which they can record child observations and make notes of the tasks that they have been asked to carry out.

Giving feedback

It is important that learners receive feedback on their performance; nobody should be unaware that they are doing well or failing. Confidence is built on praise so learners should be given recognition for the good work that they have done.

Nobody likes criticism but even more destructive to the fragile confidence that most learners have is negative criticism. Learners are bound to make mistakes; after all, even experienced people make mistakes. How these mistakes are dealt with will be very important for the learner. Unless it is a safety matter which requires immediate attention, it is better to take the learner aside to a quiet place and discuss the actions that have caused comment. This will help the supervisor to ascertain the learner's level of learning and find the reasons as to why the learner acted or failed to act as instructed. It is always a good idea to draw up an action plan with the learner so that there is a constructive conclusion to the criticism.

When supervising learners it is important to be impartial and objective and to implement the good practices of equal opportunities. It is everyone's right to have access to a fair assessment of their capabilities. Supervisors and assessors are there to make judgements upon the product not upon the personal attributes of the producer. All learners should be judged using the same standards, and special allowances should not be made for some groups; e.g. there are few males in child care and education work but those who are there must undertake the same tasks as the females and perform to the same standards. When a learner asks for help, it should be given either directly by the worker or by referring the learner to someone with the appropriate expertise.

Staff appraisal

Many posts now have in-built systems for a regular review of staff performance. In some areas of industry, payment incentives are linked to appraisal of performance. An appraisal system enables workers to assess their progress and to identify their areas of strength and weakness. Where there are formal appraisal systems it is usual for appraisal to be carried out annually. Many child care establishments, though, have informal appraisal systems, and appraisal interviews take place more regularly. The following guidelines are useful when implementing an appraisal system:

- The system must be equitable, meaning that all employees must be appraised in the same way.
- Methods of appraisal must be the same for all employees with the same job descriptions. Results of appraisals can only be made by comparing like with like.
- The method used should be simple and understood by everyone.
- The appraisal must be objective and the personality of the appraisee should only be considered if it is affecting the appraisee's performance.
- Appraisal should be a continuous process with regular feedback, whether it be praise or criticism.

It is preferable to carry out an appraisal interview rather than just hand a person a form to fill in. A lot more detail can be gleaned from an interview and it offers the opportunity for some immediate feedback. Who carries out the appraisal may be a moot point in a small organization. In large industries it is usually undertaken by the personnel or human resources department. Appraisal can be done from the 'top down', when the officer-in-charge interviews the deputy officer-in-charge, who in turn interviews the senior nursery officer, or it can be 'bottom up' when the unqualified assistant interviews the nursery nurse, who in turn interviews the nursery officer. Alternatively, a member of the management committee may undertake all the appraisal interviews. Whatever method is decided upon, it is important that staff view appraisal as a positive action which increases the smooth running of the establishment, aids efficiency and promotes good practice. The main aim of performance appraisal is to improve performance not to punish employees; however, poor performance must be dealt with.

Dealing with unsatisfactory performance

An appraisal system will direct the management to those employees who are consistently performing poorly. It is also a useful tool for recognizing when a person's performance may be slipping. There are three ways of dealing with poor or unsatisfactory performance: prevention, corrective action or drastic action. Prevention can be used when it is realized early that a person's performance may be slipping but has not yet reached the stage of being unsatisfactory. There are a number of actions that can be taken to prevent further deterioration such as delegating some of the work, giving the person more time to complete the work or assigning the person a mentor to help with the organization and carrying out of the work.

Corrective action needs to be taken when an employee is first deemed as performing in an unsatisfactory manner. This more often than not results in the employee being sent on a training course which will help particular areas of weakness.

Drastic action is usually only taken after corrective action has not resulted in any improvement in the employee's performance. Drastic action may also be taken because there has not been a regular appraisal system and the situation has only just come to light, but it has still gone too far for corrective action to be of use. Drastic action may be early retirement, sacking, redundancy or taking disciplinary action. Needless to say, which option is used needs to be carefully thought out. With legal job security under the Employment Act (1989) any employee who has been with the establishment for 2 years or more will have the right to appeal to an industrial tribunal.

Before drastic action is taken, it is only fair to give the employee a chance to improve personal performance. It is therefore useful, and often necessary, under Employment Law to give a number of warnings. Most local authorities have a disciplinary procedure which must be adhered to.

Assignments

Assignment 1

You have just taken over the local playgroup and have been asked by the chairperson of the management committee to draw up an agenda for the next committee meeting. How do you go about this and what is the agenda likely to contain?

Assignment 2

You are a nursery nurse in an infant school. A parent has made a complaint to you about the teacher that you work with. You feel that the parent is justified in her complaint. How do you handle the situation?

Assignment 3

You are in charge of a community nursery and your management committee has decided to bring in a system of appraisal. How will you explain this to your fellow workers? Draw up a plan for implementing an appraisal system.

Assignment 4

You are in charge of the local playgroup and the management committee has asked you to draw up conditions of employment for the other two workers. Draw up a model set of job descriptions, person specifications and conditions of employment for two, part-time, sessional, playgroup workers.

Assignment 5

You have been asked by your head of the family centre to prepare an estimate for a student supervision room. List the furniture and resources that you would need with appropriate costings.

REFERENCES AND FURTHER READING

Allen, R. (1995) *Winnie-the-Pooh on Management*. London: Methuen.

Andreski, R. and Nicholls, S. (1996) *Managing Your Nursery*. London: Nursery World Publications.

Cooper, C. (1981) *Psychology and Management*. London: British Psychological Society.

Dickson, A. (1984) *A Woman in Your Own Right: Assertiveness and You*. London: Quartet.

Handy, C. (1976) *Understanding Organizations*. Harmondsworth: Penguin.

Hay, S. (1997) *Essential Nursery Management*. London: Baillière Tindall.

Jenks, J. and Kelly, J. (1988) *Don't Do. Delegate! The Secret Power of Successful Management* London: Kogan Page.

Pugh, G. (1996) A policy for early childhood services. *In* Pugh, G. (Ed.) *Contemporary Issues in The Early Years, 2nd edn.* London: National Children's Bureau.

Randall, G., Shaw, R., Packard, P. and Slater, J. (1979) *Staff Appraisal*. London: Institute of Personnel Management.

Sadek, E. and Sadek, J. (1996) *Good Practice in Nursery Management*. Cheltenham: Stanley Thornes.

Vernon, J. and Smith, C. (1994) *Day Nurseries at a Crossroads*. London: National Children's Bureau.

Watt, J. (Ed.) (1994) *Early Education: the Quality Debate*. Professional Issues in Education, No. 15. Edinburgh: Scottish Academic Press.

Young, A. (1987) *The Manager's Handbook*. London: Sphere.

APPENDIX

Useful addresses

The numerals in square brackets after the name of the organization refer to the relevant chapter in this book.

Action for Sick Children [6]
First Floor, 300 Kingston Road, London, SW20 8LX
Fax: 0171 837 2110

Advisory Centre for Education (ACE) [3,4]
Unit 1B, Aberdeen Studios, 22 Highbury Grove, London, N5 2DQ
Tel: 0171 354 8321

Afro-Caribbean Education Resource Project (ACER) [8]
Acer Centre, Wyvil School, Wyvil Road, London, SW8 2TJ
Tel: 0171 627 2662   Fax: 0171 627 0278

Anti-Racist Response and Action Group (ARRAG)
c/o 112a The Green, Southall, Middlesex, UB2 4BQ
Tel: 0171 574 6019

Arthritis Research Campaign
Copeman House, St Mary's Court, St Mary's Gate, Chesterfield,
Derbyshire, S41 7TQ
Tel: 01246 558033

Association for All-Speech Impaired Children (AFASIC) [5]
347 Central Markets, Smithfield, London, EC1A 9NH
Tel: 0171 236 3632

Association for Brain Damaged Children (ABDC) [5]
Clifton House, 3 St Paul's Road, Foleshill, Coventry, CV6 5DE
Tel: 01203 665450

Association for Improvements in the Maternity Services (AIMS)
40 Kingswood Avenue, London, NW6 6LS
Tel: 0181 960 5585   Fax: 01753 654142

Association for Post-Natal Illness
25 Jerdon Place, Fulham, London, SW6 1BE
Tel: 0171 386 0868

Association for Spina Bifida and Hydrocephalus [5]
ASBAH House, 42 Park Road, Peterborough, PE1 2UQ
Tel: 01733 555988

Association of Advisers for the Under Eights and their Families (AAUEF) [1]
c/o 33 Welwood Way, Downley, High Wycombe, Buckinghamshire, HP13 5XR

Association of Breast Feeding Mothers (ABM)
PO Box 441, St Albans, Hertfordshire, AL4 0AS
Tel: 01727 859189

Association of British Paediatric Nurses (ABPN)
Worthing & Southlands Hospital NHS Trust, Southlands Hospital,
Upper Shoreham Road, Shoreham by Sea, West Sussex, BN43 6TQ
Tel: 01421 6129139 (9a.m.–5p.m.)

Association of Community Health Councils for England and Wales
30 Drayton Park, London, N5 1PB
Tel: 0171 609 8405

Association of Parents of Vaccine-Damaged Children [5]
2 Church Street, Shipston on Stour, Warwickshire, CV36 4AP
Tel: 01608 661595

BACUP [6]
3 Bath Place, Rivington Street, London, EC2A 3DR
Tel: 0171 613 2121

Barnardo's [7]
Tanner's Lane, Barkingside, Ilford, Essex, IG6 1QG
Tel: 0181 550 8822

Black Childcare Network
17 Brownhill Road, Catford, London, SE6

British Agencies for Adoption and Fostering
Skyline House, 200 Union Street, London, SE1 0LX
Tel: 0171 593 2000

British Association for Counselling
1 Regent Place, Rugby, Warwickshire, CV21 2PJ
Tel: 01788 550899

British Association for Early Childhood Education (BAECE) [3]
111 City View House, 463 Bethnal Green Road, London, E2 9QH
Tel: 0171 739 7594

British Deaf Association [5]
1–3 Worship Street, London, EC2A 2AB
Tel: 0171 588 3520

British Diabetic Association [5]
10 Queen Anne Street, London, W1M 0BD
Tel: 0171 323 1531

British Epilepsy Association [5]
Anstey House, 40 Hanover Square, Leeds, LS3 1BE
Tel: 0113 2439393

British Homeopathic Association (BHA)
27a Devonshire Street, London, W1N 1RJ
Tel: 0171 935 2163

British Medical Association (BMA)
BMA House, Tavistock Square, London, WC1H 9JP
Tel: 0171 383 6101

British Red Cross Society (BRCS)
9 Grosvenor Crescent, London, SW1X 7EJ
Tel: 0171 235 5454

Brittle Bone Society [5]
30 Guthrie Street, Dundee, DD1 5BS
Tel: 01382 204446

Brook Advisory Centres
153a East Street, London, SE17 2SD
Tel: 0171 703 7880

Cancer Relief Macmillan Fund [6]
Anchor House, 15–19 Britten Street, London, SW3 3TZ
Tel: 0171 351 7811

Carers National Association
20–25 Glasshouse Yard, London, EC1A 2JT
Tel: 0171 490 8818

Child Development Research Unit [1]
University of Nottingham, Psychology Department,
University Park, Nottingham, NG7
Tel: 0115 9515151

ChildLine [7]
Royal Mail Building, Studd Street, London, N1 0QW
Tel: 0171 239 1000

Children First [7]
Melville House, 41 Polwarth Terrace, Edinburgh, EH1 1NU
Tel: 0131 337 8539

Children's Society [7]
Edward Rudolf House, Margery Street, London, WC1X 0JL
Tel: 0171 837 4299

City and Guilds of London Institute
1 Giltspur Street, London, EC1A 9DD
Tel: 0171 294 3167

Cleft Lip and Palate Association (CLAPA)
138 Buckingham Palace Road, London, SW1W 9SA
Tel: 0171 824 8110

Coeliac Society of the UK
PO Box 220, High Wycombe, Bucks, HP11 2HY
Tel: 01494 437278

Commission for Race Equality [3]
Elliott House, 10–12 Allington House, London, SW1E 5EH
Tel: 0171 828 7022

Committee on Safety of Medicines
Market Towers, 1 Nine Elms Lane, London, SW8 5NQ
Tel: 0800 731 6789

The Compassionate Friends [6]
53 North Street, Bristol, BS3 1EN
Tel: 0117 9665202   0117 9539639 (Helpline)

Council for Awards in Children's Care and Education (CACHE)
8 Chequer Street, St Albans, Hertfordshire, AL1 3XZ
Tel: 01727 847636   Fax: 01727 867609

CRUSE [6]
The Charter House, 26 Sheen Road, Richmond, Surrey, TW9 1UR
Tel: 0181 332 7227

CRUSE is a bereavement-counselling organization with a network of branches.

Cystic Fibrosis Research Trust [6]
11 London Road, Bromley, Kent, BR1 1BY
Tel: 0181 464 7211

The Trust supplies information on cystic fibrosis and awards research grants.

Department for Education and Employment
Sanctuary Buildings, Gt Smith Street, London, SW1 3BT
Tel: 0171 925 5000

Department of Health
Richmond House, 79 Whitehall, London, SW1A 2NS
Tel: 0171 210 3000

Welsh Office
Crown Buildings, Cathays Park, Cardiff, CF1 3NQ
Tel: 01222 825111

Scottish Office
Dover House, Whitehall, London, SW1A 2AU
Tel: 0171 270 3000

Scottish Home and Health Department
St Andrew's House, Regent Road, Edinburgh, EH1 3DG
Tel: 0131 556 8400

Department of Health and Social Services, Northern Ireland
Dundonald House, Upper Newtownards Road, Belfast, BT4 2SB
Tel: 01232 543643

Department of Social Security
Richmond House, 79 Whitehall, London, SW1A 2NS
Tel: 0171 210 3000

Distance Learning Centre
103 Borough Road, London, SE1 0AA
Tel: 0171 928 8989

Down's Syndrome Association [5]
155 Mitcham Road, London, SW17 9PG
Tel: 0181 682 4001

Early Years Trainers Anti-Racist Network (EYTARN) [8]
PO Box 1870, London, N12 8JQ
Tel: 0181 446 7056   Fax: 0181 446 7591

ENABLE
6th Floor, 7 Buchanan Street, Glasgow, G1 3HL
Tel: 0141 226 4541

English National Board for Nursing, Midwifery and Health Visiting (ENB)
Victory House, 170 Tottenham Court Road, London, W1P 0HA
Tel: 0171 388 3131

Epilepsy Association of Scotland
48 Govan Road, Glasgow, G51 1JL
Tel: 0141 427 4911

Equal Opportunities Commission [3, 8]
Overseas House, Quay Street, Manchester, M3 3HN
Tel: 0161 833 9244

Exploring Parenthood [4]
4 Ivory Parade, Treadgold Street, London, W11 4BP
Tel: 0171 221 4471   Fax: 0171 221 5301

Families Anonymous (FA)
Unit 37, Charlotte Avenue, Battersea, London, SW11 5JE
Tel: 0171 498 4680

Family Planning Association (FPA)
2–12 Pentonville Road, London, N1 9FP
Tel: 0171 837 5432

Family Welfare Association
501–505 Kingsland Road, London, E8 4AU
Tel: 0171 254 6251

The Foundation for the Study of Infant Deaths
(Cot Death Research and Support)
14 Halkin Street, London, SW1X 7DP
Tel: 0171 235 1721

General Medical Council (GMC)
178 Great Portland Street, London, W1N 6JE
Tel: 0171 580 7642

Gingerbread
16–17 Clerkenwell Close, London, EC1R 0AN
Tel: 0171 336 8184

Haemophilia Society
Chesterfield House, 383 Euston Road, London, NW1 3AY
Tel: 0171 380 0600

Handicapped Adventure Playground Association (HAPA) [5]
Pryor's Bank, Bishops Park, London, SW6 3LA
Tel: 0171 736 4443

Health and Safety Executive
Rose Court, 2 Southwark Bridge, London, SE1 9HS
Tel: 0171 717 6000

Health Education Authority
Trevelyan House, 30 Great Peters Street, London, SW1P 2HW
Tel: 0171 222 5300

Health Visitors' Association (HVA) [1]
50 Southwark Street, London, SE1 1UN
Tel: 0171 378 7255   Fax: 0171 407 3521

Herpes Viruses Association (HVA)
41 North Road, London, N7 9DP
Tel: 0171 609 9061

High/Scope (UK) [3]
Research and Development Section, Barnardo's, Tanner's Lane,
Barkingside, Ilford, Essex, IG6 1QG
Tel: 0181 550 8822

Home-Start Consultancy [4]
315a London Road, Leicester, LE2 3ND
Tel: 0116 2709009

Hospice Information Service [6]
St Christopher's Hospice, 51–59 Lawrie Park Road, Sydenham,
London, SE26 6DZ
Tel: 0171 778 9252

Hyperactive Children's Support Group [5]
71 Whyte Lane, Chichester, West Sussex, PO19 2LD
Tel: 01903 725182

Institute of Child Health [1]
30 Guilford Street, London, WC1N 1EH
Tel: 0171 242 9789

Invalid Children's Aid Nationwide (ICAN) [5]
Barbican City Gate, 1–3 Dufferin Street, London, EC1Y 8NA
Tel: 0171 374 4422

Invalids at Home
17 Lapstone Gardens, Kenton, Harrow, Middlesex, HA3 0EB
Tel: 0181 907 1706

Jewish Care
Stuart Young House, 221 Golders Green Road, London, NW11 9DQ
Tel: 0171 458 3282

Jewish Social Services
Stuart Young House, 221 Golders Green Road, London, NW11 9DQ
Tel: 0171 458 3282

KIDS [5]
80 Waynflete Square, London, W10 6UD
Tel: 0181 960 6767

KIDSCAPE [7]
152 Buckingham Palace Road, London, SW1W 9TR
Tel: 0171 730 3300

King's Fund Centre (KFC)
11–13 Cavendish Square, London, W1M 0AN
Tel: 0171 307 2400

Letterbox Library [8]
Unit 2D, Leroy House, 436 Essex Road, London, N1 3QP
Tel: 0171 226 1633

Leukaemia Research Fund
43 Great Ormond Street, London, WC1N 3JT
Tel: 0171 405 0101

Leukaemia Society [6]
14 Kingfisher Court, Venny Bridge, Pinhoe, Exeter EX4 8JN
Tel: 01392 464848

The Society supplies information on childhood leukaemia and support materials for families.

London Montessori Centre
18 Balderton Street, London, W1Y 1TG
Tel: 0171 493 0165

Maternity Alliance
15 Britannia Street, London, WC1X 9JP
Tel: 0171 588 8582

MENCAP
see Royal Society for Mentally Handicapped Children and Adults

Midwifery Services
Institute of Child Health, Bristol Children's Hospital,
St Michael's Hill, Bristol, BS2 8BJ
Tel: 0117 921541

MIND (National Association for Mental Health)
Granta House, 15–19 Broadway, Stratford, London, E15 4BQ
Tel: 0181 519 2122

Minority Rights Group
379 Brixton Road, London, SW9 7DE
Tel: 0171 978 9498

Multiple Births Foundation (MBFI)
Queen Charlotte's and Chelsea Hospital, Goldhawk Road, London, W6 0XG
Tel: 0171 748 4666

Muscular Dystrophy Group of Great Britain [6]
7/11 Prescott Place, London, SW4 6BS
Tel: 0171 720 8055

An information and support network.

Myasthenia Gravis Association
Keynes House, Chester Park, Alfreton Road, Derby, DE21 4AS
Tel: 01332 290219

National Association for Gifted Children [5]
Elder House, Milton Keynes, MK9 1LR
Tel: 01908 673677

National Association for the Welfare of Children in Hospital (NAWCH) [6]
300 Kingston Road, Wimbledon Chase, London, SW20 8LX
Tel: 0181 542 4848

National Association of Bereavement Services (NABS) [6]
20 Norton Folgate, London, E1 6DB
Tel: 0171 247 1080 (24hr answerphone for referral requests);
0171 247 0617 London (Admin.)

National Association of Toy and Leisure Libraries
68 Churchway, London, NW1 1LT
Tel: 0171 387 9592

National Asthma Campaign
Providence House, Providence Place, London, NW1 0NT
Tel: 0171 226 2260

National Autistic Association [5]
393 City Road, London, EC1V 1NG
Tel: 0171 833 2299

National Board for Nursing, Midwifery and Health Visiting for Northern Ireland
RAC House, 79 Chichester Street, Belfast, BT1 4JE
Tel: 01232 238152

National Board for Nursing, Midwifery and Health Visiting for Scotland
22 Queen Street, Edinburgh, EH2 1JX
Tel: 0131 226 7371

National Centre for Play [2]
Moray House, College of Education, Cramond Road North, Edinburgh, EH4 6JD
Tel: 0131 312 6001

National Childminding Association
8 Mason's Hill, Bromley, Kent, BR2 9EY
Tel: 0181 464 6164

National Children's Bureau (NCB) [1,3,8]
Early Childhood Unit, 8 Wakley Street, London, EC1V 7QE
Tel: 0171 843 6000

The NCB has a large number of resources, especially in its Early Years Unit.

NCH Action for Children [4]
85 Highbury Park, London, N5 1UD
Tel: 0171 226 2033

National Deaf–Blind and Rubella Association (SENSE) [5]
11–13 Clifton Terrace, London, N4 3SR
Tel: 0171 272 7774

National Deaf Children's Society
15 Dufferin Street, London, EC1Y 8UR
Tel: 0171 490 8656

National Library for the Handicapped Child
Reach Resources Centre, Wellington House, Wellington Road,
Wokingham, Berkshire, RG11 2AG
Tel: 01734 891101   Fax: 01734 790989

National Playbus Association [2]
93 Whitby Road, Brislington, Bristol, NS4 3QF
Tel: 0117 977 5375

National Portage Association (NPA) [5]
12 Monks Dale, Yeovil, Somerset, BA21 3JE
Tel & Fax: 01953 71641

National Society for Epilepsy
Chalfont Centre for Epilepsy, Chalfont St Peter, Gerrards Cross, Bucks, SL9 0RJ.
Tel: 01494 601400

National Society for Mentally Handicapped People in Residential Care (RESCARE)
Rayner House, 23 Higher Hillgate, Stockport, Cheshire, SK1 3ER
Tel: 0161 474 7323

National Society for the Prevention of Cruelty to Children (NSPCC) [7]
NSPCC National Centre, 42 Curtain Road, London, EC2A 3NH
Tel: 0171 825 2500   Fax: 0171 825 2525

Northern Ireland Pre-School Playgroups Association [2,4]
Enterprise House, Boucher Crescent, Boucher Road, Belfast, BT12 6HU
Tel: 01232 662825

OMEP
☞ World Organisation for Early Childhood Education

One Parent Families Scotland
6th Floor, 7 Buchanan Street, Glasgow, G1 3HL
Tel: 0141 226 4541

Open University
Dept of Health and Social Welfare, Walton Hall, Milton Keynes, Bucks, MK7 6AA
Tel: 01908 274066

Parentline [7]
Endway House, The Endway, Hadleigh, Benfleet, Essex, SS7 2NN
Tel: 01702 554782   Fax: 01702 554911

Parent Network [4]
Room 2, Winchester House, Kennington, 11 Crammer Road, London, SW9 2EJ
Parent Line Enquiry: 0171 35 1214
Admin: 0171 735 4596   Fax: 0171 735 4692

Play Education [2]
11 Castle Lythe, Ely, Cambridgeshire, CB7 4BU
Tel & Fax: 01353 661294

Play for Life Network [2]
c/o Helga Bogish-Francis, 6 The Ridgeway, Caversham, Reading,
Berkshire, RG4 8NX

Poisons Unit
New Cross Hospital, Avonley Road, London, SE14
Tel: 0171 955 5095

Pre-school Learning Alliance [2,3,4]
69 Kings Cross Road, London, WC1X 9LL
Tel: 0171 833 0991   Helpline for Parents: 0171 837 5513   Fax: 0171 837 4942

Psoriasis Association
7 Milton Street, Northampton, NN2 7JG
Tel: 01604 711129

Qualifications and Curriculum Authority
29 Bolton Street, London, W1Y 7PD
Tel: 0171 509 5555

Royal Association in Aid of Deaf People
Walsingham Road, Colchester, CO2 7BP
Tel: 01206 509509

Royal College of Midwives (RCM)
15 Mansfield Street, London, W1M 0BE
Tel: 0171 872 5100

Royal College of Nursing (RCN)
20 Cavendish Square, London, W1M 0AB
Tel: 0171 409 3333

Royal College of Paediatrics and Child Health (RCPCH) [1]
50 Hallam Street, London, W1N 6DE
Tel: 0171 307 5600

Royal Institute for the Blind (RNIB)
224 Great Portland Street, London, W1N 6AA
Tel: 0171 388 1266

Royal National Institute for the Deaf (RNID)
19–23 Featherstone Road, London, EC1Y 8SL
Tel: 0171 296 8000

Royal Society of Health
38a St George's Drive, London, SW1V 4BH
Tel: 0171 630 0121

Royal Society for Mentally Handicapped Children and Adults (MENCAP) [5]
117–123 Golden Lane, London, EC1Y 0RF
Tel: 0171 454 0454

Royal Society for the Prevention of Accidents (ROSPA)
Edgbaston Road, Birmingham, B5 7ST
Tel: 0121 248 2000

Samaritans
17 Uxbridge Road, Slough, Berkshire, SL1 1SN
Tel: 01753 531011

Sargent Cancer Care for Children [6]
14 Abingdon Road, London, W8 6AF
Tel: 0171 565 5100

Save the Children [2]
17 Grove Lane, London, SE5 8RD
Tel: 0171 703 5400

Scoliosis Association (UK)
No. 2 Ivebury Court, 325 Latimer Road, London, W10 6RA
Tel: 0181 964 5343

Scottish Pre-School Playgroups Association [2,4]
14 Elliot Place, Glasgow, G3 8EP
Tel: 0141 221 4148

Sickle Cell Society (SCS)
54 Station Road, Harlesden, London, NW10 4BO
Tel: 0181 961 7795

SCOPE [5]
The Old School House, Main Road, Kingsley, Bordon, Hampshire, GU35 9ND
Tel: 01420 475444

Terence Higgins Trust
52–54 Gray's Inn Road, London, WC1X 8JU
Tel: 0171 242 1010

Thomas Coram Foundation [1]
40 Brunswick Square, London, WC1
Tel: 0171 278 2424

Turkish Cypriot Cultural Association (TCCA)
14a Graham Road, London, E8 1BZ
Tel: 0171 249 7410

Twins and Multiple Births Association (TAMBA)
PO Box 30, Little Sutton, South Wirral, L66 1TH
Tel & Fax: 0151 348 0026

United Kingdom Thalassemia Society
19 The Broadway, Southgate, Southgate Circus, London, N14 6PH
Tel: 0181 882 0011

Urostomy Association
'Buckland', Beaumont Park, Danbury, Essex, CM3 4DE
Tel: 01245 224294

Vegan Society
7 Battle Road, St Leonards-on-Sea, East Sussex, TN37 7AA
Tel: 01424 427393

Vegetarian Society of the UK Ltd
Parkdale, Dunham Road, Altrincham, Cheshire, WA14 4QE
Tel: 0161 928 0793

Voluntary Council for Handicapped Children (VCHC) [5]
National Children's Bureau, 8 Wakley Street, London, EC1V 7QE
Tel: 0181 843 6000

Voluntary Organisations' Liaison Council for Under Fives
77 Holloway Road, London, N7 8JZ

The Council has many materials on anti-racist child care and guidelines for good practice.

Wales Pre-School Playgroup Association [2,4]
2a Chester Street, Wrexham, Clywd, LL13 8BD
Tel: 01978 358195

Working Group Against Racism in Children's Resources (WGARCR) [2]
460 Wandsworth Road, London, SW8 3LK
Tel: 0171 627 4594

World Health Organization (WHO)
20 Avenue Appier, Geneva, Switzerland
Tel: 00 41 22 791 2111

World Organisation for Early Childhood Education (OMEP)
c/o Thomas Coram Foundation, 40 Brunswick Square, London, WC1
Tel: 0171 278 2424

Index